THY PEOPLE SHALL BE MY PEOPLE ◆ AND ◆ THY GOD MY GOD

OTHER VOLUMES IN THE SPERRY SYMPOSIUM SERIES FROM DESERET BOOK COMPANY:

The Heavens Are Open (1993)

Doctrines of the Book of Mormon (1992)

The Lord of the Gospels (1991)

A Witness of Jesus Christ (1990)

Doctrines for Exaltation (1989)

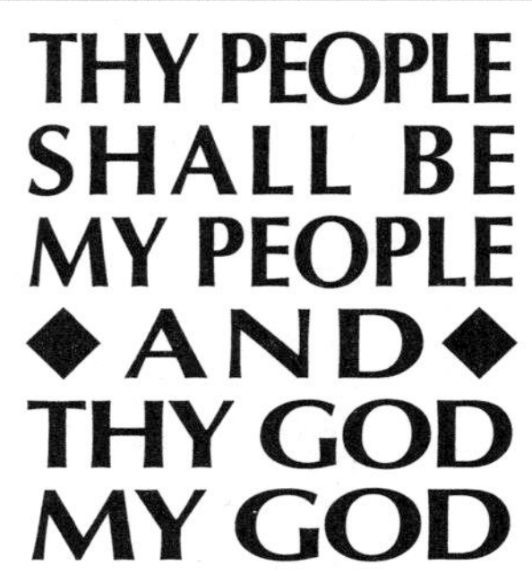

THY PEOPLE SHALL BE MY PEOPLE ◆ AND ◆ THY GOD MY GOD

THE 22D ANNUAL SIDNEY B. SPERRY SYMPOSIUM

DESERET BOOK COMPANY
SALT LAKE CITY, UTAH

Library of Congress Cataloging-in-Publication Data

Sperry Symposium (22nd : 1993 : Brigham Young University)
Thy people shall be my people and thy God my God : the 1993 Sperry Symposium on the Old Testament.
p. cm.
Proceedings of the 22nd Sperry Symposium, Nov. 1993, Brigham Young University.
Includes bibliographical references (p. xxx–xxx) and index.
ISBN 0-87579-831-4
1. Bible. O.T.—Criticism, interpretation, etc.—Congresses.
2. Church of Jesus Christ of Latter-day Saints—Doctrines—Congresses. 3. Mormons—Doctrines—Congresses. I. Title.
BS1171.2.S67 1993
221.6—dc20 93-47598
CIP

Printed in the United States of America

10 9 8 7 6 5 4 3 2 1

CONTENTS

PREFACE

This volume is dedicated with gratitude to Dr. Sidney B. Sperry, who, during his twenty-nine years at Brigham Young University, taught at least two generations of young students to love and appreciate the Old Testament. As the student of one of those students, I am a recipient of Brother Sperry's legacy, which I gratefully acknowledge.

Brother Sperry received his doctorate in biblical languages and literature in 1931 from the University of Chicago and promptly left for a year of postdoctoral work at the American School of Oriental Research in Jerusalem. It was after this thorough training that he began a distinguished teaching and writing career at Brigham Young University. During the years that followed, with unflinching loyalty both to the Restoration and to scholarly rigor, he helped his students to study the scriptures and to develop a passion for all Holy Writ. It was therefore most appropriate that when Brother Sperry passed away in 1977, President Ezra Taft Benson of the Quorum of the Twelve Apostles presided at the funeral services held in the auditorium of the original Joseph Smith building on the campus of BYU.

The essays in this volume are a fitting tribute to Sidney B. Sperry because, like Brother Sperry himself, they display a wide range of interest and scholarship as they view the Old Testament through the lens of the restored gospel. Because it is not always apparent how the Old Testament bears witness of Jesus Christ and his redeeming work, these essays discuss for the Latter-day Saint audience several ways in which that sacred volume speaks of the gospel of Christ both in ancient times and in the latter days.

This volume is thus dedicated to the memory of Dr. Sidney B. Sperry and offered to all students of the scriptures.

Paul Y. Hoskisson
Editor

CHAPTER ONE

OUR HERITAGE FROM JOSEPH OF ISRAEL

ROBERT J. MATTHEWS

There is something wonderful and exciting about our ancient ancestor Joseph the son of Jacob, who is generally known as Joseph of Egypt. More correctly, he is Joseph of Israel, who lived in Egypt. He is a hero in many ways and is one of the outstanding seers of all time. So great was he in the work of the Lord that the name of Joseph has a quality of reverence about it; just hearing the name causes spiritual echoes and visual images to come to mind. His faithfulness thirty-six hundred years ago, from boyhood to old age, led to promises and covenants and blessings being given to him personally and has influenced the writing of scripture and the work of the Church right up to this very moment. This heritage from Joseph will continue to influence us throughout the eternities to come.

THE BIBLICAL ACCOUNT OF JOSEPH

The Bible contains no book of Joseph, but the book of Genesis has a great deal of information about him. It is instructive to analyze its contents. The word *Genesis* means "beginning" (Bible Dictionary, "Genesis"); the book derives its title from its first three words: "In the beginning." Genesis tells of many beginnings: the beginning, or creation, of the earth, the beginning of man, of animals, of sin, of the preaching of the gospel, of families, tribes, and nations, and the beginning of the house of Israel. The book of Genesis introduces the rest of the Bible and was written to give the Israelites, just out of Egypt, a knowledge of who they were, the purposes of God, and the origin of things in the world. Genesis gives background essential to recognizing the hand of God in the Creation, the establishment of a covenant with Abraham, and the founding of the house of Israel as the Lord's special people among the nations. It is through Israel that

□ □ □ □ □

Robert J. Matthews is professor emeritus of ancient scripture at Brigham Young University.

the name of the Lord is to be preserved and the gospel is to be taught throughout the earth among all peoples.

A chapter-by-chapter analysis of Genesis shows that not all things were treated equally. For example, the amount of space given to the stories of Abraham and Joseph is disproportionate to the length of time each one lived.

Genesis 1 and 2 cover the creation of the earth and the origin of life on the earth. Thousands and thousands of years are covered in just two chapters.

Genesis 3 through 5 deal with the fall of man and the history of early families from Adam to Noah—at least fifteen hundred years are covered in three chapters, averaging more than five hundred years per chapter.

Genesis 6 through 11 cover the events from the birth of Noah through the tower of Babel—possibly five hundred years in six chapters, averaging almost one hundred years per chapter.

Genesis 12 through 27 introduce Abraham, Isaac, and Jacob. Two hundred years is covered in sixteen chapters—fewer than fourteen years per chapter.

Genesis 28 through 36 relate the life of Jacob, his marriages, and the beginnings of the tribes of Israel. Eight chapters cover no more than one hundred years—twelve years per chapter.

Genesis 37 through 50 detail the life of Joseph. Chapter 38 is about Judah, leaving thirteen chapters for the story of Joseph from age seventeen to one hundred ten —ninety-three years are covered in those thirteen chapters, averaging fewer than eight years per chapter.

The book of Genesis covers seventy-eight pages in my copy of the Bible. If we deduct four pages for the account of the Creation, that leaves seventy-four pages to cover the time from the fall of Adam to the death of Joseph, a period of about twenty-three hundred years. The ninety-three years of Joseph's life from age seventeen to one hundred ten are covered in twenty-four pages; in other words, 30 percent of Genesis covers only 5 percent of the time period. That proportion ought to give us an idea of how Moses, the inspired author of Genesis, felt about the importance of Joseph's story.

THE NAME OF JOSEPH

According to *The Interpreter's Dictionary of the Bible,* the name *Joseph* means "to add" or "may God add," as adding to one's life through a posterity.[1] The Egyptian name given to Joseph was *Zaphnath-paaneah* (see Genesis 41:45), which experts say could mean "God speaks" or "God reveals."[2] *Unger's Bible Dictionary* interprets that name to mean "sustainer of life."[3] Others have felt the name *Joseph* is an adaptation of the name *Asaph,* meaning "to gather." What we know about Joseph fits all of these interpretations very well.

JOSEPH'S LIFE ON EARTH

Joseph was chosen in the Grand Council before the world was.[4] He is one of the "noble and great ones" seen in vision by Abraham (Abraham 3:22–23) and was foreordained to become a ruler on the earth and in eternity.

As to his mortal life, Joseph was the eleventh son of Jacob and the first child of Rachel. He seems to have been considerably younger than his half-brothers Reuben, Simeon, Levi, and Judah, the sons of Jacob's first wife, Leah. It is likely that Jacob was in his early nineties when Joseph was born. Joseph was thirty years of age when he was made overseer of Egypt (see Genesis 41:46); seven years later the famine began, and two years later still Joseph made himself known to his brothers, making him about thirty-nine at that time (see Genesis 45:6). A short time later Jacob went to Egypt and met the Pharaoh, who asked Jacob his age; Jacob responded that he was 130 (see Genesis 47:9). If we can trust that information given in the text of Genesis, we would conclude that Jacob must have been approximately ninety-one when Joseph was born.

When Reuben, who was Jacob's firstborn, lost the birthright because of transgression (see Genesis 35:22; 49:4; 1 Chronicles 5:1), the blessing went to the firstborn of the second wife, Rachel. And thus Joseph was given the birthright in his father's house—the house of Israel. The birthright carried with it certain prerogatives and responsibilities. It entailed an inheritance of land; but more important, it meant the right to preside in the family after the death of the father. Birthright is presidency and leadership.

Our understanding of the office associated with the birthright is enhanced by our knowledge of the holy priesthood and the keys to preside. The priesthood and the requisite keys descended in regular succession by lineage from Adam and were conferred upon Abraham, by Abraham to Isaac, by Isaac to Jacob, and by Jacob to Joseph. Such power and prerogatives were not mere tribal custom and folklore, as some scholars would have us believe, but were the priesthood powers designed to regulate and set in order the affairs of the kingdom of God on the earth and are the channel through which God revealed his will to his prophets.

JOSEPH AND THE GOSPEL

Little is said in the scriptures about Joseph's having the gospel and knowing the doctrine of Jesus Christ, but we know from other scripture (see Jacob 4:4–5; Mosiah 13:33–35) that all of the prophets believed in Jesus, who was to come, and of necessity they were baptized, confirmed, ordained, and called according to the proper order of the kingdom. All true prophets and seers have been witnesses for the Lord Jesus Christ, even though our current Bibles lack that information.[5]

As a young man, Joseph had several dreams that foreshadowed his earthly mission and his leadership in the family. One dream was of his brothers' sheaves of grain bowing down to his sheaf. Some of his dreams are recorded in Genesis 37:5–11, and a partial fulfillment is noted in Genesis 42:6–9, when his brothers bowed before him in Egypt. Joseph's belief in the gospel of Jesus Christ, including his reliance on dreams and visions, is another part of our heritage from him.

JOSEPH'S INTEGRITY

The life of Joseph illustrates the truth that when the Lord wants something done, he has a particular baby born who will grow up and do it. That is true of all the prophets and apostles and was true of Joseph. The Lord foresaw the need to preserve the house of Israel during a widespread famine and through other dangers, and he had Joseph waiting and ready, able to do the work.

The story of Joseph exemplifies the Lord's knowledge of the situation of all His children and His awareness of their individual circumstances. He often proves and tries them to the uttermost, tempering and strengthening them to accomplish very difficult tasks. Perhaps the most significant test of Joseph's faithfulness and love of God came through his experience with Potiphar's wife, who day by day sought to have him "lie" with her in carnal immorality. Joseph's response was that he would not do so because his master, her husband, trusted him, and he could not do this great wickedness and sin against God. Thereupon, the woman, frustrated in her efforts to seduce him, falsely accused him of trying to seduce her, and he was thrown into prison (see Genesis 39:3–20). That must have been a very discouraging turn of events to be so treated for obeying the Lord's law of chastity. Joseph's experiences with his older brothers who sold him as a slave, the false accusation by Potiphar's wife, Joseph's leadership in the prison, and finally, the God-given inspiration to interpret the Pharaoh's dream—all signify that the Lord does not make our paths easy, but he does help those who trust in him. Joseph would not have had the wisdom, and perhaps not even the opportunity, to use his wisdom if he had not been blessed of the Lord for his faithfulness in times of adversity. The Lord, who looketh on the heart, knew of Joseph's integrity.

Thus, part of our heritage from Joseph is his good example. Joseph's life reminds us of the Lord's promises in the Doctrine and Covenants, which were spoken to all of us:

"For thus saith the Lord—I, the Lord, am merciful and gracious unto those who fear me, and delight to honor those who serve me in righteousness and in truth unto the end.

"Great shall be their reward and eternal shall be their glory.

"And to them will I reveal all mysteries, yea, all the hidden mysteries of my kingdom from days of old, and for ages to come, will I make known unto them the good pleasure of my will concerning all things pertaining to my kingdom.

"Yea, even the wonders of eternity shall they know, and things to come will I show them, even the things of many generations.

"And their wisdom shall be great, and their understanding reach to heaven; and before them the wisdom of the wise shall perish, and the understanding of the prudent shall come to naught.

"For by my Spirit will I enlighten them, and by my power will I make known unto them the secrets of my will—yea, even those things which eye has not seen, nor ear heard, nor yet entered into the heart of man" (D&C 76:5–10).

These words assure us that the Lord will help all who sincerely obey him. He may not make everyone prime minister of Egypt, but he will not overlook anyone; he will rescue and generously reward each of us in his own time and in his own way. I believe that what the Lord does for us will be better than if we had dictated the terms ourselves.

THE CONSEQUENCES OF SIN

The record of Joseph's brothers also demonstrates that unrighteous acts that remain uncorrected leave a residue in our consciousness that at some future time will surface to our sorrow and shame. Remember that when Joseph's brothers arrived in Egypt looking for food, he recognized them and temporarily confined them. They didn't know him, nor did they know the cause of their imprisonment, but their imaginations became active. They began to argue among themselves, and Reuben said, in effect, "I told you that you should not have mistreated our younger brother those many years ago. When we saw his anguish at our plan to sell him, and he pleaded for mercy, you should have listened" (see Genesis 42:21–22). That was twenty years after the selling of Joseph, but in that crisis, it all came back to trouble them. What they didn't know was that Joseph was listening to them in their plight and could understand them.

Later, when Joseph made himself known to his brothers and sent them back to Canaan to get their father, Jacob, and to tell him that Joseph was yet alive, the problem was increased for the elder brothers—Joseph wanted Jacob to come to Egypt to see him and live out the famine. This development presented certain difficulties to them. After selling Joseph, they had taken his coat of many colors, dipped it in goats' blood, and asked their father if he recognized it. He at once came to the conclusion that a vicious animal had slain the boy. The brothers didn't actually say that, but they arranged the evidence in such a way that it led to their father's wrong conclusion. They beheld their father's sorrow and long mourning, and yet they let him believe a lie for more than twenty years while they professed innocence. Now all that would change. Jacob would go to Egypt, and Joseph would be able to tell him how it really happened. Circumstances have a way of surfacing, no matter how carefully and deeply concealed. That is true of good deeds as well as of bad. All things shall, at some time, be manifest to our glory and honor or to our shame. The lesson of the need for repentance, taught by this episode in the lives of his brothers, is also part of our heritage from Joseph.

Joseph was aware of the discomfort his brothers were feeling. The account reads: "And Joseph said unto his brethren, I am Joseph; doth my father yet live? And his brethren could not answer him; for they were troubled at his presence.

"And Joseph said unto his brethren, Come near to me, I pray you. And they came near. And he said, I am Joseph your brother, whom ye sold into Egypt.

"Now therefore be not grieved, nor angry with yourselves, that ye sold me hither: for God did send me before you to preserve life" (Genesis 45:3–5).

Seventeen years later, when their father, Jacob, died and was buried at Hebron, the brothers feared that Joseph might then take action against them for their misdeeds. Joseph's magnanimity was again demonstrated:

"And when Joseph's brethren saw that their father was dead, they said, Joseph will peradventure hate us, and will certainly requite us all the evil which we did unto him.

"And they sent a messenger unto Joseph, saying, Thy father did command before he died, saying,

"So shall ye say unto Joseph, Forgive, I pray thee now, the trespass of thy brethren, and their sin; for they did unto thee evil: and now, we pray thee, forgive the trespass of the servants of the God of thy father. And Joseph wept when they spake unto him.

"And his brethren also went and fell down before his face; and they said, Behold, we be thy servants.

"And Joseph said unto them, Fear not: for am I in the place of God?

"But as for you, ye thought evil against me; but God meant it unto good, to bring to pass, as it is this day, to save much people alive.

"Now therefore fear ye not: I will nourish you, and your little ones. And he comforted them, and spake kindly unto them" (Genesis 50:15–21).

Before Jacob died, he gave each of his sons a father's blessing, or in other words, a patriarchal blessing. That was not only a blessing regarding each son but a prophecy and explanation of the posterity of each one. Of Joseph, Jacob said:

"Joseph is a fruitful bough, even a fruitful bough by a well; whose branches run over the wall:

"The archers have sorely grieved him, and shot at him, and hated him:

"But his bow abode in strength, and the arms of his hands were made strong by the hands of the mighty God of Jacob; (from thence is the shepherd, the stone of Israel:)

"Even by the God of thy father, who shall help thee; and by the Almighty, who shall bless thee with blessings of heaven above, blessings of the deep that lieth under, blessings of the breasts, and of the womb:

"The blessings of thy father have prevailed above the blessings of my progenitors unto the utmost bound of the everlasting hills: they shall be on the head of Joseph, and on the crown of the head of him that was separate from his brethren" (Genesis 49:22–26).

I want to pay particular attention to the last sentence, which speaks of the "everlasting hills" and the blessings upon him who was "separate from his brethren." The land of the everlasting hills we regard as the Western Hemisphere—North and South America. The matter of Joseph's being separate from his brethren was partially fulfilled by the Nephites' and Lamanites' dwelling for many centuries in the Western Hemisphere, separate from the other tribes of Israel. Moreover, there will be further fulfillment of this separation, for we learn from Ether 13:2–11 and 3 Nephi 20–21 that Joseph's seed shall build and inhabit the New Jerusalem on the American continent, whereas the other tribes of Israel will find inheritances in and around the old Jerusalem. This separation was explained by President Joseph Fielding Smith: "Because of his faithfulness and integrity, Joseph received greater blessings than the progenitors of Jacob and was rewarded with the land of Zion. His brothers, with malicious intent, separated him and cast him out from among them. The Lord, in rewarding him, separated him from his brothers—the other tribes of Israel—and gave him an inheritance in a land that is choice above all other lands, which, we have learned from the *Book of Mormon* and modern revelation, is America."[6] Thus, the events in Joseph's own life foreshadowed the more permanent arrangement of his posterity, who will remain separate from the other tribes by divine decree and special blessing in the land choice above all other lands.

Nephi, speaking of the ancient Joseph, said: "He truly prophesied concerning all his seed. And the prophecies which he wrote, there are not many greater" (2 Nephi 4:2). And father Lehi said: "I am a descendant of Joseph who was carried captive into Egypt. And great were the covenants of the Lord which he made unto Joseph. Wherefore, Joseph truly saw our day" (2 Nephi 3:4–5).

Joseph saw the times of Lehi, Nephi, and the Book of Mormon peoples, and he also saw our day in the nineteenth and twentieth centuries. He prophesied of Moses, of Aaron, and of the Messiah, and he also prophesied of Joseph Smith, Sr., Joseph Smith, Jr., and Oliver Cowdery.

We know that more of Joseph's prophecies were contained on the plates of brass. Parts of them are cited in the Book of Mormon (see 2 Nephi 3), and additional information is given in Joseph Smith's translation of Genesis 50. The Prophet knew of even further information coming from ancient Joseph, particularly about the restoration of the priesthood to Joseph Smith and his scribe, Oliver Cowdery. The account was written in Oliver's handwriting in 1835 in the patriarchal blessing book of Joseph Smith, Sr., and is preserved in the Church archives. A portion of Oliver's record reads as follows: "Therefore we repaired to the woods, even as our father Joseph said we should, that is, to the bush, and called upon the name of the Lord, and he answered us out of the heavens. And while we were in the heavenly vision, the angel came down and bestowed upon us this priesthood; and then, as I have said, we repaired to the water and were baptized. After this, we received the high and holy priesthood; but an account of this will be given elsewhere, or in another place."[7]

Elder Joseph Fielding Smith commented on this little-known prophecy: "In this statement, made by Oliver, reference is made to a prophecy by Joseph of old, son of Jacob, in which he declared that the priesthood should be restored in the last days through the administration of an angel 'in the bush.' In the Book of Mormon we are given a glimpse at the prophecy uttered by Joseph concerning the restoration, but the prophecy has only been given in part unto us, and is yet to be revealed. Without doubt, it was made known to the Prophet in connection with many other things which have not yet been given to the world. The Prophet has, however, added some light concerning this prophecy, and has revealed to us the manner of the ordination to the Melchizedek priesthood of himself and Oliver Cowdery.

"On the 18th day of December, 1833, when the Prophet blessed his father, and ordained him to the Patriarchal priesthood, he also blessed a number of others, among whom was Oliver Cowdery. After pronouncing Oliver's blessing, the Prophet said:

" 'These blessings shall come upon him [Oliver] according to the blessings of the prophecy of Joseph in ancient days, which he said should come upon the seer of the last days and the scribe that should sit with him, and that should be ordained with him, by the hands of the angel in the bush, unto the lesser priesthood, and *after* receive the holy priesthood *under the hands* of those who had been held in reserve for a long season, *even those who received it under the hands of the Messiah*, while he should dwell in the flesh upon the earth, and should receive the blessings with him, even the seer of the God of Abraham, Isaac and Jacob, saith he, even Joseph of old.' "[8]

Elder Smith explained further that this information was copied by Oliver into the record under the date of 2 October 1835.[9]

I have been particular on this point to emphasize the precise knowledge that ancient Joseph possessed about the doings of Joseph Smith and his scribe Oliver Cowdery in the last days.

THE WRITINGS OF JOSEPH

There is not today a book of Joseph in the standard works, but we can be very certain that Joseph did write and there will yet be a book of his writings available to the Church. Nephi said that there were not many prophecies greater than those Joseph had written (see 2 Nephi 4:2). Furthermore, when Joseph Smith obtained the two Egyptian papyri scrolls from Michael Chandler in 1835 at Kirtland, the Prophet identified one of them as containing the writings of Joseph of Egypt.[10] The Prophet did not publish a translation from the Joseph scroll, but he must have examined it and formed an idea of its contents, for Oliver Cowdery wrote an extensive and detailed account of it, which was published in the *Messenger and Advocate* in Kirtland, Ohio, in December 1835.[11] We assume that Oliver obtained his detailed information about the Joseph scroll from the Prophet. It appears from Brother Cowdery's description that several of the pieces of papyri the Church obtained from the New York Metropolitan Museum in 1967 are from the Joseph scroll. Surely we can look forward to a time to come when the Church will have a complete record and translation of all of Joseph's writings.

THE POSTERITY OF JOSEPH TODAY

We are given to understand, without equivocation, that Joseph Smith, Jr., was a direct descendant of Joseph of Egypt. The Book of Mormon so declares in 2 Nephi 3:7–15. President Brigham Young often spoke on this theme, stating emphatically that Joseph Smith was a literal, biological descendant of ancient Joseph. For example, on 9 October 1859 he said: "It was decreed in the counsels of eternity, long before the foundations of the earth were laid, that he [Joseph Smith] should be the man, in the last dispensation of this world, to bring forth the word of God to the people, and receive the fulness of the keys and powers of the Priesthood of the Son of God. The Lord had his eye upon him, and upon his father, and upon his father's father, and upon their progenitors clear back to Abraham, and from Abraham to the flood, from the flood to Enoch, and from Enoch to Adam. He has watched that family and that blood as it has circulated from its fountain to the birth of that man."[12]

On an earlier occasion President Young had said: "You have heard Joseph say that the people did not know him; he had his eyes on the relation to blood-relations. Some have supposed that he meant spirit, but it was the blood-relation. This is it that he referred to. His descent from Joseph that was sold into Egypt was direct, and the blood was pure in him. That is why the Lord chose him and we are pure when this blood-strain from Ephraim comes down pure. The decrees of the Almighty will be exalted—that blood which was in him was pure and he had the sole right and lawful power, as he was the legal heir to the blood that has been on the earth and has come down through a pure lineage. The union of various ancestors kept that blood pure. There is a great deal the people do not understand, and many of the Latter-day Saints have to learn all about it."[13]

We have already noted that events in the life of Joseph were typical or symbolic of events in the lives of his posterity, as in his being separate from his brethren. The comparison can be carried further. Just as Joseph saved his people with corn (literally, cornbread) in Egypt, so the family of Joseph today has the "bread of life," the priesthood and the gospel of Jesus Christ, to feed to a spiritually famished world, to gather scattered Israel, and to restore them to the true church and fold of God. We can benefit from President Young's words on this subject: "[God] foreknew what Joseph, who was sold into Egypt, would do. Joseph was foreordained to be the temporal saviour of his father's house, and the seed of Joseph are ordained to be the spiritual and temporal saviours of all the house of Israel in the latter days. Joseph's seed has mixed itself with all the seed of man upon the face of the whole earth. The great majority of those who are now before me are the descendants of that Joseph who was sold. Joseph Smith, junior, was foreordained to come through the loins of Abraham, Isaac, Jacob, Joseph, and so on down through the Prophets and Apostles; and thus he came forth in the last days to be a minister of salvation, and to hold the keys of the last dispensation of the fulness of times."[14]

It is not by accident nor by coincidence that most of the members of the Church today are literal descendants of ancient Joseph. Such lineage is plainly declared in their individual patriarchal blessings and in the revelations of the Lord. The descent from Joseph is actual, literal, and biological in the bloodstreams of Church members. We read in the Doctrine and Covenants, "Ye are lawful heirs, according to the flesh," and the priesthood "must needs remain through you and your lineage" (D&C 86:9–10).

A number of years ago, Elder Mark E. Petersen, of the Quorum of the Twelve Apostles, reported the results of a survey of a large number of patriarchal blessings of Church members in specific geographical areas. His conclusions were published in 1981 and are quite instructive: "Patriarchal blessings clearly point out that it is the tribe of

Joseph that is carrying forward the last dispensation. And how could it be otherwise? . . .

"So it is Joseph who is doing the present-day work through The Church of Jesus Christ of Latter-day Saints. Patriarchal blessings give the lineage of Church members receiving the blessings, and they are predominantly of Joseph.

"For example, three different patriarchs in Great Britain report that of their blessings, very few indeed show a lineage other than that of Ephraim. One of those patriarchs has given more than six hundred blessings, another five hundred, and the third more than three hundred. Each reports that of all his blessings, not more than half a dozen declare a lineage other than of Ephraim.

"This clearly shows that Great Britain is a land of Ephraim. But the same thing may be said of other European countries. They too are Ephraim. Converts by the thousands have come from there. It is not expected, of course, that all of the millions in Europe will join the Church. . . . But those who do come are primarily of Ephraim. And Ephraim is a son of Joseph.

"Throughout the Polynesian islands and Latin America the blood of Manasseh is dominant.

"In Mexico, patriarchs report that 75 percent of the blessings indicate the lineage of Manasseh and 25 percent, of Ephraim. Only two or three blessings out of hundreds given mention any other tribe.

"In Peru one patriarch in a given period gave 95 blessings, of which 90 indicated the blood of Manasseh, 3 of Ephraim, and 2 of Abraham.

"Another patriarch in the same area gave 347 blessings in a given period, of which 122 were of Ephraim, 130 of Manasseh, 90 of Joseph, 2 of Asher, 2 of Benjamin, and 1 of Levi.

"Another patriarch in that land has given over nine hundred blessings, of which 90 percent are of Manasseh and the rest of Ephraim, except for a half dozen referring to other tribes.

"In New Zealand virtually all of the Europeans are declared to be of Ephraim and the Polynesians of Manasseh, with a few declared simply to be of Joseph.

"In Tonga the patriarchs report that 75 percent of their blessings show a lineage of Manasseh and 25 percent of Ephraim. Out of many blessings given, only 4 were related to other tribes.

"It is interesting to see how the blessings occur in still other lands. In Hong Kong, out of 326 blessings, 323 were of Ephraim and 3 of Manasseh.

"In Taiwan, out of a group of 210 blessings, all were of Ephraim. In the Philippines every blessing given by the patriarchs there declared a lineage of Ephraim.

"In Japan, out of 2,641 blessings, 1,326 were shown to be of Joseph, 444 specifically of Ephraim, and 871 of Manasseh. No other tribes were mentioned.

"In Italy, out of 150 blessings, all were declared of Ephraim. No exceptions.

"In France one patriarch reported on 300 blessings of which 280 were of Ephraim and the rest of Manasseh except a few of Judah.

"Another French patriarch gave 94 blessings, all showing a line of Ephraim except one of Judah. A third French patriarch just beginning his work said that all of his blessings thus far showed the line of Ephraim.

"In Argentina, out of 100 blessings given, 66 were of Ephraim and 33 of Manasseh, with one from another tribe.

"Out of 100 blessings in Chile, 60 were of Ephraim and 40 of Manasseh. From 100 blessings given in Uruguay, 21 were of Ephraim, 76 of Manasseh, and 3 from other tribes. In North America nearly all Indians are shown to be of Manasseh. The sifting of the blood of Joseph and his sons Ephraim and Manasseh to all parts of the world is nothing short of miraculous. And it is likewise obviously an act of Providence that the Latter-day Saints being brought into the Church in all parts of the world are overwhelmingly of the blood of Joseph.

"It is highly significant in the light of the prophecies concerning Joseph and his latter-day mission."[15]

On the subject of our lineage, President Spencer W. Kimball said with great clarity: "The Lamanite is a chosen child of God, but he is not the only chosen one. There are many other good people including the Anglos, the French, the German, and the English, who are also of Ephraim and Manasseh. They, with the Lamanites, are also a chosen people, and they are a remnant of Jacob. The Lamanite is not wholly and exclusively the remnant of the Jacob which the Book of Mormon talks about. We are *all* of Israel! We are of Abraham and Isaac and Jacob and Joseph through Ephraim and Manasseh. We are *all of us* remnants of Jacob."[16]

Some may think that present-day, Latter-day Saints are descendants of Joseph only by assignment or by adoption, but such a conclusion is not in harmony with the scriptures, the promises to the ancient prophets, nor the teachings of the latter-day prophets. We must understand that our descent from Joseph is literal. Elder Bruce R.

McConkie, speaking at a Brigham Young University summer session on 8 August 1967, was asked whether we, as Latter-day Saints, are literal descendants of Israel or Israelites by adoption. His answer, which I have on audiotape, was as follows: "We are literally of the seed of Abraham. Let's just drill it into ourselves! We are literally of the seed of Abraham. We are natural heirs according to the flesh. We are not adopted nor anything else. I don't know how there could be language more express than these revelations, 'natural heirs according to the flesh,' 'lawful heirs,' 'the literal seed of the body.' You see He [the Lord] just goes out of his way to make it literal. The literal seed of your body has the right to the priesthood and the gospel, and that is us. Now, granted that somebody can be adopted in but they are so few and far between up to now, that we can just about forget about them."[17]

That most Latter-day Saints are descended from ancient Joseph is reflected in an address delivered by President Ezra Taft Benson on 2 May 1976 in Calgary, Alberta, Canada, to an audience that included many Jewish people. President Benson titled his discourse, "A Message to Judah from Joseph."[18]

Thus we see that our earthly lineage is another part of our heritage from ancient Joseph. We have the same gospel of Jesus Christ that he had, the same priesthood, the same Abrahamic covenant, the same blood in our veins, and a similar responsibility to feed the bread of life to our fellow beings in the world. When Joseph's brothers went into Egypt, they did not know him. Yet he knew who he was. That is similar to the way it is today. The world does not know who we are—that we are Joseph's seed. What a tragedy it would have been if Joseph had not known himself who he was. It will likewise be tragic if we ourselves do not recognize and appreciate our true identity.

DIGNITY OF THE NAME OF JOSEPH

In view of the greatness of ancient Joseph and the many righteous Josephs in sacred history, such as Joseph the husband of Mary, Joseph Smith, Sr., Joseph Smith, Jr., Joseph F. Smith, Joseph Fielding Smith, and many others, the name Joseph has a certain dignity about it. Along this line, there is an account of Joseph Smith talking with an unfriendly minister of religion, who said to the Prophet:

" 'Why, I told my congregation the other Sunday that they might as well believe Joe Smith as such theology as that.'

" 'Did you say Joe Smith in a sermon?' [asked Joseph Smith].

" 'Of course I did. Why not?'

"The Prophet's reply was given with a quiet superiority that was overwhelming: 'Considering only the day and the place it would have been more respectful to have said Lieutenant General Joseph Smith.' "[19]

Further, in 1909 President Joseph F. Smith wrote to one of his daughters about his feelings about the name *Joseph*. A portion of the letter reads as follows: "Somehow the name *Joseph* has fixed in my mind a *sense* of sacredness, as being the name of the *Prophet* that would not permit me to abbreviate it even if it were borne by my worst enemy. Aside from that . . . it is very sacred to me, and I cannot think, with any pleasure of her *nick-naming* her husband, when to do so seems to cast not only a slight on his name but on the whole line of *Josephs* reaching back to him who was sold into Egypt."[20]

As far as salvation in the celestial kingdom is concerned, it makes no difference what our name or our lineage is, for Christ died for all mankind, and salvation comes by the grace of Christ and our willing obedience. However, promises were made to the ancient prophets and patriarchs that the gospel would be offered to their posterity. In the Lord's orderly manner of doing things, He has called upon the biological descendants of ancient Joseph to be the ones who would hold those blessings first in the last days and to be the leaders in building the dispensation of the fulness of times and in extending the blessings of the gospel to others. All persons of other tribes will have equal opportunity, through obedience to the gospel. However, they will receive the gospel, the priesthood, and the ordinances through the agency of the descendants of Joseph, which is the birthright tribe, for that is the way the Lord has chosen to do it. May we appreciate our heritage I pray in the name of Jesus Christ, amen.

NOTES

1. *The Interpreter's Dictionary of the Bible* (Nashville: Abingdon Press, 1962), 2:979.
2. *Interpreter's Dictionary of the Bible,* 4:934.
3. Merrill F. Unger, *Unger's Bible Dictionary* (Chicago: Moody Press, 1985), p. 1179.
4. Joseph Smith, *Teachings of the Prophet Joseph Smith,* sel. Joseph Fielding Smith (Salt Lake City: Deseret Book Co., 1938), p. 365.
5. Smith, *Teachings of the Prophet Joseph Smith,* pp. 168, 264, 308.
6. Joseph Fielding Smith, *Doctrines of Salvation,* comp. Bruce R. McConkie (Salt Lake City: Bookcraft, 1956), 3:68.
7. Smith, *Doctrines of Salvation,* 3:100.

8. Smith, *Doctrines of Salvation,* 3:100–101.
9. Smith, *Doctrines of Salvation,* 3:100–101.
10. Joseph Smith, *History of The Church of Jesus Christ of Latter-day Saints,* 2d ed. rev., edited by B. H. Roberts (Salt Lake City: The Church of Jesus Christ of Latter-day Saints, 1965), 2:236.
11. Oliver Cowdery, "To the Elders of the Church of the Latter Day Saints," *Latter Day Saints' Messenger and Advocate,* 2 (December 1835): 236–37.
12. Brigham Young, in *Journal of Discourses* (London: Latter-day Saints' Book Depot, 1860), 7:289–90.
13. Brigham Young, *The Utah Genealogical and Historical Magazine,* 11 (July 1920): 107; discourse delivered 8 Jan. 1845.
14. Young, in *Journal of Discourses,* 7:290.
15. Mark E. Petersen, *Joseph of Egypt* (Salt Lake City: Deseret Book Co., 1981), pp. 15–17.
16. Spencer W. Kimball, *The Teachings of Spencer W. Kimball,* ed. Edward L. Kimball (Salt Lake City: Bookcraft, 1982), pp. 600–601.
17. Original audiotape in the author's possession.
18. See Ezra Taft Benson, *A Message to Judah from Joseph* (Salt Lake City: The Church of Jesus Christ of Latter-day Saints, n.d.).
19. Edwin F. Parry, *Stories about Joseph Smith* (Salt Lake City: Deseret News Press, 1934), p. 122.
20. Joseph Fielding Smith, *Life of Joseph F. Smith* (Salt Lake City: Deseret News Press, 1938), p. 435.

CHAPTER TWO

ISAIAH'S IMAGERY OF PLANTS AND PLANTING

TERRY BALL

During his second visit as the resurrected Messiah, the Savior commanded the faithful Nephites gathered at the temple in Bountiful: "And now, behold, I say unto you, that ye ought to search these things. Yea, a commandment I give unto you that ye search these things diligently; for great are the words of Isaiah" (3 Nephi 23:1). This admonition by the Son of God specifically to study the writings of Isaiah affords that prophet's teachings a place of distinction among canonized literature. The Savior further explained to the Nephites why Isaiah's writings were so deserving of special attention: "For surely he spake as touching all things concerning my people which are of the house of Israel; therefore it must needs be that he must speak also to the Gentiles. And all things that he spake have been and shall be, even according to the words which he spake" (3 Nephi 23:2–3).

The Savior's exhortation to "search" Isaiah's writings "diligently" is instructive. His choice of words suggests that more than a casual reading of the text is required to best comprehend and be blessed by the prophet's message. Rather than a quick and superficial "frisk" of text, the Lord is asking for a thorough and careful investigation, looking for clues, insights, and evidences that will edify and enhance our understanding. In such a search of Isaiah's writings, one rewarding avenue of investigation is the imagery of plants and planting that the prophet incorporated into his writings. The book of Isaiah contains more than three hundred references to plants or plant parts, representing at least twenty different kinds of vegetation (see Table 1). Isaiah used the plants metaphorically to teach the covenant people and their neighbors about their relationship to God, their need for

□ □ □ □ □

Terry Ball is assistant professor of ancient scripture at Brigham Young University.

repentance, their future according to His plan, and the ministry of their Messiah. Analyzing Isaiah's botanical metaphors, along with the characteristics of the plants and plant parts that Isaiah drew upon to create them, can offer insights into the prophet's message.

JEHOVAH AS THE GOOD HUSBANDMAN

The metaphor of the nurturing husbandman, Jehovah, caring for his crops, Israel, is one of the most significant of the images related to vegetation. The metaphor of the nurturing husbandman illustrates both the efforts the Lord has made to raise a covenant people and the ways those people have responded and will respond to his care.

The Vine and the Vineyard

The fifth chapter of Isaiah speaks of Jehovah and the vines of his vineyard. The common grape, or biblical vine, *Vitis vinifera,* has a long history of cultivation in Israel. It is the first cultivated plant to be identified by name in the Bible (see Genesis 9:20) and continues to be an important crop in modern Israel. It was an important source of food and beverage in the ancient Near East. In ancient Israel the September grape harvest was a time of feasting, joy, and song.[1]

In the Holy Land, the grapevine can be an exceptionally robust plant, capable of developing trunks up to one and one-half feet in diameter. They typically produce clusters of grapes weighing from ten to twelve pounds, although some approach thirty pounds in weight.[2] To reach this fruit-producing potential, however, the vine requires a tremendous amount of care and attention. If left untended, it seldom survives.[3] These characteristics made the vine an ideal metaphor for Israel.

"Now will I sing to my wellbeloved a song of my beloved touching his vineyard. My wellbeloved hath a vineyard in a very fruitful hill:

"And he fenced it, and gathered out the stones thereof, and planted it with the choicest vine, and built a tower in the midst of it, and also made a winepress therein: and he looked that it should bring forth grapes, and it brought forth wild grapes.

"And now, O inhabitants of Jerusalem, and men of Judah, judge, I pray you, betwixt me and my vineyard.

"What could have been done more to my vineyard, that I have not done in it? wherefore, when I looked that it should bring forth grapes, brought it forth wild grapes?

"And now go to; I will tell you what I will do to my vineyard: I will take away the hedge thereof, and it shall be eaten up; and break down the wall thereof, and it shall be trodden down:

"And I will lay it waste: it shall not be pruned, nor digged; but there shall come up briers and thorns: I will also command the clouds that they rain no rain upon it.

"For the vineyard of the Lord of hosts is the house of Israel, and the men of Judah his pleasant plant: and he looked for judgment, but behold oppression; for righteousness, but behold a cry" (Isaiah 5:1–7).

This metaphor of the Lord's vineyard commences as a song, possibly like those sung by the men of Judah during the grape harvest. The husbandman of the vineyard is referred to as the "wellbeloved," who is identified as Jehovah, while the vineyard itself is clearly the house of Israel.

From the very beginning, it is evident that the "wellbeloved" invested all the care requisite for an abundant harvest from this vineyard. He planted it in an ideal location, on a *keren ben-shemen* (Heb., which is translated as "a very fruitful hill" in the KJV). Literally, *keren* means "a horn" and probably refers to a hornlike mountain peak[4] or hillside.[5] By planting the vineyard on such a *keren,* the wise husbandman would ensure that his vineyard would not be shadowed from essential sunlight. The phrase *ben-shemen* means, literally, "a child of fatness" and might refer to a location with exceptionally fertile soil. The husbandman prepared the soil by digging about it carefully[6] and removing the stones. He then planted the vineyard, not with ordinary vines, or *gephen,* but rather with *soreq,* which is thought to be a variety of grapevine that produces one of the choicest of bluish-red grapes.[7] To protect the vineyard, he built a watchtower and apparently placed a hedge or wall around it. Both the tower and the protective walls would probably be constructed from the stones gathered out of the fields.[8] In anticipation of an abundant harvest, he even hewed out a winepress in the vineyard.

Surely the wellbeloved could have done nothing more to guarantee production from his vineyard. How bitter must his disappointment have been when, rather than bringing forth sweet juicy grapes—a faithful covenant people—the well-tended vineyard brought forth "wild grapes," or *beushim,* literally meaning "stinking, worthless things."[9]

In frustration the husbandman determined to lay waste the vineyard but not by personally destroying the vines. Rather, he decided to cease taking care of the vineyard and withdraw his protection from it.

Accordingly, he stopped pruning and cultivating the vineyard and commanded the clouds to rain no longer upon it. He also removed the protective wall from around it, thus allowing the vines to be trampled and ravaged. Eventually the vines were displaced from their choice location by noxious vegetation, including briars and thorns (see Isaiah 7:23). Thus, the metaphor gives a powerful warning to Israel. If they do not respond to the nurturing direction and loving kindness of Jehovah, he will abandon them and allow another people to possess their choice land.

In a vineyard song, the Lord promises that Jacob will not be left forsaken:

"In that day sing ye unto her, A vineyard of red wine.

"I the Lord do keep it; I will water it every moment: lest any hurt it, I will keep it night and day.

"Fury is not in me: who would set the briers and thorns against me in battle? I would go through them, I would burn them together.

"Or let him take hold of my strength, that he may make peace with me; and he shall make peace with me.

"He shall cause them that come of Jacob to take root: Israel shall blossom and bud, and fill the face of the world with fruit" (Isaiah 27:2–6).

Here Jehovah promises to burn those briars and thorns that refuse to "make peace" with him. He also promises to protect the vineyard night and day, see that it is watered "every moment," and cause Jacob to take root once again. Israel will then blossom, bud, and finally "fill the face of the world with fruit" (Isaiah 27:2–6).

The Wise Farmer and the Field

The book of Isaiah contains another metaphor featuring a husbandman who is instructed by God on how to prepare for, plant, and thresh a number of different plants:

"Give ye ear, and hear my voice; hearken, and hear my speech.

"Doth the plowman plow all day to sow? doth he open and break the clods of his ground?

"When he hath made plain the face thereof, doth he not cast abroad the fitches, and scatter the cummin, and cast in the principal wheat and the appointed barley and rie in their place?

"For his God doth instruct him to discretion, and doth teach him.

"For the fitches are not threshed with a threshing instrument, neither is a cart wheel turned about upon the cummin; but the fitches are beaten out with a staff, and the cummin with a rod.

"Bread corn is bruised; because he will not ever be threshing it, nor break it with the wheel of his cart, nor bruise it with his horsemen.

"This also cometh forth from the Lord of hosts, which is wonderful in counsel, and excellent in working" (Isaiah 28:23–29).

This metaphor begins with a series of rhetorical questions. They make the point that a wise farmer does not spend all his time plowing his field over and over again, but rather, when the ground has been broken open *(patach)* and harrowed *(sadad),* he proceeds to level *(shiwah)* it and then to sow the seeds. This wise farmer sows five different kinds of seeds, each in the manner that best suits its growth requirements and relative value.

Nutmeg flower and cumin. The first two types of seeds sown are fitches and cumin. Fitches *(qetsach)* have been variously identified as dill, vetches, caraway, and poppies but are now usually understood to be *Nigella sativa,* a plant commonly called nutmeg flower or black cumin.[10] It is an annual herb that grows to be about twelve inches tall and has finely incised leaves. Its branches end in a showy flower that varies from white to blue. The mature fruit is a capsule that contains a profusion of very small black seeds.[11] The aromatic seeds are as pungent as pepper and are thought to predate pepper in their use as a spice. In the Holy Land and in Egypt, they are sprinkled over breads and pastries or added to curries and other dishes.[12] Cumin *(Cuminum cyminum)* also produces small pungent seeds that are used as a flavoring for breads and dishes. The seeds have a taste similar to that of caraway seeds and have been used in folk medicine as an antispasmodic. They are also the source of an oil used in perfumes. Cumin is an annual herb of the carrot family with highly dissected leaves. It grows from one to two feet tall and produces clusters of flowers that vary from white to pink.[13] Both nutmeg flower and cumin have plentiful and relatively small seeds that do not require special spacing in their planting, so the wise farmer sows them by merely throwing *(zaraq)* and scattering *(hephitz)* them over the earth.

Wheats and barley. The wise farmer next planted three different kinds of cereal grains, two wheats and one barley. The first, *chittah,* was most likely the bread wheat *Triticum aestivum,* which was the most common wheat grown in Isaiah's time.[14] This remarkable wheat produces seed heads that do not spontaneously shatter, and yet with only a minimal amount of threshing yield an abundance of naked kernels. A superior bread flour is made from its high-gluten grains. The wise farmer sows these valuable seeds much more cautiously. Rather than haphazardly broadcasting them, he carefully places *(sam)* them in furrows to ensure adequate spacing for germination and watering.[15]

The next grain, barley *(seorah),* was also to be sown in this prudent manner in its "appointed" *(nisman)* place. Three types of barley are known to have been cultivated in biblical times: common barley *(Hordeum vulgare),* two-rowed barley *(H. distichum),* and six-rowed barley *(H. hexastichum).*[16] Barley was generally considered inferior to wheat for human consumption, but it was grown for animal feed in locations where the soil, moisture, and temperature would not support the less-tolerant wheats.[17]

The last cereal grain mentioned, translated as *rie* in the King James Version, was probably a type of spelt wheat, that is, one in which the seed is firmly encased in the chaff and is thus not easily threshed.[18] This inferior wheat, which was used mainly for animal fodder, was planted by the wise farmer "in their place," the Hebrew for which, *gebulto,* is better translated as "in its [the field's] edges or borders."

Just as the wise farmer planted each kind of seed in the field in the most efficacious manner, he also threshed the plants in the way that would yield the best results. The delicate herbs, cumin and nutmeg flower, were not threshed with threshing sledges or cart wheels but rather were carefully beaten out with a stick. The more robust cereal grains were threshed with a cart but not to the extent that the kernels were crushed.[19]

Thus in his preparation, sowing, and harvesting, the wise farmer treated each plant in the best manner. The metaphor therefore suggests that Jehovah acts in the same way. He has prepared for each people a place that is best for their growth and development and has placed them there in the fashion that best suits their needs and his plans for them. When it comes time for threshing—chastising, separating out, or gathering—the Lord will do it not so vigorously as to destroy them but rather in a fashion that will maximize his harvest of saved souls.

APOSTASY

Despite all that the good husbandman did to raise up and bless his people, some refused to develop into what he desired. Isaiah used imagery of plants to teach those individuals as well.

Pride and Worldliness

Trees, briars, and thorns. Trees in general were highly valued by the inhabitants of the ancient Near East as sources of food, fuel, and building material. Indeed, Moses taught the children of Israel that "the tree of the field is man's life"[20] and that fruit trees especially should not be destroyed when a city was besieged (Deuteronomy 20:19–20). The loftiness of trees, along with the great value men placed upon them, made trees an ideal metaphor for arrogance and materialism.

In the same fashion, characteristics of the lowly briars and thorns render them an appropriate metaphor for pride and worldliness. More than seventy species of thorned and spiny plants are indigenous to Israel. They range from heavily armed trees such as the Christ thorn, *Ziziphus spina-christi,* to spiny shrubs such as the thorny burnet, *Sarcopoterium spinosum,* to herbaceous annuals such as Spanish thistle, *Centaurea iberica.*[21] It is difficult to know exactly what thorny species Isaiah intended in the metaphor,[22] but all thistles have some characteristics in common. They are invasive, noxious, and unruly, doing harm to any that would touch them—traits commonly found in the proud and worldly as well.

Isaiah coupled the lowly briars and thorns with the lofty trees of the forest to illustrate and foretell the fate of the ungrateful, rebellious, and worldly, be they rich or poor, great or small. For example, in speaking of the destruction of the boastful Assyrians, Isaiah prophesied that the flame of the Holy One would devour Assyria's thorns and briars "in one day" and also "consume the glory of his [Assyria's] forest," so that the remaining trees would be so few even a child could count them (see Isaiah 10:17–19). In the same chapter he further warned Assyria that "the Lord of hosts, shall lop the bough with terror: and the high ones of stature shall be hewn down, and the haughty shall be humbled. And he shall cut down the thickets of the forest" (Isaiah 10:33–34). Fulfillment of this prophecy can be seen in the subsequent conquest of Assyria by the Babylonians and the Medes, after which the proud Assyrians ceased to be a people.[23] Likewise, Isaiah warned Israel that their wickedness would burn them and devour their briars and thorns as well as their forests (see Isaiah 9:18).[24] Then, in a triumphant song, the Lord declared that any briars and thorns invading his vineyard would be burned (see Isaiah 27:4), and apostates would be burned like thorns cut up (see Isaiah 33:12).

The cedars of Lebanon and the oaks of Bashan. The cedars of Lebanon, *Cedrus libani,* were an especially appropriate species to liken to pride and worldliness. These were the noblest, tallest, and most massive trees the Israelites knew.[25] Unlike the small and shrubby junipers called "cedars" in the Rocky Mountain West, these true cedars were monarchs of the forest, reaching heights of 120 feet and diameters of up to eight feet.[26] They were once common in the mountains of Lebanon and parts of Cilicia and can still be found there in reduced numbers today. They were esteemed for the fragrance and durability of their wood, which was fit for palaces and temples, thrones and altars.[27] Likewise, the oaks of Bashan, most likely *Quercus aegilops,* were impressive trees. Bashan is a fertile region east of Galilee and today is called the Golan Heights. In Bashan the oaks reached heights of up to fifty feet. In biblical times they were prized as a source of food, dye, and tanning agents.[28] Isaiah likened these cedars and oaks to arrogant Israel as he warned that "the day of the Lord of hosts shall be upon every one that is proud and lofty, and upon every one that is lifted up; and he shall be brought low: and upon all the cedars of Lebanon, that are high and lifted up, and upon all the oaks of Bashan" (Isaiah 2:12–13).

Isaiah also condemned the inhabitants of Ephraim, Samaria, and Assyria who metaphorically used cedars to boast of their own strength (see Isaiah 9:9–10; 37:24; Ezekiel 31:3–9).

Fine linen. Another metaphor Isaiah employed for worldliness and vanity was "fine linen," or *pishtim seriqim.* The linen plant *Linum usitatissimum* was an important source of textiles in the ancient Near East. The plant itself is an annual that grows rapidly to about three feet in height and produces beautiful blue flowers. The fibers for fine thread are extracted from the stems of young plants; tough fibers for rope come from more mature plants.[29] Linen is made in several grades, but the fine-carded variety is the most costly and highly esteemed and therefore an appropriate metaphor for vanity. Isaiah warned the worldly daughters of Zion that the Lord would take away from them all the material things they valued more than righteousness, including their garments of "fine linen," or *sadinim* (Isaiah 3:23), and further prophesied that when the Lord smote Egypt, he would confound all those that "work in fine flax" (Isaiah 19:9).

Adultery and Idolatry

Trees and wood. Trees were a symbol of life and fertility for peoples of the ancient Near East, for where trees could grow, there was water—and where there was water, there was life.[30] This association may have led to the use of groves as sites for the idolatrous fertility rites and worship to which Israel frequently apostatized (see Isaiah 57:5; 17:8; 27:9; Jeremiah 17:2; 1 Kings 14:15).[31] Isaiah mocked those who carved idols out of trees, pointing out the silliness of worshipping the same wood they also used to build fires for warmth and to bake bread and roast flesh upon (see Isaiah 44:13–19; 37:19; 40:20; 45:20).

Apparently the oaks, *Quercus sp.,* and the terebinths, or teils, *Pistacia sp.,* were the trees most often made into idols.[32] Species of both are common in Israel and are renowned for their stature and longevity.[33] Isaiah warned Judah that when Zion is redeemed "they shall be ashamed of the oaks which ye have desired" (Isaiah 1:29).

RETRIBUTION

Isaiah taught that because of wickedness, rebellion, and apostasy, Jehovah would punish the offenders with destruction and abandonment, leaving only a remnant behind. He often used botanical metaphors to warn of those impending acts of retribution.

Destruction of the Wicked

As discussed above, Isaiah prophesied that Jehovah planned to destroy the briars, thorns, and trees—the wicked among the people (see Isaiah 9:18; 10:17; 27:4; 33:12). He used botanical metaphors to teach that this destruction would be sudden, timely, and thorough.

Sudden destruction: chaff and stubble. On blustery days after the harvest, the Israelite farmer took advantage of the wind to winnow his threshed grain. The threshed mixture of chaff, chopped stubble, and seed would be gathered upon a winnowing board or fork and tossed into the air. There the wind would catch the light chaff and stubble and blow it away while the heavy, clean kernels would fall back to the earth for the farmer to collect.[34] Once the grains were removed, the remaining chaff and stubble would be dispersed by the wind or burned in a fire that was extremely hot, fast, and furious. Isaiah saw the fleeting chaff and stubble as a type of the temporality of the wicked. He warned that just as the "chaff of the mountains" is chased "before the wind" (Isaiah 17:13) and as the "fire devoureth the stubble, and the flame consumeth the chaff" (Isaiah 5:24), so shall Jehovah destroy the enemies of the covenant people and the apostates of Israel (see Isaiah 29:5; 33:11; 40:24; 41:2, 15; 47:14).

Grass, herbs, and flowers. Isaiah saw the transient appearance of grass, herbs, and flowers as an image for the destruction of the wicked. Much of the Holy Land is arid and can support an abundance of vegetation only during the rainy seasons from about November to April. Many plants begin to grow during the colder, winter months, but most do not mature and flower until the warmer weeks of spring from February to April. During those few short weeks, land that is usually barren can be covered with grasses, herbs, and flowers; but with the end of the rains, most of the vegetation withers and dies. By June the land that was once verdant is bleak and bare.[35] Moreover, occasionally an east wind, heated by the desert sands of Arabia, will sweep across the country, withering the vegetation as if in a furnace. In Isaiah this phenomenon is used as a type of the brief existence of mortality: "The voice said, Cry. And he said, What shall I cry? All flesh is grass, and all the goodliness thereof is as the flower of the field: the grass withereth, the flower fadeth: because the spirit of the Lord bloweth upon it: surely the people is grass. The grass withereth, the flower fadeth: but the word of our God shall stand for ever" (Isaiah 40:6–7; see also 51:12).

The phenomenon is also used as a type of the sudden destruction of the Lord's enemies: "Therefore their inhabitants were of small power, they were dismayed and confounded: they were as the grass of the field, and as the green herb, as the grass on the housetops, and as corn blasted before it be grown up" (Isaiah 37:27; see also 5:24; 15:6; 28:1–4; 42:15).

An especially graphic example of a metaphor of sudden destruction is found in Isaiah 17. Here Isaiah warned that when God rebukes the nations that are enemies of Israel, they shall be chased "like a rolling thing before the whirlwind" (v. 13). The word *galgal,* translated in the King James Version as *rolling thing,* is also translated as *tumbleweed* (NIV) and has been identified with Tournefort's gundelia, *Gundelia tournefortii.*[36] The first tender leaves and young flower buds of this rapidly growing plant appear in March. At this stage, its foliage can be used as a potherb in cooking, but at maturity the plant is a leathery thistle reaching heights of twelve to twenty inches.[37] The change from a tender herb to a "thorny monster" covered with "wickedly sharp thorns" occurs within a few short weeks.[38] Strangely, when the plant seems to be thriving most, a separation forms at the base of its stalk and "with one puff [of] a summer wind" it is blown away. The message to Israel is clear: although your enemies look formidable and heavily armed at the moment, when the time is right, God will remove them with a quick blast.[39] "And behold at eveningtide trouble; and before the morning he is not" (Isaiah 17:14).

Timely destruction. Isaiah taught that the retribution dealt to the wicked would be not only sudden but timely. "For so the Lord said unto me, I will take my rest, and I will consider in my dwelling place like a clear heat upon herbs, and like a cloud of dew in the heat of harvest. For afore the harvest, when the bud is perfect, and the sour grape is ripening in the flower, he shall both cut off the sprigs with pruning hooks, and take away and cut down the branches" (Isaiah 18:4–5).

This warning is poignant. Isaiah declared to the wicked that God will allow them to prosper in the world for a time but will not permit them to enjoy the fruit of their iniquities. Rather, in a timely way just before their harvest is to occur, when the "sour grape is ripening," Jehovah will enter their vineyards and not only destroy the twigs bearing evil fruit but also "cut down the branches" of their evil.[40] Similarly, Isaiah warned those who had forgotten the God of their salvation that although their plants may grow and their seeds may flourish, their harvest would be "a heap in the day of grief and of desperate sorrow" (Isaiah 17:10–11).

Thorough destruction: roots. Using imagery of plants, Isaiah taught that the destruction of Jehovah's enemies would be thorough. He prophesied that when Messiah delivers his people, even the poor of the righteous would enjoy peace and prosperity, whereas the unrepentant enemies of Jehovah would be left without "root" or remnant (Isaiah 14:30). The metaphor of thoroughly removing the wicked, clear down to the roots, is also found in Isaiah's warning to apostate Israel. He declared that in the day of the Lord's retribution He not only will burn their chaff and stubble but also will cause their roots to decay (see Isaiah 5:24).

Abandonment of the Peoples

Isaiah used several botanical images to teach various peoples that their iniquities would cause Jehovah to abandon them. He warned Israel, as discussed above, that Jehovah would cease digging and pruning and watering in His vineyard and would remove the protective wall and tower from around it (see Isaiah 5:5–7). Isaiah prophesied that the "daughter of Zion" would find herself as a "cottage in a vineyard" and a "lodge in a garden of cucumbers," both of which are left empty and neglected after the harvest is over, thus becoming bleak reminders to Israel of more prosperous times (Isaiah 1:8).[41] Moreover, Israel's strong cities would be like the forsaken woods *(choresh),* that is, woods that no one cares about, and as an "uppermost branch," one that is overlooked or untended because it is too difficult to reach or manage (Isaiah 17:9). As a result, the covenant people would fade like an oak leaf and as "a garden that hath no water" (Isaiah 1:30). Animals would come into the fields and feed upon the crops with no one and nothing to stop them (see Isaiah 5:5; 27:10). Eventually, briars and thorns would take over the lands that were once productive and become so thick that no one would dare enter them unarmed (see Isaiah 7:23–25; 5:6; 32:13; 34:13).

Isaiah gave similar warnings to other nations. He told Egypt that when they were forsaken by Jehovah and given over into the hand of "a cruel lord," the waters—God's blessings—would fail and the reeds, flags, rushes, and crops would wither—that is, their kingdoms, glories, and sustenance would disappear (Isaiah 19:4–7). He also rebuked Moab for their pride and prophesied that their fields and vines would languish and the joy and song of the vineyard would cease (see Isaiah 16:6–10).

THE REMNANT AND THE RESTORATION

The Remnant

After the wicked had been forsaken and destroyed, a remnant of the covenant people would still persist. Isaiah saw a type of that result in the harvesting practices of his time. Mosaic law prohibited the Israelite from harvesting every cluster of grapes from his vineyard. Rather, after the harvest, he was to leave any he had missed for strangers, orphans, and widows (see Deuteronomy 24:21). Thus a few hidden and scattered grapes would be left on the vines. Likewise, when olives were harvested, those that were too high to be picked by hand were either knocked down with sticks or shaken from the tree.[42] Consequently, a few would always be left in the uppermost branches. Isaiah taught that these remaining fruits or individuals were a type of the remnant that would be left of Israel. "Yet gleaning grapes shall be left in it, as the shaking of an olive tree, two or three berries in the top of the uppermost bough, four or five in the outmost fruitful branches thereof, saith the Lord God of Israel" (Isaiah 17:6; see also 24:13).

The Restoration

Isaiah knew that the Lord's forsaking the covenant people would not last forever but that a time of restoration and reconciliation would come. He used metaphors from the plant world to illustrate those occurrences.

The oak and terebinth. Isaiah associated the oak and the terebinth not only with apostasy but also with restoration. Both kinds of trees are robust and cannot be destroyed merely by chopping them down, for the remaining stumps will regenerate the tree by sending forth new shoots. "And the Lord have removed men far away, and there be a great forsaking in the midst of the land. But yet in it shall be a tenth, and it shall return, and shall be eaten: as a teil tree, and as an oak, whose substance is in them, when they cast their leaves: so the holy seed shall be the substance thereof" (Isaiah 6:12–13).

Accordingly, Isaiah taught that a part of Israel would return like the oak and terebinth, which, though they are eaten or consumed *(hayetah lebaer)* right to their substance or stumps *(matzebeth),* yet they possess a seed in them that can regenerate (see Isaiah 6:13). Isaiah also indicated that the regenerated branch would be both beautiful and fruitful (see Isaiah 4:2).

Revegetation. Isaiah likened the restoration to a revegetation of lands that were left barren and dry. He promised that in the formerly desolate wilderness or desert, the Lord would plant such valuable trees as the cedar, the *shittah (Acacia sp.),* the myrtle *(Myrtus communis),* the oil, or olive *(Olea europaea),* the fir, or Aleppo pine *(Pinus halepensis),*[43] the box *(Buxus longifolia),* and other pine species *(Pinus sp.).* "I will open rivers in high places, and fountains in the midst of the valleys: I will make the wilderness a pool of water, and the dry land springs of water. I will plant in the wilderness the cedar, the shittah tree, and the myrtle, and the oil tree; I will set in the desert the fir tree, and the pine, and the box tree together" (Isaiah 41:18–19; see also 60:13).

These trees, restored to the wilderness, typified the restoration of God's people to their promised land. Through Isaiah, the Lord promised he would aid the revegetation/restoration of Jacob by pouring "water upon him that is thirsty," "floods upon the dry ground," even his "spirit upon thy seed," so that they would "spring up as among the grass, as willows by the water courses" (Isaiah 44:2–4). As a result, water-loving plants—those that thrive on the blessings of Jehovah—such as willows *(Salix sp.),* reeds *(Arundo donax* or *Cyperus papyrus),* and rushes *(Juncus sp.* or *Scirpus sp.),* would flourish (see Isaiah 35:7; 55:10; 61:11). Eventually, restored

Jacob would "blossom as the rose," *chabatzaleh,* which likely means some showy native flower such as the narcissus *(Narcissus tazetta)* or crocus *(Crocus sp.)* (Isaiah 35:1).

Not only would all this new vegetation grow but it would replace the old, undesirable vegetation—sinners and apostates: "Instead of the thorn shall come up the fir tree, and instead of the brier shall come up the myrtle tree: and it shall be to the Lord for a name, for an everlasting sign that shall not be cut off" (Isaiah 55:13; see also 9:10). Eventually, this restored people would again produce and enjoy good fruit as a covenant people nurtured by Jehovah should. "And the remnant that is escaped of the house of Judah shall again take root downward, and bear fruit upward" (Isaiah 37:31; see also 3:10; 27:6; 37:30; 55:10; 62:8; 65:21).

Isaiah prophesied that during this time mankind's values would be changed, causing the people to esteem fruitful fields as they had formerly valued their apostate forests (see Isaiah 29:17; 32:15). In fact, even such proud trees as the cedar and the fir would rejoice at the fall of the king of Babylon (Isaiah 14:8) and applaud the redemption of Israel (see Isaiah 44:23; 55:12).

THE MESSIAH

Isaiah used imagery from the plant kingdom to describe the Messiah. He taught that the Messiah would be a descendant or "stem of Jesse" (Isaiah 11:1; see also D&C 113:1). He taught of the mortal Messiah's humble beginnings as "a tender plant, and as a root out of a dry ground" (Isaiah 53:2). He prophesied that although Jesus Christ would bring forth judgment and truth, he would not condemn the feeble or afflicted. He would not break even a "bruised reed" nor extinguish a dimly burning flaxen wick (Isaiah 42:3).[44]

CONCLUSION

Isaiah used imagery from the plant world to teach Israel and their neighbors about their relationship to God, their need for repentance, their future according to God's plan, and the mission and message of their Messiah. Through careful study of the plants Isaiah knew and the metaphors he used, we can gain a better understanding of this marvelous prophet and his message. It is a message so important that Christ specifically pleaded with us to search the words of Isaiah (see 3 Nephi 23:1).

TABLE 1

PLANT IMAGERY IN ISAIAH[45]

General Plants and Plant Parts

Trees, Forests, Woods, Thickets. 7:2; 9:18; 10:15, 18, 19, 34; 21:13; 29:17; 30:33; 32:15, 19; 37:19, 24; 40:20; 44:14, 19, 23; 45:20; 55:12; 56:3, 9; 57:5; 60:17; 65:22

Branch, Bough, Rod, Stem, Sprout. 4:2; 9:14; 10:33; 11:1; 14:19; 16:8; 17:6, 9; 18:5; 19:15; 25:5; 27:10, 11; 60:21

Plant, Herbs. 5:7; 16:8; 17:10; 18:4; 26:19; 37:27; 42:15; 53:2; 66:14

Grass, Hay, Chaff, Stubble. 5:24; 15:6; 17:13; 29:5; 33:11; 37:27; 40:7, 8, 24; 41:2, 15; 44:4; 47:14; 51:12

Fruit. 3:10; 4:2; 10:12; 13:18; 14:29; 16:9; 27:6, 9; 28:4; 37:30, 31; 65:21

Root, Take Root. 5:24; 11:1, 10; 14:29, 30; 27:6; 37:31; 40:24; 53:2

Leaf. 1:30; 34:4; 64:6

Seed.[46] 5:10; 6:13; 17:11; 30:23; 44:3; 55:10

Bud, Blossom, Flower. 5:24; 18:5; 27:6; 28:1, 4; 40:6, 7, 8; 55:10; 61:11

Specific Plants

Thorns, Thistles, Briars, Nettles. 5:6; 7:19, 23, 24, 25; 9:18; 10:17; 27:4; 32:13; 33:12; 34:13; 55:13

Reeds, Rushes, Flags, Bulrushes. 9:14; 19:6, 7, 15; 35:7; 36:6; 42:3; 58:5

Grapes, Vines, Vineyards. 1:8; 3:14; 5:1, 2, 3, 4, 5, 7, 10; 7:23; 16:8, 9, 10; 17:6; 18:5; 24:7, 13; 27:2; 32:12; 34:4; 36:16, 17; 37:30; 65:21

Other Forbs (showy, flowering herbs). Cucumber: 1:8; *Rose:* 35:1;[47] *Cumin:* 28:25, 27; *Fitches:* 28:25, 27;[48] *Flax, Linen:* 3:23; 19:9; 42:3

Wheat, Corn, Barley, Rye.[49] 17:5; 21:10; 28:25, 28; 36:17; 37:27; 47:2; 55:10

Trees and Shrubs. Cedars: 2:13; 9:10; 14:8; 37:24; 41:19; 44:14; *Oaks, Terebinths, Groves:*[50] 1:29, 30; 2:13; 6:13; 17:8; 27:9; 44:14; *Olive:* 17:6; 24:13; *Myrtle:* 41:19; 55:13; *Fig:* 34:4; 36:16; 38:21; *Sycamore:*[51] 9:10; *Cypress:* 44:14;[52] *Shittim* or *Acacia:* 41:19; *Pine:* 41:19; 60:13; *Fir:*[53] 14:8; 41:19; 55:13; 60:13; *Willow:* 44:4; *Box:* 41:19; 60:13

NOTES

1. Michael Zohary, *Plants of the Bible* (Tel-Aviv: Sadan Publishing House Ltd., 1982), p. 54.
2. Harold N. Moldenke and Alma L. Moldenke, *Plants of the Bible* (Waltham, Mass.: Chronica Botanica Co., 1952), p. 243.
3. Moldenke and Moldenke, *Plants of the Bible,* p. 244.
4. Franz Delitzsch, *Biblical Commentary on the Prophecies of Isaiah* (Grand Rapids, Mich.: Eerdmans Publishing Co., 1965; originally published in Edinburgh by T&T Clark, 1890), 1:160–61.
5. John D. W. Watts, *Word Biblical Commentary* (Waco, Tex.: Word Books, 1985), 24:55.
6. The KJV translates the verb root *azaq* as *to fence,* possibly in an effort to explain the appearance of hedges and walls in Isaiah 5:5. It is commonly thought today that *azaq* means "to dig about or hoe." In this context it appears in its intensified Piel form, hence "to dig about carefully." See Francis Brown, *The New Brown-Driver-Briggs-Gesenius Hebrew and English Lexicon* (Christian Copyrights, 1983; originally published in New York by Houghton Mifflin, 1906), p. 740.
7. Delitzsch, *Commentary on the Prophecies of Isaiah,* 1:161; Watts, *Word Biblical Commentary,* 24:55.
8. F. Nigel Hepper, *Baker Encyclopedia of Biblical Plants* (London: Three's Co., 1992), p. 96.
9. Brown, *Hebrew and English Lexicon,* p. 92. Moldenke and Moldenke (*Plants of the Bible,* p. 239) suggest that *beushim* refers to the wild grape, *Vitis orientalis,* but the message of the metaphor is intensified if it is not a new species of grape that has invaded the vineyard and thus produced bad fruit but rather the very vines that received all the attention from the good husbandman that yet still betrayed him by bringing forth stinking things.
10. Moldenke and Moldenke, *Plants of the Bible,* p. 152.
11. Zohary, *Plants of the Bible,* p. 91.
12. Moldenke and Moldenke, *Plants of the Bible,* pp. 152–53.
13. Moldenke and Moldenke, *Plants of the Bible,* p. 89; Zohary, *Plants of the Bible,* p. 88.
14. Hepper, *Baker Encyclopedia of Biblical Plants,* p. 85.
15. *Sorah,* the word translated as *principle* in the KJV, is enigmatic. The Modern Language Bible translates it as *rows* or *furrows,* as does Delitzsch (*Biblical Commentary on the Prophecies of Isaiah,* 2:15), probably reading *shurah* rather than *sorah*. Brown (*Hebrew and English Lexicon,* p. 965) suggests the word is either dittographical for barley, *seorah,* or refers to some unknown kind of cereal grain. In any case, the use of the verb *sam,* meaning "to put or place," suggests a careful sowing of the seeds.
16. Moldenke and Moldenke, *Plants of the Bible,* p. 112.
17. Hepper, *Baker Encyclopedia of Biblical Plants,* p. 86.
18. The wheat referred to here, *cusemeth,* is not our modern spelt, or *Triticum spelta* (see Hepper, *Baker Encyclopedia of Biblical Plants,* p. 86), but probably some other wheat that does not easily yield naked grains upon threshing.

Such grains are generically called spelts and include the Einkorn *(T. monococcum)* and Emmer *(T. dicoccon)* varieties.

19. Victor L. Ludlow, *Isaiah: Prophet, Seer, and Poet* (Salt Lake City: Deseret Book Co., 1982), p. 266.
20. Some translators interpret the Hebrew word that begins this phrase as an interrogative rather than the definite article, in which case the meaning would be "Are trees men that they should be besieged?"
21. Zohary, *Plants of the Bible,* pp. 153–67.
22. Isaiah referred to thorny plants by such generic terms as *shamir, shayith,* and *kotz*. These are probably loose collective terms and, as in our own language, can be used to refer to different varieties. For a discussion of the problem, see Zohary, *Plants of the Bible,* p. 153.
23. Ludlow, *Isaiah,* p. 163.
24. It has been suggested that the use of briars and thorns in contrast to forests in this metaphor illustrates not the destruction of the high and the low nor the useful and the useless of the proud but rather first the destruction of individual sinners—briars and thorns—followed by the nation as a whole—the forest. See Delitzsch, *Biblical Commentary on the Prophecies of Isaiah,* 1:261.
25. Moldenke and Moldenke, *Plants of the Bible,* p. 68.
26. Moldenke and Moldenke, *Plants of the Bible,* p. 68.
27. Zohary, *Plants of the Bible,* p. 104.
28. Moldenke and Moldenke, *Plants of the Bible,* p. 197.
29. Hepper, *Baker Encyclopedia of Bible Plants,* pp. 166–67.
30. Kirsten Nielsen, "There Is Hope for a Tree: The Tree as Metaphor in Isaiah," *Journal for the Study of the Old Testament,* supp. ser. 65 (1989): 79–80.
31. Nielsen, "There Is Hope for a Tree," p. 80. The word frequently translated as *grove* or *green tree* in the KJV is *asherah,* which also happens to be the name of an important female fertility deity in the Canaanite pantheon. Edifices dedicated to her apparently consisted of a treelike pole or living trees.
32. Zohary (*Plants of the Bible,* pp. 108–10) suggests that the words interchangeably translated in the KJV as *oak* and *terebinth—allon, elon, elah,* and *alah*—share the same root as the Hebrew word for god, *el.* Zohary is convinced that *allon* and *elon* should be translated as *oak,* whereas *elah* and *alah* should be translated as *terebinth*. For a contrasting opinion, see under the entries for *ayil, alah, allon* in Brown, *Hebrew and English Lexicon,* pp. 18, 47. See also Moldenke and Moldenke, *Plants of the Bible,* pp. 195–99.
33. Moldenke and Moldenke, *Plants of the Bible,* p. 178.
34. Hepper, *Baker Encyclopedia of Bible Plants,* p. 90.
35. Hepper, *Baker Encyclopedia of Bible Plants,* p. 43.
36. Zohary, *Plants of the Bible,* p. 163.
37. Zohary, *Plants of the Bible,* p. 163.
38. Nogah Hareuveni and Helen Frenkley, *Ecology in the Bible* (Kiryat Ono, Israel: Neot Kedumim Ltd., 1974), p. 18.
39. Hareuveni and Frenkley, *Ecology in the Bible,* p. 18.
40. Delitzsch, *Biblical Commentary on the Prophecies of Isaiah,* 1:352–53. Ludlow (*Isaiah,* p. 208) sees this passage as referring to a special pruning away of

the wicked rather than an annihilation of the vineyard. He suggests that the pruning serves to strengthen and make room for the good vines that remain—a thought that makes excellent sense in the context of the rest of the chapter.

41. Ludlow, *Isaiah,* p. 75.
42. Hepper, *Baker Encyclopedia of Bible Plants,* p. 107.
43. Moldenke and Moldenke, *Plants of the Bible,* p. 176. The identity of this tree, *berosh,* translated in the KJV as *fir tree* is uncertain. Many feel the Aleppo pine is a good candidate, but the cypress *Cupressus sempervirens* is also likely.
44. Monte S. Nyman, *Great Are the Words of Isaiah* (Salt Lake City: Bookcraft, 1980), p. 156.
45. This table does not generally include metaphorical uses of plant products such as wine, strong drink, oil, and incense. For additional information, see "Flora," in *Anchor Bible Dictionary,* ed. David Noel Freedman (New York: Doubleday, 1992), pp. 803–17.
46. The Hebrew word for seed, *zera,* also means offspring. Only those references that clearly refer to plant seeds are included in this list.
47. The Hebrew word *chabatzaleth,* translated as *rose,* most likely refers to some showy native flower such as crocus or narcissus.
48. The Hebrew word *qetsach,* translated as *fitches,* most likely refers to nutmeg flower.
49. See note 18. *Dagan,* the word most commonly translated *corn,* refers to the kernels of a cereal grain, not the New World maize.
50. See note 32. It is generally believed that the groves used for idolatry were either oaks or terebinths or both.
51. Probably the sycamore fig, or *Ficus sycomorus.*
52. The Hebrew word *tirtzah,* translated as *cypress,* probably refers to a native tree such as the plane tree or the Holm tree.
53. See note 43.

CHAPTER THREE

MELCHIZEDEK: SEEKING AFTER THE ZION OF ENOCH

FRANK F. JUDD, JR.

The shadowy figure of Melchizedek entices the student of the scriptures. Next to Enoch, Melchizedek is perhaps the most enigmatic figure in the Bible. His life and mission are covered in only a few brief verses in the Bible, yet of all God's holy high priests, "none were greater" (Alma 13:19). What made Melchizedek such a great high priest? The debates are endless about the few verses in Genesis that speak of him. Many scholars come to erroneous conclusions about Melchizedek, king of Salem. For example, some believe that Melchizedek worshipped not Jehovah but a different god named *El Elyon* or *Most High God*.[1] This and other false conclusions result from a lack of adequate sources and information.

Latter-day Saints, however, are blessed with scriptural insights provided through the Prophet Joseph Smith. For instance, in the Book of Mormon, Alma the Younger delivered a masterful discourse devoted in part to the life and ministry of Melchizedek. Several sections of the Doctrine and Covenants discuss important biographical facts relating to Melchizedek. The Joseph Smith Translation of the Bible (JST) restores valuable knowledge not found in the Old and the New Testament concerning the role of the priesthood in Melchizedek's life. Modern prophets also supply pertinent doctrines relative to Melchizedek and the priesthood. As we study the Bible in light of these Restoration scriptures, a significant pattern emerges. Just as we seek to emulate our Savior by following the examples of righteous leaders today, those who lived anciently also sought to emulate their promised Messiah by following the patterns set by their righteous predecessors and peers. It is possible that Melchizedek used the pattern set by Enoch and his people as a pattern for seeking after the

□ □ □ □ □

Frank F. Judd, Jr., is an instructor in ancient scripture at Brigham Young University.

Lord and establishing a Zion society. On that subject, Elder Bruce R. McConkie said: "Enoch built Zion, a City of Holiness, and Melchizedek, reigning as king and ministering as priest of the Most High God, sought to make Jerusalem [Salem], his capital city, into another Zion. As we have seen, Melchizedek himself was called by his people the Prince of peace, the King of peace, and the King of heaven, for Jerusalem [Salem] had become a heaven to them."[2]

Joseph Smith's translation of Genesis states that Melchizedek was ordained after the same order of the priesthood as Enoch and that "every one being ordained after this order" (JST Genesis 14:30) had the power to do the things that Enoch did (see JST Genesis 14:27). Thus, Elder McConkie observed, "Abraham, Isaac, and Jacob sought an inheritance in the City of Zion, as had all the righteous saints from Enoch to Melchizedek."[3] As Melchizedek and his people "sought for the city of Enoch which God had before taken" (JST Genesis 14:34), Melchizedek was privileged to lead a life remarkably similar to Enoch's. Both of these great men held the same priesthood authority, performed similar miracles, received the same temple blessings, established Zion communities, and were, along with their people, eventually translated and taken up to heaven.

THE ORDER OF THE PRIESTHOOD

Melchizedek and Enoch were both ordained after the order of the greater priesthood. In addition, Melchizedek and his priesthood authority have a closer tie to Enoch than may be seen at first glance. The Doctrine and Covenants states that "Abraham received the priesthood *from Melchizedek,* who received it through the lineage of his fathers, even till Noah; And from Noah *till Enoch,* through the lineage of their fathers" (D&C 84:14–15; italics added). This greater priesthood was originally called *"the Holy Priesthood, after the Order of the Son of God"* (D&C 107:3; italics in original). To avoid disrespect for the Lord by too frequent repetition of his holy name, this priesthood, in the days of the king of Salem, was "called the Melchizedek Priesthood . . . because Melchizedek was such a great high priest" (D&C 107:2; see also v. 4).

But that is not the only time the Lord has called this order of the priesthood after a mortal high priest. Melchizedek "was ordained an high priest after the order of the covenant which God made with Enoch" (JST Genesis 14:27). According to the Doctrine and Covenants, the high priesthood was called "after the order of Melchizedek, which was after the order of Enoch, which was after the order of the Only Begotten Son" (D&C 76:57). This high priesthood provides the means whereby the righteous may "commune with the general assembly and church of the Firstborn" (D&C 107:19). More specifically, those who receive and keep sacred covenants relating to the priesthood of Melchizedek become part of "the general assembly and church of Enoch, and of the Firstborn" (D&C 76:67). Thus, the king of Salem and the greater priesthood, which currently bears his name, have a very close connection with Enoch that may go unnoticed.

POWER FROM ON HIGH

The higher priesthood gave Melchizedek the power to perform many of the same types of miracles Enoch had performed. The Lord, in promising this power to Enoch, had said, "the mountains shall flee before you, and the rivers shall turn from their course" (Moses 6:34). Consequently, Enoch became a mighty man of miracles. According to the restored scriptural account, he "spake the word of the Lord, and the earth trembled, and the mountains fled, even according to his command; and the rivers of water were turned out of their course; and the roar of the lions was heard out of the wilderness; and all nations feared greatly, so powerful was the word of Enoch, and so great was the power of the language which God had given him" (Moses 7:13).

The Lord had previously made a covenant with Enoch that not only he but "every one" (JST Genesis 14:30) who received the greater priesthood would have power—if he was faithful—to perform miracles, namely, "to break mountains, to divide the seas, to dry up waters, to turn them out of their course; to put at defiance the armies of nations, to divide the earth, to break every band, to stand in the presence of God; to do all things according to his will, according to his command, subdue principalities and powers; and this by the will of the Son of God which was from before the foundation of the world" (JST Genesis 14:30–31).

When Melchizedek was but a child, he "stopped the mouths of lions, and quenched the violence of fire" (JST Genesis 14:26). Moreover, because "Melchizedek was a priest of this order" (v. 33), meaning the order of Enoch, he had the ability to perform the same types of miraculous deeds Enoch had while Melchizedek and his people "sought for the city of Enoch" (v. 34).

LIFE AND MINISTRY OF PEACE

The lives and ministries of Melchizedek and Enoch were very

similar. Enoch's mortal father, Jared, taught him "in all the ways of God" (Moses 6:21; see also v. 41). The principle of faith was an important concept that Jared, a preacher of righteousness, taught his son (see Moses 6:23). The scriptures say that "so great was the faith of Enoch that he led the people of God" (Moses 7:13). As their leader, Enoch was able to establish peace among his people. First, he preached repentance. The Lord had specifically told Enoch to "prophesy unto this people, and say unto them—Repent" (Moses 6:27; see also 7:10). So Enoch did. He exhorted the people to change their ways and come unto the Lord (see Moses 6:37; 7:12). A few people hearkened, and they created a small righteous society under the peaceful leadership of Enoch. As Elder Ezra Taft Benson observed: "Small numbers do not insure peace; only righteousness does. . . . the whole city of Enoch was peaceful; and it was taken into heaven because it was made up of righteous people."[4]

The second means whereby Enoch established peace was righteous military defense. Because of Enoch's faithfulness, "he led the people of God, and their enemies came to battle against them; and he spake the word of the Lord, . . . and all nations feared greatly, so powerful was the word of Enoch, and so great was the power of the language which God had given him. There also came up a land out of the depth of the sea, and so great was the fear of the enemies of the people of God, that they fled and stood afar off and went upon the land which came up out of the depth of the sea. And the giants of the land, also, stood afar off; and there went forth a curse upon all people that fought against God; And from that time forth there were wars and bloodshed among them; but the Lord came and dwelt with his people, and they dwelt in righteousness" (Moses 7:13–16).

As recorded in the book of Revelation, John the Revelator saw an individual on a white horse who "went forth conquering, and to conquer" (Revelation 6:2). Elder Bruce R. McConkie said that at least some of these military experiences belong to Enoch: "Excluding, as we necessarily must, the events surrounding the creation and the fall, it is clear that the most transcendent happenings involved Enoch and his ministry. And it is interesting to note that what John saw [in the book of Revelation] was not the establishment of Zion and its removal to heavenly spheres, *but the unparalleled wars in which Enoch, as a general over the armies of the saints, 'went forth conquering and to conquer.' . . . Truly, never was there a ministry such as Enoch's, and never a conqueror and general who was his equal!* How appropriate that he should ride the white horse of victory in John's apocalyptic vision!"[5]

Elder Mark E. Petersen also taught that Enoch "fought off enemies."[6] Therefore, it seems that Enoch, with the help of the Lord, established peace among his people by means of preaching repentance and by defeating the enemies of God in battle, that they might "dwell in safety forever" (Moses 7:20).

Melchizedek's ministry was strikingly parallel to Enoch's. Alma said that Melchizedek, as king of Salem, "did reign under his father" (Alma 13:18). It is probable that Melchizedek's father also taught him to have faith in the Lord. This righteous parental instruction possibly assisted Melchizedek in gaining approval from God even as a young child (see JST Genesis 14:26–27), because, like all of us, Melchizedek needed to learn obedience to the commandments of God. Paul said that "though he were a Son, yet learned he obedience by the things which he suffered" (Hebrews 5:8). A note on the manuscript of Joseph Smith's translation of this verse makes clear that this is a reference to Melchizedek (see Hebrews 5:7*a*). Both the Book of Mormon and Joseph Smith's translation of Genesis state that Melchizedek was a man of great faith (see JST Genesis 14:26; Alma 13:18). According to Alma, Melchizedek used this faith to bring about peace among his people and in his land.

Just as Enoch had done, Melchizedek established peace among his people in two ways. First, because the people of the land of Salem were terribly wicked, Melchizedek went on the spiritual offensive. "Melchizedek was a king over the land of Salem; and his people had waxed strong in iniquity and abomination; yea, they had all gone astray; they were full of all manner of wickedness; But Melchizedek having exercised mighty faith, and received the office of the high priesthood according to the holy order of God, did preach repentance unto his people" (Alma 13:17–18).

This preaching affected the people of Salem as it had the people of Enoch—they repented of their evil ways and humbled themselves before the Lord (see Alma 13:14, 18). Thus, in this way "Melchizedek did establish peace in the land in his days; therefore he was called the prince of peace" (Alma 13:18).

The other method by which Melchizedek established peace was defending his people, just as Enoch had done. The Lord's covenant with Enoch—that "every one" ordained after this order of the priesthood would be able "to put at defiance the armies of nations . . . [and to] subdue principalities and powers" (JST Genesis 14:30–31)—

applied to Melchizedek. The apostle Paul, who sometimes quoted records that were available to him but lost until the restoration of the gospel through the Prophet Joseph Smith, spoke of biblical prophets "who through faith subdued kingdoms, wrought righteousness, obtained promises, stopped the mouths of lions, quenched the violence of fire, escaped the edge of the sword, out of weakness were made strong, waxed valiant in fight, [and] turned to flight the armies of the aliens" (Hebrews 11:33–34). Elder McConkie said of these verses, "This language is, of course, a paraphrase, a quotation, and a summary of what Genesis once contained relative to Melchizedek, which makes it perfectly clear that the Melchizedek material was still in Genesis when Paul wrote to his Hebrew brethren."[7] It seems evident that the life and ministry of Melchizedek were very similar to those of Enoch. Both of these prophets were able to establish peace by means of preaching repentance and by means of righteous military defense.

TEMPLE BLESSINGS IN ZION

The scriptures indicate that Melchizedek and Enoch received temple blessings during the process of establishing Zion. When Enoch climbed Mount Simeon, he was "clothed upon with glory" (Moses 7:3) and was privileged to see and converse with the Lord, face to face (see Moses 7:4). Following that sacred experience in the presence of God, Enoch and the people of God "were blessed upon the mountains, and upon the high places, and did flourish" (Moses 7:17). In the ancient world, mountains were associated with sacred space, specifically with temple experiences.[8] President Brigham Young believed that there were temples in the city of Enoch. He said, "I will not say but what Enoch had Temples and officiated therein, but we have no account of it."[9] Similarly, concerning the possibility of temples in the city of Enoch, Elder Franklin D. Richards said, "I expect that in the city of Enoch there are temples; and when Enoch and his people come back, they will come back with their city, their temples, blessings and powers."[10] Initially, only Enoch walked before God, but eventually "Enoch and all his people walked with God, and he dwelt in the midst of Zion" (Moses 7:69). President Ezra Taft Benson said of the temple experiences of Enoch and his people: "Adam and his descendants entered into the priesthood order of God. Today we would say they went to the House of the Lord and received their blessings.

"The order of priesthood spoken of in the scriptures is sometimes referred to as the patriarchal order because it came down from father to son.

"But this order is otherwise described in modern revelation as an order of family government where a man and woman enter into a covenant with God—just as did Adam and Eve—to be sealed for eternity, to have posterity, and to do the will and work of God throughout their mortality.

"If a couple are true to their covenants, they are entitled to the blessings of the highest degree of the celestial kingdom. These covenants today can only be entered into by going to the House of the Lord.

"Adam followed this order and brought his posterity into the presence of God. He is the greatest example for us to follow.

"Enoch followed this pattern and brought the Saints of his day into the presence of God."[11]

This evidence indicates that Enoch and his Zion society did indeed enjoy temple blessings, such that the Son of God revealed himself and thereby dwelt with his people in Zion.

As Melchizedek and his people established their city of Zion, it seems that they, too, enjoyed temple blessings. Josephus, a Jewish historian who lived in the first century after Christ, knew of a tradition that Melchizedek, not Solomon, was the first person to build a temple of the Lord in Palestine. "Its [Salem's] original founder was a Canaanite chief, called in the native tongue 'Righteous King' [or Melchizedek]; for such indeed he was. In virtue thereof he was the first to officiate as priest of God and, being the first to build the temple, gave the city, previously called Solyma [or Salem], the name of Jerusalem."[12]

There are also modern references to Melchizedek and temple blessings. From Joseph Smith's translation of Genesis, it seems that Melchizedek received his priesthood blessings when he was "ordained an high priest after the order of the covenant which God made with Enoch, it being after the order of the Son of God; which order came, not by man, nor the will of man; neither by father nor mother; neither by beginning of days nor end of years; but of God" (JST Genesis 14:27–28; emphasis added).

But what does entering into this order of the priesthood have to do with receiving temple blessings? President Ezra Taft Benson explained what it means to enter into the order of the Son of God: "Adam and his posterity were commanded by God to be baptized, to receive the Holy Ghost, and to enter into the order of the Son of God.

"To enter into the order of the Son of God is the equivalent today of entering into the fullness of the Melchizedek Priesthood, which is only received in the house of the Lord.

"Because Adam and Eve had complied with these requirements, God said to them, 'Thou art after the order of him who was without beginning of days or end of years, from all eternity to all eternity' " (Moses 6:67).[13]

This order of the priesthood authorized Melchizedek "to stand in the presence of God" (JST Genesis 14:31). According to the Doctrine and Covenants, that is the reason temples are built, namely, "that the Son of Man might have a place to manifest himself to his people" (D&C 109:5). Therefore, it seems that the society of Melchizedek, like the society of Enoch, enjoyed priesthood blessings similar to those we enjoy today in the temple of the Lord.

THE TRANSLATION OF ZION INTO HEAVEN

The last point of similarity between the lives of Melchizedek and Enoch is their establishment of their Zion community and eventual translation into heaven. One scriptural definition of Zion is "THE PURE IN HEART" (D&C 97:21). Most of our information about Zion societies comes from the scriptures that describe the experience of Enoch and his people. The society of Enoch was called Zion "because they were of one heart and one mind, and dwelt in righteousness; and there was no poor among them" (Moses 7:18).

But Zion is not only righteous people; Zion is also a place. As Enoch and his people continued in righteousness, they "built a city that was called the City of Holiness, even ZION" (Moses 7:19). Stephen E. Robinson has commented on the use of the term *Zion* to designate a people and a place: "Zion is wherever the pure in heart dwell. . . . Zion is a spiritual category, which may in different contexts mean Salt Lake City, Far West, Jerusalem, or the city of Enoch."[14] After the Lord came and dwelt with his Zion people in the city of Zion, they, "in process of time, [were] taken up into heaven" (Moses 7:21), that is, they were translated (see Moses 7:23). Later, the scripture states, "Zion was not, for God received it up into his own bosom; and from thence went forth the saying, ZION IS FLED" (Moses 7:69). Therefore, after Enoch established a community that was pure in heart and dwelt with the Lord on earth, the entire society, including the people and the city itself, was received up into heaven.

Enoch's people were not the only ones who were granted such a sacred privilege. The scriptures state that after Enoch was translated, "the Holy Ghost fell on many, and they were caught up by the powers of heaven into Zion" (Moses 7:27). In other words, those who achieved purity in their hearts were received into the city of Enoch to enjoy fellowship with those righteous people. Elder Bruce R. McConkie said that "righteous men, after the flood, not only sought an inheritance in Enoch's Zion, but also began the process of building their own City of Holiness in earth."[15] Melchizedek and his people were among those righteous people who actively "sought for the city of Enoch which God had before taken, separating it from the earth" (JST Genesis 14:34). As Melchizedek did so, and because of priesthood power and mighty faith, he performed miracles, preached righteousness, and established Zion, as Enoch had done before him.

In the Zion society of Melchizedek, the storehouse was not to provide for him but "for the poor" (JST Genesis 14:38). By that means they were able to live as had the people of Enoch, who had "no poor among them" (Moses 7:18). Melchizedek and his people were blessed greatly for their diligence and righteousness, for they "obtained heaven" (JST Genesis 14:34). Elder McConkie declared: "That this process of translating the righteous saints and taking them to heaven was still going on after the flood among the people of Melchizedek is apparent from the account in the Inspired Version of the Bible. . . . As far as we know, instances of translation since the day of Melchizedek and his people have been few and far between. After recording that Enoch was translated, Paul says that Abraham, Isaac, and Jacob, and their seed after them (they obviously knowing what had taken place as pertaining to the people of Melchizedek and others) 'looked for a city which hath foundations, whose builder and maker is God' (Heb. 11:5–10), that is, they 'sought for the city of Enoch which God had before taken' (*Inspired Version,* Gen. 14:34)."[16]

Elder John Taylor interpreted those verses in the same manner: "The fact of Enoch's translation was generally known by the people who lived immediately after the flood. It had occurred so short a time before, that it was almost a matter of personal recollection with the sons of Noah. They must also have been acquainted with the fact that others were caught up by the power of heaven into Zion, and it would appear strongly probable that Melchizedec and many of his people were also translated. Revelation does not state this in so many words, but the inference to be drawn from what is said, points clearly in that direction."[17]

The apostle Paul, once again using biblical sources we did not have until the restoration of the gospel, said that Melchizedek "offered up prayers and supplications with strong crying and tears unto him [God] that was able to save him [Melchizedek] from death, and was heard" (Hebrews 5:7). The manuscript of the Joseph Smith Translation makes note that this verse indeed refers to Melchizedek (see Hebrews 5:7*a*). The statement "to save him from death" could refer to salvation from spiritual death by means of the Atonement or to salvation from physical death by means of translation. I believe that Paul had both interpretations in mind. Melchizedek and his people wanted to enjoy the same blessings Enoch's society had received. As a result, Melchizedek sought after the Zion of Enoch, and eventually Melchizedek and his society were also translated and received into the heavenly Zion.

ENOCH AND MELCHIZEDEK ARE TYPES OF CHRIST

Melchizedek followed the pattern of righteous living set by his noble ancestor Enoch. The scriptures indicate that Melchizedek and his people sought after the Zion of Enoch and actually achieved it. It is significant that much of the information about the ministries of Melchizedek and Enoch was among the plain and precious parts taken from the scriptures (see 1 Nephi 13:23–29). Concerning these parts of the Bible, the Lord said to Moses, "And in a day when the children of men shall esteem my words as naught and take many of them from the book which thou shalt write, behold, I will raise up another like unto thee; and they shall be had again among the children of men—among as many as shall believe" (Moses 1:41). This man "like unto [Moses]" was the Prophet Joseph Smith,[18] who brought forth the restoration of these words through the Book of Mormon, the Doctrine and Covenants, the Pearl of Great Price, and his inspired revision of the Bible.

The Prophet Joseph Smith said, "The building up of Zion is a cause that has interested the people of God in every age; it is a theme upon which prophets, priests and kings have dwelt with peculiar delight."[19] Elder McConkie taught that establishing Zion is a goal for which many righteous people have sought: "Abraham, Isaac, and Jacob sought an inheritance in the City of Zion, as had all the righteous saints from Enoch to Melchizedek—an inheritance which would have been but prelude to gaining exaltation in the Celestial Zion where God and Christ are the judge of all. Since it is no longer the general order for the saints to be translated—their labors in the next sphere now being to preach the gospel to the spirits in prison, rather than to act as ministering servants in other fields—today's saints seek a heavenly country and a celestial city in the sense of striving for an inheritance in the Celestial City of exalted beings."[20]

The Prophet Joseph Smith also directly applied this principle to us when he taught that "we ought to have the building up of Zion as our greatest object."[21] Elder Orson Pratt summarized one of the reasons: "The Latter-Day Zion will resemble, in most particulars, the Zion of Enoch: it will be established upon the same celestial laws—be built upon the same gospel, and be guided by continued revelation. Its inhabitants, like those of the antediluvian Zion, will be the righteous gathered out from all nations: the glory of God will be seen upon it; and His power will be manifested there, even as in the Zion of old. All the blessings and grand characteristics which were exhibited in ancient Zion will be shown forth in the Latter-Day Zion."[22]

As the Prophet Joseph said, it is important for us to do as the ancient patriarchs did. Brigham Young taught the Saints: "If we obtain the glory that Abraham obtained, we must do so by the same means that he did. If we are ever prepared to enjoy the society of Enoch, Noah, Melchizedek, Abraham, Isaac, and Jacob, or of their faithful children, and of the faithful Prophets and Apostles, we must pass through the same experience, and gain the knowledge, intelligence, and endowments that will prepare us to enter into the celestial kingdom of our Father and God."[23]

We also must strive to build up Zion, as they did. Revelation through modern prophets teaches us how the ancient Saints sought after and obtained Zion. If we pattern our lives after theirs, just as Melchizedek did with Enoch's, we too can reach the same goals. If we are to go where the prophets are going, we must follow their righteous examples.

During one of his sermons of which we have record, Enoch wrote that the Lord said, "And behold, all things have their likeness, and all things are created and made to bear record of me, both things which are temporal, and things which are spiritual; . . . all things bear record of me" (Moses 6:63). Similarly, Nephi said that "all things which have been given of God from the beginning of the world, unto man, are the typifying of [Christ]" (2 Nephi 11:4). It seems that not only things but also people are types of the true Messiah. Elder McConkie taught that all prophets are types of Christ: "All the ancient prophets and all righteous men who preceded our Lord in birth were, in one sense or another, patterns for him. . . . many of them lived in special situations or did particular things that singled them out as types and patterns and shadows of that which was to be in the life of him who is our Lord."[24]

Both of the great patriarchs Enoch and Melchizedek were thus types of the coming Savior. Elder John Taylor taught: "There is yet another source from which the ancients obtained their ideas of the life and mission of the Son of God. It is to be found in the translation of Enoch and his city."[25] In addition, the apostle Paul referred to the Lord Himself as coming "after the similitude of Melchisedec" (Hebrews 7:15).

All of the similarities we have identified between Enoch and Melchizedek are important aspects of the mission of Jesus Christ. Enoch and Melchizedek were ordained after the same order of the priesthood, and they were types of the Savior who, as Paul wrote, was the "High Priest of our profession" (Hebrews 3:1). As the great patriarchs Enoch and Melchizedek were great miracle workers, so the true and living Miracle Worker was the One of whom King Benjamin prophesied: "For behold, the time cometh, and is not far distant, that with power, the Lord Omnipotent who reigneth, who was, and is from all eternity to all eternity, shall come down from heaven among the children of men, and shall dwell in a tabernacle of clay, and shall go forth amongst men, working mighty miracles, such as healing the sick, raising the dead, causing the lame to walk, the blind to receive their sight, and the deaf to hear, and curing all manner of diseases. And he shall cast out devils, or the evil spirits which dwell in the hearts of the children of men" (Mosiah 3:5–6). Those two patriarchs even established peace in their respective societies, but the real "Prince of Peace" (Isaiah 9:6) gave unto us the ultimate peace that we, through him, might "overcome the world" (John 16:33; see also 14:27).

Lastly, Enoch and Melchizedek sought for and obtained Zion and were translated into heaven. But even they anticipated then, as we do now, that wonderful day when the Savior would come in power and glory and the righteous saints would be "caught up in the cloud to meet [the Lord], that we may ever be with the Lord" (D&C 109:75).

It is even more fitting that we follow those ancient patriarchs because they were types of Jesus Christ. Elder McConkie summarized our duty when he explained that all righteous saints "should be a type of Christ. Those who lived before he came were types and shadows and witnesses of his coming. Those who have lived since he came are witnesses of such coming and are types and shadows of what he was."[26] Truly there is no better example, for as our Perfect Master said, "Therefore, what manner of men ought ye to be? Verily I say unto you, even as I am" (3 Nephi 27:27).

NOTES

1. For different views of Melchizedek, see Michael C. Astour, "Melchizedek," in *Anchor Bible Dictionary,* ed. David Noel Freedman (New York: Doubleday, 1992), 4:684–86.
2. Bruce R. McConkie, *The Mortal Messiah: From Bethlehem to Calvary* (Salt Lake City: Deseret Book Co., 1979), 1:86.
3. Bruce R. McConkie, *Doctrinal New Testament Commentary* (Salt Lake City: Bookcraft, 1973), 3:205.
4. Ezra Taft Benson, in Conference Report, Apr. 1969, p. 12.
5. McConkie, *Doctrinal New Testament Commentary,* 3:477–78; emphasis added.
6. Mark E. Petersen, *Noah and the Flood* (Salt Lake City: Deseret Book Co., 1982), p. 24.
7. McConkie, *Mortal Messiah,* 1:271.
8. John M. Lundquist, "The Common Temple Ideology of the Ancient Near East," in *The Temple in Antiquity,* ed. Truman G. Madsen (Provo, Utah: BYU Religious Studies Center, 1984), pp. 56, 59–60.
9. Brigham Young, in *Journal of Discourses* (London: Latter-day Saints' Book Depot, 1854–86), 18:303.
10. Franklin D. Richards, in *Journal of Discourses,* 25:237.
11. Ezra Taft Benson, "What I Hope You Will Teach Your Children about the Temple," *Ensign,* Aug. 1985, p. 9.
12. Josephus, *The Jewish War* 6.10.1, trans. H. St. J. Thackeray (London: Cambridge University Press, 1928), 3:501, 503.
13. Benson, "What I Hope You Will Teach Your Children about the Temple," p. 8.
14. Stephen E. Robinson, "Early Christianity and 1 Nephi 13–14," *The Book of Mormon: First Nephi, The Doctrinal Foundation* (Provo, Utah: BYU Religious Studies Center, 1988), p. 183.
15. McConkie, *Mortal Messiah,* 1:85.
16. McConkie, *Doctrinal New Testament Commentary,* 3:202–3.
17. John Taylor, *The Mediation and Atonement* (Salt Lake City, 1882; reprint, 1975), p. 203.
18. Young, in *Journal of Discourses,* 7:289–90.
19. Joseph Smith, *Teachings of the Prophet Joseph Smith,* sel. Joseph Fielding Smith (Salt Lake City: Deseret Book Co., 1938), p. 231.
20. McConkie, *Doctrinal New Testament Commentary,* 3:205.
21. Smith, *Teachings of the Prophet Joseph Smith,* p. 160.
22. Orson Pratt, *The Seer,* May 1854, p. 265.
23. Brigham Young, in *Journal of Discourses,* 8:150.

24. Bruce R. McConkie, *The Promised Messiah: The First Coming of Christ* (Salt Lake City, Deseret Book Co., 1978), p. 448.
25. Taylor, *Mediation and Atonement,* p. 203.
26. McConkie, *Promised Messiah,* p. 451.

CHAPTER FOUR

THE LORD WILL REDEEM HIS PEOPLE: "ADOPTIVE" COVENANT AND REDEMPTION IN THE OLD TESTAMENT

JENNIFER CLARK LANE

In singing the hymn "Redeemer of Israel," I have always enjoyed the message of the Lord's sustaining and protecting power, but until recently, I had never asked myself, What does it mean that the Lord is the Redeemer of Israel? What does it mean to be a redeemer? Why is he the Redeemer of Israel? When and how did he become Israel's redeemer?

Likewise, biblical scholarship has not often addressed these questions. Some scholars have briefly noted a correlation between redemption and covenant, but questions such as why, when, and how the Lord became the Redeemer of Israel are not frequently asked. The Lord's characterization as redeemer is usually seen by scholars as a vague reference to his desire to help his people. More specific study of his role as redeemer is rarely made.

An examination of the text of the Old Testament, however, suggests that the Lord's acts of redemption involve far more than simply an exercise of strength for a people he loves. The role of a redeemer in ancient Israelite society carried with it specific responsibilities and a very specific relation to the person redeemed. To the Israelites, a redeemer was a close family member responsible for helping other family members who had lost their property, liberty, or lives by buying them out of their bondage or avenging them. The family relationship was the reason the redeemer acted on behalf of his enslaved kinsman.[1]

The Old Testament further indicates that those people for whom

□ □ □ □ □

Jennifer Clark Lane is a graduate student in ancient Near Eastern studies at Brigham Young University.

the Lord acts as redeemer likewise have established a familial relationship with him. Covenants in the Old Testament are repeatedly associated with the giving of a new name, which indicates a new character and a new relationship. Those covenants are the means by which individuals, or Israel as a people, are "adopted" into a new relationship and receive a new name. They become part of the family of the Lord and, as their kinsman, he becomes their redeemer. I refer to this idea of familial ties being created by covenant and expressed in the giving of a new name as "adoptive redemption."

As Latter-day Saints, we recognize that we are the spirit children of our Father in Heaven. Through our own sins, we separate ourselves from our Father and enslave ourselves spiritually. Christ, also known as Jehovah, the God of the Old Testament, can act as our intermediary to redeem us from spiritual bondage, if we make and keep covenants with him. When we covenant with Christ and take his name upon us, we become his "adopted" children and he becomes our spiritual Father. King Benjamin explained: "Because of the covenant which ye have made ye shall be called the children of Christ, his sons, and his daughters" (Mosiah 5:7). Thus, the Book of Mormon supports the Old Testament connection between the making of a covenant and the receiving of a new name, whereby the Lord allows people to enter into an "adoptive" relationship with him so that he can act as their redeemer. An overview of the use of *redemption, name,* and *covenant,* combined with an examination of critical biblical passages, demonstrates how the covenantal relationship between the Lord and his people binds the two parties together and permits the Lord to act as the Redeemer of Israel.

REDEMPTION IN THE OLD TESTAMENT: DEFINITIONS AND USAGE

In the Old Testament, two words, *ga'al* and *padah*, are usually translated as *redeem* in English. Both express the idea of "buy[ing] back" or "releas[ing] by the payment of a price"[2] and are often used interchangeably, illustrating the concept of salvation through a commercial or legal transaction. Both verbs also imply a mortal danger or a fatal situation from which one needs to be redeemed.[3]

Although these two terms are often used interchangeably, there are several clear differences in connotation between the two. *Padah* is essentially a commercial term that shares a common root with words in other Semitic languages, such as the Arabic *fidan* ("ransom money") or the Akkadian *padû* ("to set free").[4] *Padah* refers only to the change of ownership from "evil" ownership (slavery) to "good" ownership (being repurchased by a family member) and freedom. The motive for the redemption is not essential to the meaning of the word; this idea of redemption does not suggest prerogative, right, or duty.[5] The classic distinction between *ga'al* and *padah* is that *ga'al* is used in connection with family law, whereas *padah* is linked mainly with commercial law.[6]

Unlike *padah*, *ga'al* has no Semitic cognates; therefore, the base meaning cannot be traced etymologically. Some have suggested root meanings such as "to cover," "to protect," "to lay claim to someone or to something," "to redeem," and "to repurchase."[7] *Ga'al* carries a sense of duty (for the redeemer) or right (for the person redeemed). This duty is based on familial ties to the person or object (usually land) to be redeemed and can be understood as a recuperation or a restoration.[8] The person who carries this responsibility is known as the *gō'el*, which is the participle form of *ga'al*.

THE ROLE OF THE *GO'EL*

The *gō'el* was a person's closest relative who was "responsible for standing up for him and maintaining his rights,"[9] a responsibility based on feelings of tribal unity. In a sense, the *gō'el* represents the clan, exemplifying the ancient Hebrew concept of vicarious solidarity.[10] Basic duties of the *gō'el* were to buy back sold property; to buy back a man who had sold himself to a foreigner as a slave; to avenge blood and kill a relative's murderer; to receive atonement money; and, figuratively, to be a helper in a lawsuit.[11] Michael S. Moore makes several perceptive observations about the spiritual implications of the role of redeemer. He suggests that the *gō'el*'s temporal responsibilities can be understood only in light of spiritual relationships. He argues that "all the legal material which deals with the duties of the *gō'el* is predicated by Israel's relationship to Yahweh."[12]

Moore describes the *gō'el* as the "cultural gyroscope" of Israel, whose purpose is to restore equilibrium, and claims that the social and economic situations of Israel must be seen in light of their relationship with the Lord. Israel's responsibility is to obey the Lord's statutes and ordinances; in return for their obedience, they will be blessed with economic and social equilibrium. Events that disrupt the social equilibrium, such as manslaughter, the death of one's husband or male children, or the obligation in time of poverty to sell one's ancestral estate, affect the whole of the kinship group. Thus "the *gō'el* functions as a restorative agent whenever there is a breach in the clan's corporate life."[13]

The need to restore the social equilibrium can help us understand the role of the *gō'el* as the avenger of blood (*gō'el ha-dam*). It has been argued etymologically that the root meaning of *ga'al* is "to revenge" or "to protect" and that the basic duty of the family was to avenge the death of a kinsman.[14] Moore insists that what western minds may see as excessive vengeance must be understood in an Israelite context. He writes that whereas "western societies restore justice by means of external laws imputed by the State, ancient Israelite society restored justice by means of the divinely appointed agent of restoration (Leviticus 25:25ff.)."[15] Another scholar claims that the "vengeance of blood . . . acts less as a vengeance than as a recuperation,"[16] suggesting that the blood of the murderer acts as compensation for the life of his victim.[17]

THE LORD AS THE *GO'EL* OF ISRAEL

All of the various duties of the redeemer are at different times assumed by the Lord, who acts as the *gō'el* of Israel in the Old Testament. The idea of intimate kinship, essential to the role of the *gō'el*, is connected with the Lord in Isaiah 63:16, where Isaiah cries out, "Doubtless thou art our father, though Abraham be ignorant of us, and Israel acknowledge us not: thou, O Lord, art our father, our redeemer; thy name is from everlasting." The Lord's protection of orphans and widows is described in Proverbs 23:10–11 and Isaiah 54:4–5. He is also portrayed as the redeemer of individuals, as the worshipper in Lamentations 3:52–58 states: "Mine enemies chased me sore, like a bird, without cause. They have cut off my life in the dungeon, and cast a stone upon me. Waters flowed over mine head; then I said, I am cut off. I called upon thy name, O Lord, out of the low dungeon. Thou hast heard my voice: hide not thine ear at my breathing, at my cry. Thou drewest near in the day that I called upon thee: thou saidst, Fear not. O Lord, thou hast pleaded the causes of my soul; *thou hast redeemed my life*" (emphasis added).

REDEMPTION AS A SUBCLASS OF SALVATION

In addition to questions about meaning and usage of *ga'al* and *padah*, there is a confusion about the use of the English words *save* and *redeem*. Although they seem to be used interchangeably and are sometimes assumed to be synonyms because they both do convey the meaning of "deliver," nonetheless *redeem* is a subclass of *save*. In both English and Hebrew, there is a clear difference in meaning:

save means any kind of deliverance, and *redeem* means, specifically, deliverance based upon a payment. The English word *save* is from the Latin *salvare* ("to save") and *salvus* ("safe"), and its basic meaning is "to deliver or rescue from peril or hurt; to make safe, put in safety."[18] There is no intrinsic indication of how this rescue is performed. With *redeem,* on the other hand, the Latin root specifically means "to buy back," *re(d)* + *emere*. Accordingly, the basic meaning in English is "to buy back (a thing formerly possessed); to make payment for (a thing held or claimed by another)."[19]

Although the meaning of Hebrew words may not be as clear as English words because of our limited information on etymology and usage, the words used to express the general concept of salvation are different from those used to refer to salvation through a specific means. The most common Hebrew root meaning "save" is *yasa*. W. L. Liefeld notes that "whereas other terms describe specific aspects of salvation (e.g., redemption), *yasa* is a general term. . . . The root idea seems to be that of enlargement . . . removing that which restricts."[20] Other Hebrew words that express a general concept of delivering include *nasal, palat,* and *malat*. Those terms clearly differ from *ga'al* and *padah*, which refer to deliverance through the payment of a ransom.

NAME GIVING AND COVENANT MAKING

To understand the significance in the Old Testament of giving a name, it is essential to appreciate the importance of names to the Israelites.[21] The Hebrew word *sem,* usually translated *name,* can also be rendered *remembrance* or *memorial,* indicating that the name acts as a reminder to its bearers and others. The name shows both the true nature of its bearer and the relationship that exists between people. The Old Testament records several instances when names were changed to indicate a corresponding change in character and conduct, thus illustrating the Hebrew belief that names represent something of the essence of a person. A new name, therefore, shows a new status or a new relationship. That new relationship may express the dependent state of the person who receives a new name; at the same time, renaming may also indicate a type of adoption.[22]

To the Israelites, covenant making symbolized the formation of a new relationship. In a discussion of the establishment of the covenant at Sinai—and the associated ritual meal of Moses and the elders of Israel with the Lord—in Exodus 24:9–11, Dennis J. McCarthy comments: "To see a great chief and eat in his place is to join his family in the root sense of that Latin word *[gens]:* the whole group related by blood or not which stood under the authority and protection of the father. One is united to him as a client to his patron who protects him and whom he serves. . . . Covenant is something one makes by a rite, not something one is born to or forced into, and it can be described in family terms. God is patron and father, Israel servant and son."[23]

By making a covenant with the Lord, the people of Israel enter into his family and protection. That concept is explicitly expressed in terms of adoption when the Lord tells Moses: "I will take you to me for a people, and I will be to you a God" (Exodus 6:7).

OLD TESTAMENT EXAMPLES OF "ADOPTIVE" REDEMPTION

An examination of biblical passages that include redemption, covenant making, and name giving illuminates the "adoptive" aspect of covenantal redemption and demonstrates that it is this creation of an "adoptive" relationship by covenant that is the basis for the Lord's acts of redemption. The story of the covenant of Abraham, for example, is central both to the Old Testament and to subsequent religious traditions. It gives a sense of identity to many religious groups that look to Abraham as their father. Even the Lord repeatedly refers to that covenant, calling himself the God of Abraham, Isaac, and Jacob. The central text for this covenant and the name change from Abram to Abraham is found in Genesis 17:1–8. This passage does not touch on redemption specifically, but it contains two elements that are central to the covenant-redemption relationship: renaming and adoption.

In this passage, as part of the covenant, Abram is called by a new name, Abraham, "father of a multitude," denoting a change in nature and character. In addition, there is a specific promise of adoption. The Lord says, "I will establish my covenant between me and thee and thy seed . . . to be a God unto thee, and to thy seed after thee" (Genesis 17:7). This adoptive covenant makes Abraham and his descendants the people of the Lord. It establishes a sense of possession, a familial relation that allows the Lord to act as a *gō'el* and redeem, or buy back, his people from slavery. Though the concept of redemption is not specifically related to Abraham in this passage, it may have been understood, as we infer from a statement made hundreds of years later by Isaiah, who referred to God as the redeemer of Abraham: "Therefore thus saith the Lord, *who redeemed Abraham*, concerning the house of Jacob" (Isaiah 29:22; emphasis added).

These same elements—renaming and establishing a covenant—are combined with the idea of redemption in the story of Jacob and the angel. The texts that relate this story are found in both Genesis 32:24–30 and Genesis 48:14–16. The first passage tells of Jacob's wrestling with the angel and receiving a new name. The second passage is the blessing that Jacob (Israel) gave to his grandchildren Ephraim and Manasseh, in which he referred to his experience with the angel when he received his new name. In the second passage, which represents Jacob's commentary on the original incident, Jacob clearly identifies his experience as an act of redemption. When Jacob refers to "the Angel which redeemed me from all evil" (Genesis 48:16), it could be argued that he is referring to the Lord Himself. He "called the name of the place Peniel: for I have seen God face to face" (Genesis 32:30) and declared that his life had been preserved. In the Hebrew text, the angel is called *ha-gō'el,* "the redeemer" or "the one redeeming." In both passages, the concept of renaming or passing on a name is central. In the original description, Jacob is blessed in response to his request by being given the new name *Israel.* Then, in Genesis 48, Jacob blesses his grandsons Ephraim and Manasseh, recalling his redemption, and asks for the angel's blessing to be upon the boys, giving them his name and the names of Abraham and Isaac.

In the account of the deliverance out of Egypt, we find another clear connection between redemption and covenant. In Exodus 5, Moses speaks to the Lord, reporting on his unsuccessful efforts to convince Pharaoh to release the children of Israel. The Lord responds that he has "heard the groaning of the children of Israel" (Exodus 6:5) and remembered the covenant that he made with Abraham, Isaac, and Jacob. Because of this covenant, he promises to act as a redeemer: "I will bring you out from under the burdens of the Egyptians, and I will rid you out of their bondage, and I will redeem you with a stretched out arm, and with great judgments" (Exodus 6:6). This connection between covenant and redemption is clearly explained in Deuteronomy 7:8: "Because he would keep the oath which he had sworn unto your fathers, hath the Lord brought you out with a mighty hand, and redeemed you out of the house of bondmen, from the hand of Pharaoh king of Egypt."

After the promise of redemption from bondage in Egypt because of previous covenants, the Lord promises to establish that adoptive relationship with the house of Israel as a people. The phrase "I will take you to me for a people, and I will be to you a God" (Exodus

6:7) is reminiscent of a sense of adoption in the individual covenants the Lord made with Abraham and Isaac. The adoption to become the people of the Lord suggests a sense of family obligation that is the basis of the redemption provided by the *gō'el* in Hebrew legal practice. Interestingly, because the *gō'el* has the responsibility to both redeem family members out of slavery and also to restore land to those who have lost it, this passage contains the promise that the land will be given as "a heritage" by the Lord.

The story of the redemption from Egypt remained a powerful image to later Old Testament prophets. In Psalm 74:1–2, the psalmist cries out to the Lord for help and recalls the memory of his redemption and adoption of Israel: "O God, why hast thou cast us off for ever? why doth thine anger smoke against the sheep of thy pasture? Remember thy congregation, which thou hast purchased of old; the rod of thine inheritance, which thou hast redeemed; this mount Zion, wherein thou hast dwelt." Here again, the purchase of Israel is cited as a source of connection with the Lord that allows present-day Israel to call for divine help.

The Lord is repeatedly identified as the *gō'el* of Israel in the writings of Isaiah, where the redemption of Israel is portrayed as both a past and a future event. In Isaiah 43:1–3, the redemption and adoption of Israel are cited as sources of comfort for present fears: "But now thus saith the Lord that created thee, O Jacob, and he that formed thee, O Israel, Fear not: for I have redeemed thee, I have called thee by thy name; thou art mine. When thou passest through the waters, I will be with thee; and through the rivers, they shall not overflow thee: when thou walkest through the fire, thou shalt not be burned; neither shall the flame kindle upon thee. For I am the Lord thy God, the Holy One of Israel, thy Saviour: I gave Egypt for thy ransom, Ethiopia and Seba for thee." Here again the redemption *gō'el* of Israel is connected with both the giving of a name and the creating of a tie between the Lord and Israel: "Thou art mine" (Isaiah 43:1). The mention of the Lord's position as redeemer assures that he will be with Israel in future troubles and trials.

The comfort of past redemption and the promise of future deliverance are combined in Isaiah 63. To demonstrate the goodness and mercy of the Lord for the house of Israel, Isaiah refers to the redemption out of Egypt: "In all their affliction he was afflicted, and the angel of his presence saved them: in his love and in his pity he redeemed them; and he bare them, and carried them all the days of old. . . . As a beast goeth down into the valley, the Spirit of the Lord caused him to rest: so didst thou lead thy people, to make thyself a glorious name" (vv. 9, 14). Isaiah specifically refers to this act of the Lord as a redemption rather than simply a deliverance. He explains the motive for this action twice, once in speaking about the Lord and the other time in direct address, saying that the Lord did it "to make himself an everlasting name" (v. 12). Even though this particular phrase does not specifically connect to the common theme of giving Israel a name, that concept is part of the fundamental role of the *gō'el,* who was to redeem his kinsmen in order to protect the family name. Isaiah's mention of "the angel of his presence" that saved them is reminiscent of Jacob's reference to the "Angel which redeemed me from all evil" (Genesis 48:16). More likely, however, Isaiah refers to the angel in the promise the Lord made to Israel as they left Egypt: "I send an Angel before thee, to keep thee in the way, and to bring thee into the place which I have prepared. Beware of him, and obey his voice . . . for my name is in him" (Exodus 23:20–21). Interestingly, in both situations—Jacob's struggle and the deliverance of the house of Israel—there is an association with angels, a name, and redemption.

In all of these Old Testament passages, whether descriptions of original events or commentaries by later prophets, the Lord's acts of redemption are connected to covenant making and name giving. Like an ancient Israelite *gō'el,* by whose title he is called, the Redeemer of Israel acts to save his "adoptive" kinsmen from bondage. Those "adoptive" family ties with both individuals and the house of Israel are created by the "rebirth" provided by covenant and indicated in the giving of a new name.

"ADOPTIVE" REDEMPTION IN THE BOOK OF MORMON

The distinctive Israelite concept of a redeemer as a close family member is seen in the Book of Mormon as well as in the Old Testament.[24] As in the Old Testament, redemption is a central theme of the Book of Mormon. The concept of redemption in the Book of Mormon fits the ancient Near Eastern practice of buying someone out of slavery and bondage. That redemption is often expressed in spiritual terms, as seen in references to the "chains of hell" (Alma 5:7), "the captivity of the devil" (1 Nephi 14:4), and others. Just as the writers of the Book of Mormon saw captivity in spiritual terms, so they also saw redemption as a spiritual matter and sought to persuade people that Jesus Christ is the Redeemer (see Alma 37:5–10).

The concept of a redeemer in the Book of Mormon clearly

matches the Israelite concept of the *gō'el*, a family member who had the responsibility to redeem his kinsmen from bondage. The Lord's acts of redemption are connected to covenants that establish an "adoptive" relationship with a person or a people; when they enter into an "adoptive" covenantal relationship and receive a new name, Christ becomes their *gō'el* and is able to redeem them from spiritual captivity.

One clear and concise textual example of the connection between covenant and redemption is found in Mosiah 18, in which Alma talks to the subjects of King Noah who have come into the wilderness to hear him teach the words of Abinadi. We are told that, in the city, Alma taught the people "concerning the resurrection of the dead, and the redemption of the people, which was to be brought to pass through the power, and sufferings, and death of Christ, and his resurrection and ascension into heaven" (Mosiah 18:2). Those who believed his teachings went to the waters of Mormon, where he "did preach unto them repentance, and redemption, and faith on the Lord" (Mosiah 18:7). When they were ready to enter into a covenant with the Lord, Alma addressed them in a famous discussion of the duties of the Saints associated with the baptismal covenant.

Alma's speech is even more interesting when we notice the explicit connection among covenant, adoption, and redemption. In Mosiah 18:8–9, Alma mentions the people's desire "to come into the fold of God, and to be called his people" and "to bear one anothers' burdens, that they may be light, . . . that ye may be redeemed of God, and be numbered with those of the first resurrection, that ye may have eternal life." This passage explicitly states that coming "into the fold of God" and being "called his people" (v. 8) are necessary in order to be redeemed of God. In Mosiah 18:10, Alma explains how this adoption is possible, saying that "if this be the desire of your hearts, what have you against being baptized in the name of the Lord, as a witness before him that ye have entered into a covenant with him." The baptismal covenant acts here as an adoption, which allows the Lord to become the redeemer, or *gō'el*, of the individual who has taken His name upon him and covenanted with Him.

CONCLUSION

Knowing that an Israelite redeemer was a close family member fulfilling family responsibility gives a new perspective on the Lord's actions as the Redeemer of Israel. It is through covenants and the reception of a new name that individuals are adopted into the family of the Lord and are eligible to be redeemed. Paralleling the Israelite concept of the *gōʼel* as a close relative whose responsibility was to redeem his kinsmen, this "adoptive" covenant can be understood as the basis for the Lord's redemptive actions as the *gōʼel* of Israel.

An understanding of the role of covenants in creating an "adoptive" relationship with the Lord, allowing him to act as *gōʼel*, is more than a scriptural or historical footnote. The concept of "adoptive" redemption explains the importance of making covenants to qualify for redemption through the atonement of Christ. This understanding is crucial for Latter-day Saints as a modern covenant people. To fully appreciate the importance of covenants, we must recognize that we are in bondage and that, like the ancient Israelites, we need a *gōʼel* to redeem us. We need Christ to become our spiritual father and ransom us from spiritual bondage, understanding that "were it not for the redemption which he hath made for his people, which was prepared from the foundation of the world, . . . all mankind must have perished" (Mosiah 15:19). To appreciate the power of our covenants, we must recognize not only that we are in bondage but also that our *gōʼel* has already paid the price of redemption, that "he suffered the pains of all men, yea, the pains of every living creature, both men, women, and children" (2 Nephi 9:21). With the knowledge that our *gōʼel* has paid the ransom price, we can claim the redemptive power of the Lord because we have established an "adoptive" relationship with him through our covenants. We must believe in the reality of that relationship and "exercise faith in the redemption of him who created [us]" (Alma 5:15).

NOTES

1. *"Ga'al,"* in *Theological Dictionary of the Old Testament,* ed. G. Johannes Botterweck and Helmer Ringgren (Grand Rapids, Mich.: Eerdmans Publishing Co., 1975), pp. 351–52.
2. J. Murray, "Redeemer; Redemption," *The International Standard Bible Encyclopedia,* ed. Geoffrey W. Bromiley (Grand Rapids, Mich.: Eerdmans Publishing Co., 1979), 4:61.
3. Evode Beaucamp, "Aux origines du mot 'rédemption' le 'rachat' dans l'ancien testament," *Laval Théologique et Philosophique* 34 (1978): 50–51.
4. Gerhard Kittel, ed., *Theological Dictionary of the New Testament* (Grand Rapids, Mich.: Eerdmans Publishing Co., 1967), 330–31, s.v. "Luo."
5. Beaucamp, "Aux origines," p. 53.
6. Johann Jakob Stamm, *Erlösen und Vergeben im Alten Testament* (Bern: A. Francke A.-G, 1940), p. 30.

7. Botterweck and Ringgren, *Theological Dictionary of the Old Testament,* p. 351. An interesting discussion of these different root meanings is found in Michael S. Moore, "*Haggo'el:* The Cultural Gyroscope of Ancient Hebrew Society," *Restoration Quarterly* 23, no. 1 (1988): 27–28.
8. Beaucamp, "Aux origines," p. 53.
9. Botterweck and Ringgren, *Theological Dictionary of the Old Testament,* p. 351.
10. Cuthbert Lattey, "Vicarious Solidarity in the Old Testament," *Vetus Testamentum* 1 (October 1951): 267–74.
11. Botterweck and Ringgren, *Theological Dictionary of the Old Testament,* pp. 351–52.
12. Moore, *"Haggo'el,"* p. 29.
13. Moore, *"Haggo'el,"* p. 31.
14. Mario Cimosa, "Translating *Gō'el Ha-dam,*" *The Bible Translator* 41 (July 1990): 319–26.
15. Moore, *"Haggo'el,"* p. 33. "Such total vengeance is difficult for western minds to comprehend and may underlie much of the Occidental world's attempts to see a different God in the Old Testament from the God revealed in the pages of the New Testament."
16. Beaucamp, "Aux origines," p. 54. "Il s'agit moins d'une vengeance, que d'une récupération." Translation mine.
17. Beaucamp, "Aux origines," p. 54.
18. *Oxford English Dictionary,* 2d ed., s.v. "Save."
19. *Oxford English Dictionary,* 2d ed., s.v. "Redeem."
20. W. L. Liefeld, "Salvation," *International Standard Bible Encyclopedia,* 4:288.
21. G. F. Hawthorne, "Name," *International Standard Bible Encyclopedia,* 3:481–83; D. Stuart, "Names, Proper," *International Standard Bible Encyclopedia,* 3:483–88.
22. Bruce H. Porter and Stephen D. Ricks, "Names in Antiquity: Old, New, and Hidden," in *By Study and Also by Faith* (Salt Lake City: Deseret Book Co., 1990), pp. 504–5.
23. Dennis J. McCarthy, *Treaty and Covenant: A Study in the Ancient Oriental Documents and in the Old Testament* (Rome: Biblical Institute Press, 1978), p. 266.
24. For a further discussion of "adoptive" covenant and redemption in the Book of Mormon, see my paper, "The Lord Will Redeem His People: 'Adoptive' Covenant and Redemption in the Old Testament and the Book of Mormon," *Journal of Book of Mormon Studies* 2 (Fall 1993): 39–62.

CHAPTER FIVE

ELIJAH'S MISSION: HIS KEYS, POWERS, AND BLESSINGS FROM THE OLD TESTAMENT TO THE LATTER DAYS

E. DALE LEBARON

In this, the dispensation of the fulness of times, when there is to be a "restitution of all things" (Acts 3:21), the mission of Elijah, the last prophet in the Old Testament to hold the keys of the priesthood, is very significant.[1] The Lord has given that important status to Elijah's latter-day mission, for each of the standard works contains prophecies of Elijah's important work.

The last verses of the Old Testament focus on Elijah's mission, as Malachi concluded his writings with "Behold, I will send you Elijah the prophet before the coming of the great and dreadful day of the Lord: And he shall turn the heart of the fathers to the children, and the heart of the children to their fathers, lest I come and smite the earth with a curse" (Malachi 4:5–6).

The New Testament records that Elijah bestowed the keys of the sealing power on Peter, James, and John when they were with the Savior on the Mount of Transfiguration (see Mark 9:1–9).[2] Jesus later taught these three apostles that Elijah would return in the last days to "restore all things" (Matt. 7:11, 1–13; see also Mark 9:2–13; Luke 9:28–36).[3]

The Book of Mormon records that the Savior quoted Malachi's prophecy of Elijah (see 3 Nephi 25:5–6). He told the Nephites, "These scriptures, which ye had not with you, the Father commanded that I should give unto you" (3 Nephi 26:2).

Malachi's prophecy of Elijah is also found in the Pearl of Great

□ □ □ □ □

E. Dale LeBaron is associate professor of Church history and doctrine at Brigham Young University.

Price, as it was part of Moroni's instructions to the Prophet Joseph Smith (see JS–H 1:38–39).

Elijah's mission is discussed several times in the Doctrine and Covenants (2:1–3; 27:9; 35:4; 110:13–16; 128:17; 138:46–47). The earliest revelation received by the Prophet Joseph Smith that is recorded in the Doctrine and Covenants states: "Behold, I will reveal unto you the Priesthood, by the hand of Elijah the prophet, before the coming of the great and dreadful day of the Lord. And he shall plant in the hearts of the children the promises made to the fathers, and the hearts of the children shall turn to their fathers. If it were not so, the whole earth would be utterly wasted at his coming" (D&C 2:1–3). According to the headnote, this is "an extract from the words of the angel Moroni to Joseph Smith the Prophet . . . on the evening of September 21, 1823." It is noteworthy that during this eventful night Moroni visited young Joseph three times, quoting many scriptures and giving much revelation. But of all the passages of scripture Moroni quoted that night, the only verses we know of that the Lord had the Prophet Joseph Smith include in the Doctrine and Covenants were three verses prophesying of Elijah's mission.

The last verses of the Old Testament and the earliest passage of scripture recorded in the Doctrine and Covenants are both prophecies of Elijah's mission. Malachi's prophecy of Elijah's mission forms a scriptural and a spiritual bridge between the last prophet of the Old Testament and the first prophet of this dispensation.

THE IMPORTANCE OF ELIJAH'S MISSION

Events that occurred in the Kirtland Temple were very important. The temple was dedicated 27 March 1836. It was a season of pentecost, with an outpouring of the Spirit of the Lord. Before Elijah and other heavenly messengers restored vital priesthood keys on 3 April 1836, the Savior himself appeared to Joseph Smith and Oliver Cowdery to accept the temple and the sacrifices the Saints had made.

Earlier the Lord had declared that if Elijah's mission were not accomplished as prophesied, "the whole earth would be utterly wasted at his coming" (D&C 2:3). The Prophet Joseph Smith taught, "How shall God come to the rescue of this generation? He will send Elijah the prophet. . . . Elijah shall reveal the covenants to seal the hearts of the fathers to the children, and the children to the fathers. . . . What is this office and work of Elijah? It is one of the greatest and most important subjects that God has revealed. . . . The power of Elijah is sufficient to make our calling and election sure."[4]

President Joseph Fielding Smith explained: "Elijah restored to this Church . . . the keys of the sealing power; and that sealing power puts the stamp of approval upon every ordinance that is done in this Church and more particularly those that are performed in the temples of the Lord. . . . Some members of the Church have been confused in thinking that Elijah came with the keys of baptism for the dead or of salvation for the dead. Elijah's keys were greater than that. They were the keys of sealing, and those keys of sealing pertain to the living and embrace the dead who are willing to repent."[5] President Smith further stated, "This priesthood holds the keys of binding and sealing on earth and in heaven of all the ordinances and principles pertaining to the salvation of man, that they may thus become valid in the celestial kingdom of God."[6]

Without the keys that Elijah conferred upon the Prophet Joseph Smith in the Kirtland Temple, no ordinance of the gospel would be binding beyond this life. All sealings would be null and void, including eternal marriages and eternal families. And because eternal marriage is a prerequisite for exaltation, our purpose for coming to this earth would be thwarted. The Lord has stated that marriage and families are necessary for the earth to "answer the end of its creation" (D&C 49:15–17). Thus, without the sealing powers Elijah restored, truly "the whole earth would be utterly wasted at [the Lord's] coming" (D&C 2:3).

Soon after the keys were restored in Kirtland, the Saints were forced to flee, leaving their beloved temple. Elder Boyd K. Packer gave us this perspective on those events: "You might think the Lord would protect His temple with thunderbolts or earthquakes, if necessary. He did not! The Saints lost the Kirtland Temple. . . . The Church does not have the Kirtland Temple now. *But we have the keys we received within it.*"[7]

FATHERS, CHILDREN, AND PROMISES

The words of Malachi's prophecy concerning Elijah's return vary somewhat in the several scriptural records, but their essence is the same in all, for they speak of fathers, children, and hearts of children turning to their fathers. In addition, Moroni's words to Joseph Smith refer to promises made to the fathers by the children.

Who are the fathers and the children referred to? President Joseph Fielding Smith said: "The fathers are our dead ancestors who died without the privilege of receiving the gospel, but who received the promise that the time would come when that privilege would be granted them. The children are those now living who are preparing genealogical data and who are performing the vicarious ordinances in the temples."[8]

What are the promises? The prophets have taught that we made sacred covenants before we came to this earth. President Spencer W. Kimball said, "We made vows, solemn vows, in the heavens before we came to this mortal life. . . . We have made covenants. We made them before we accepted our position here on earth. . . . We committed ourselves to our Heavenly Father, that if He would send us to the earth and give us bodies and give to us the priceless opportunities that earth life afforded, we would keep our lives clean and would marry in the holy temple and would rear a family and teach them righteousness. This was a solemn oath, a solemn promise."[9]

Elder John A. Widtsoe said of the specific promises we made to our fathers: "In our preexistent state, in the day of the great council, we made a certain agreement with the Almighty. The Lord proposed a plan, conceived by him. We accepted it. Since the plan is intended for all men, we become parties to the salvation of every person under that plan. We agreed, right then and there, to be not only saviors for ourselves but measurably, saviors for the whole human family. We went into a partnership with the Lord. The working out of the plan became then not merely the Father's work, and the Savior's work, but also our work. The least of us, the humblest, is in partnership with the Almighty in achieving the purpose of the eternal plan of salvation."[10]

Moroni's account of Elijah's mission is especially significant. Moroni says: "And he shall *plant in the hearts* of the children the promises made to the fathers, and the hearts of the children shall turn to their fathers" (D&C 2:2; emphasis added). Because we do not remember our experiences before birth, the verb *plant* should be given careful consideration. The mission of Elijah plants in our hearts the awareness of our responsibilities to be saviors to our fathers. It then becomes our responsibility to nourish the tender plant so that it grows and produces fruit. Some of us excuse ourselves from genealogical and temple work, saying, "I just can't get interested" or "Others in the family have done it all."

Alma used a powerful analogy that can be applied here. He taught that after the seed is planted, we should desire to believe and not cast it out. He promised, "If ye nourish it with much care it will get root, and grow up, and bring forth fruit. But if ye neglect the tree, and take no thought for its nourishment, behold it will not get any root; . . . and ye pluck it up and cast it out. Now, this is not because the seed was not good, neither is it because the fruit thereof would not be desirable; but it is because your ground is barren, and ye will not nourish the tree, therefore ye cannot have the fruit thereof. . . . But if ye will . . . nourish the tree as it beginneth to grow, by your faith with great diligence, and with patience, looking forward to the fruit thereof, it shall take root; and behold it shall be a tree springing up unto everlasting life" (Alma 32:37–41).

With respect to planting promises in our hearts—promises made to our forefathers—the growth is up to us. There are specific things we can do to cause this growth, as President Ezra Taft Benson has stated: "When you attend the temple and perform the ordinances that pertain to the House of the Lord, certain blessings will come to you:

"You will receive the spirit of Elijah, which will turn your hearts to your spouse, to your children, and to your forebears.

"You will love your family with a deeper love than you have loved before.

"Your hearts will be turned to your fathers and theirs to you.

"You will be endowed with power from on high as the Lord has promised.

"You will receive the key of the knowledge of God. (See D&C 84:19.) You will learn how you can be like Him. Even the power of godliness will be manifest to you. (See D&C 84:20.)

"You will be doing a great service to those who have passed to the other side of the veil in order that they might be 'judged according to men in the flesh, but live according to God in the spirit.' (D&C 138:34.)"[11]

ELIJAH'S MISSION MANIFEST

There are many ways in which the spirit and power of Elijah are manifest today. We may not even be aware when they happen. Let me share a few of them.

Missionary work on the earth. Because of Elijah's mission, missionaries are led to descendants of those who have accepted the gospel in the spirit world. Elder Melvin J. Ballard observed: "It was made known to me that it is because the righteous dead who have received the Gospel in the spirit world are exercising themselves, and in answers to their prayers elders of the Church are sent to the homes of their posterity so that the Gospel might be taught to them, and that descendant in the flesh is then privileged to do the work for his dead kindred. I want to say to you that it is with greater intensity that the hearts of the fathers and mothers in the spirit world are turned to their children now in the flesh than that our hearts are turned to them."[12]

A pair of missionaries in the South Africa Johannesburg Mission had an experience that demonstrates this principle. While driving near the outskirts of town, they passed an elderly gentleman standing at the side of the road. The missionaries felt strongly impressed to stop and speak to him. They told him that Jesus Christ had sent them to him with an important message. The elders bore strong testimony of Joseph Smith and the Restoration. They gave him a pamphlet with their names and phone number and urged him to read the material and contact them.

About three weeks later, the elderly gentleman phoned the missionaries. He asked them to come to his home and pray for his wife, who was very ill. At the home, which was so far out of town that they never would have stopped at that house during their regular proselyting, the elders administered to the wife, and she was healed immediately. She then asked the missionaries to teach her and her husband. Three weeks later, the couple were baptized. The elderly sister told the missionaries the following story:

"Some time ago my husband came home and told me that he met two young men who said that the Lord had sent them to him.

"Three days later I had a dream. I dreamed that I was with my mother who died thirty-five years ago. I have never before dreamed of my mother. The dream was vivid, just as if it was real.

"My mother said to me, 'My child, I cannot rest.' I replied, 'Why, Mom, why can't you rest?' She answered, 'Because you don't belong to the right church.' I was surprised because I am in the church which my mother and father raised me in. Then the scene changed and we were standing next to a beautiful clear pool of water that had three steps leading down into the water. My mother said, 'My child, go down into the water and I will follow.' I hesitated and said, 'No Mom, you go first and then I will follow.' Then my mother said, 'No, my child, you must go first! Then I will come after.'

"When I woke, I wondered what the dream meant. Then I became sick and you came out and blessed me. You taught us the gospel. I learned about the spirit world and that my parents may have heard the gospel. Then we were baptized. When I stood before the steps of the baptismal font I remembered my dream. It was the same pool of water that I had seen in my dream."[13]

Missionary work in the spirit world. There may be occasions when missionary work and mission calls are correlated on both sides of the veil. President Joseph F. Smith said, "I beheld [in a vision] that the faithful elders of this dispensation, when they depart from mortal life, continue their labors in the preaching of the gospel . . . in the great world of the spirits of the dead" (D&C 138:57).

As the work expands in the spirit world, specially qualified servants may be required to move the work forward there, as President Wilford Woodruff explained: "I have felt of late as if our brethren on the other side of the vail had held a council, and that they had said to this one, and that one, 'Cease thy work on earth, come hence, we need help,' and they have called this man and that man. It has appeared so to me in seeing the many men who have been called from our midst lately."[14]

When Sister LeBaron and I returned from presiding over the South Africa Johannesburg Mission fourteen years ago, we were honored to join a close-knit group of former South Africa mission presidents and their wives. Every three months we have met together to visit and keep current about the land and people of Africa. Fourteen years ago, the group was large and most of us were in good health. But since 1984, nine of those former mission presidents have died, some within three or four months of each other. I feel that that is more than coincidental. There may well be a connection between the passing of these great men and the rapid expansion of missionary work in Africa.

A statement Elder Neal A. Maxwell made at the dedication of the Toronto Temple helps explain how missionary work on the earth is connected with missionary work on the other side of the veil. "[The Lord] will hasten His work in its time. (See D&C 88:73.) When He hastens His work, He hastens it on both sides of the veil. This is why, of course, the holy temples are so crucial especially at this time in human history. The constituency in the spirit world, by the way, is many times larger, numerically, than here. Whenever we open new nations on this side of the veil, as is now happening, we have simultaneously opened the door to thousands beyond the veil. The temple provides the precious spiritual linkage."[15]

It was during our mission in South Africa that the revelation on the priesthood was received. Shortly after that historic revelation of 1978, many African nations were dedicated to the preaching of the gospel. The growth of the Church on that continent has accelerated greatly since then. As the gospel has gone forth among the people of Africa, the work among their African ancestors in the spirit world has also moved ahead. Valiant workers may well be called from this earth to help in that effort.

Sacred records. The Lord preserves and makes available treasured records so that saving ordinances can be performed for his children. Inspired leaders are instruments in God's hands to preserve these records.

In October 1976, Brother Ted Powell, from the Church Genealogical Department, was planning a trip to the Orient when Elder Boyd K. Packer, who was responsible for the family history work, asked him to change his plans and leave immediately for southern Africa. Elder Packer had received a strong prompting and said that there were records there that needed to be microfilmed as soon as possible. The stake and mission leaders in southern Africa asked the Saints to fast and exercise their faith that this urgent project might be completed. The mission president recorded in his journal: "Indeed, this is the most crucial time in the history of this great part of the world as far as genealogy is concerned. The momentous decisions about to be made will determine whether the records are preserved."[16]

Brother Powell and the mission president traveled to Rhodesia to meet with Prime Minister Ian Smith. Because he was out of the country, they met instead with the acting prime minister. A letter of introduction from President Ezra Taft Benson, who knew the prime minister personally, gave them needed credibility. The acting prime minister agreed that microfilming the records was a good idea, but he did not feel he had authority to approve it. For three frustrating days, Brother Powell talked with other high government officials who also agreed that it was a good idea but felt they did not have the authority to approve the project. It seemed hopeless. Brother Powell pleaded with the Lord for help. After a day of pondering and prayer, he heard the voice of the Spirit say: "Ted Powell, who do you think you are? Whose errand are you on?" He was then directed about what to say and do.

Through a sequence of miracles, the way was opened for microfilming to begin. The project moved along quickly, considering the limited equipment and personnel available. Within days of the last roll of microfilm being safely stored in the Church vaults in Cottonwood Canyon, the government of Ian Smith collapsed and a Marxist government took over the country. The national archivist and government officials who had been very cooperative and friendly during the project were immediately removed from office. The new government destroyed many of the records that had been microfilmed and made it difficult for the Church to operate in that country.

Temple ordinances. Temple ordinances are at the heart of Elijah's mission. Those in the spirit world who have accepted the gospel may be involved when their ordinances are performed for them in the temple. Elder Melvin J. Ballard said that while witnessing baptisms for the dead performed in the Logan Temple, he saw a vision of a great congregation of spirits witnessing their ordinances. He had never seen such happy people in his life. From that time Elder Ballard taught that departed spirits are permitted to witness and accept the ordinances performed in their behalf.[17]

There are many manifestations of spirits witnessing their ordinances being performed by proxy in temples. One example is from the life of President Edward J. Wood, the first president of the Alberta Temple. In 1931 a group of Saints traveled from Portland, Oregon, to the Alberta Temple. One sister, a convert to the Church, was in the sealing room waiting to be sealed to her husband and children who had passed away. Friends were acting as proxy for the husband and children. As President Wood was about to seal the children to the parents, he asked the sister if the information he had been given was complete. After being assured that it was, he again began the ceremony. Again he stopped and asked if this sister had other children whose names should be included. She said she had other living adult children who were not members of the Church, but that was all. A third time President Wood started the ceremony, but again he stopped, saying he had heard a voice quite distinctly say, "I am her child." Once more he asked the mother if she had another child who was not listed on the sheet. She explained, with tears running down her face, that she did indeed have another daughter, one who had died twelve days after birth and had been overlooked in preparing the information. "All in the room shed tears of joy to realize the closeness of kindred dead."[18]

ETERNAL FAMILIES TODAY

Building an eternal family is surely our ultimate partnership with our Heavenly Father, but doing so depends upon each family member's responding to the spirit of Elijah. President Harold B. Lee said: "When the full measure of Elijah's mission is understood, . . . the hearts of the children will be turned to the fathers, and the fathers to the children. It applies just as much on this side of the veil as it does to the other side of the veil. If we neglect our families here in having family home night and we fail in our responsibility here, how would heaven look if we lost some of those [we love] through our own neglect? Heaven would not be heaven until we have done everything we can to save those whom the Lord has sent through our lineage. So, the hearts of you fathers and mothers must be turned to your children right now, if you have the true spirit of Elijah, and not think that it applies merely to those who are beyond the veil. Let your hearts be turned to your children, and teach your children; but you must do it when they are young enough to be schooled. And if you are neglecting your family home evening, you are neglecting the beginning of the mission of Elijah just as certainly as if you were neglecting your research work of genealogy."[19]

All things that help turn the hearts of children to their parents and the hearts of parents to their children are of great importance. Recent as well as historical family records can help us reach that eternal goal and thus are important to the Lord. I learned that through an experience we had while we were presiding over the South Africa Johannesburg Mission.

One Sunday afternoon Sister LeBaron became ill. She took some medicine and went to bed while I took the children to sacrament meeting. After the meeting, I received an urgent message that the mission home was on fire. I raced the three or four miles to our home, the smoke rising above the trees. I was terrified, not knowing whether my wife was still asleep in the house.

By the time I arrived, the fire was spreading through the upper story of the beautiful mansion. I raced into the house, calling my wife's name. I ran to our upstairs bedroom, which was filled with smoke. My wife was not there. I ran back down the winding stairway to the foyer, and then I heard her calling from outside. At that moment an explosion above me sent the huge chandelier crashing to the hardwood floor at my feet.

I dashed into my office. What should we do? All the significant records for the Church in Africa were housed in the mission home and office. They were invaluable. My mind raced as I tried to think of what to do.

Then the thought came that I should use my priesthood to pronounce a blessing upon those records. They were the Lord's. I should leave them in his hands. I felt impressed to bless everything in the home and office that was either of great value or irreplaceable that it would be preserved. As I said amen, I felt a spirit of peace and calm that was every bit as strong as my feelings of terror and fear had been a few moments earlier. I took our family picture from my desk, put it into my briefcase, and calmly walked out of the mission home to join my family outside.

That night we comforted the children by pointing out that we still had everything that was important in our lives. Their mother's life had been spared, we had the gospel, our family was together, and we had not lost anything that really mattered. I shared with them my experience in giving the priesthood blessing and assured them that the irreplaceable things of great value had not been lost. I assured them that the Lord had granted that blessing and that none of the valuable Church records had been burned.

Then one child asked about our family photo album. It was a large leather album my wife had given me early in our marriage, and it contained portraits of our children at various ages. Like the Church records, it also was of great value and irreplaceable. Had it been preserved? I did not have an answer.

The next morning we went back into the mission home. It was painful to see this once-beautiful mansion a shell with no roof. Our children tried to be as positive as they could. One of them said, "Dad, you can tell the Brethren that last night we had a fireside and today we have an open house."

My main objective was to answer my child's question from the night before—what about the family photo album? I got a digging fork and carefully went up the concrete stairs to the family room where our photo album had been. This was the room where the fire had started, and the heat had been so intense that the television set had melted. I could see nothing but blackened walls and about four feet of ashes and rubble. I went to the area where the album had been lying on a table, and I began to dig. As I got near the floor level, the fork hit something solid. I carefully dug around it and lifted it up with the fork. It was a large black blob. I gingerly carried it down the stairs and outside into the cool morning. I called my family together; they were puzzled about what I had. Carefully I removed layers of blackened and burned material until we saw the photographs. Every picture had been preserved, although some of the edges were singed. Our children were ecstatic as they exclaimed, "Dad, look! Our pictures have been antiqued!"

I am so grateful that a loving Heavenly Father cared about our family portraits and preserved them for us. But more miraculous and meaningful even than that experience has been the spirit and power that touched a precious daughter's heart and brought her back to our eternal family. Although too personal and sacred to relate, that has brought a witness and gratitude to each family member's heart of the power and blessing of Elijah's mission and the Savior's atonement.

CONCLUSION

Truly, the more clearly we are able to see eternity, the more monumental Elijah's mission becomes. President Benson has said: "God bless us to receive all the blessings revealed by Elijah the prophet so that our callings and election will be made sure."[20] Some years ago, at the dedication of the temple in Buenos Aires, Argentina, Elder Boyd K. Packer said: "We are dedicating a monument to [the] resurrection and exaltation of the human family. If the outside knew about what was happening here, the cars would stop, planes would not take off, and people would gather to see what the Lord hath wrought. This work we have a part in; it is cause for great rejoicing."[21]

Indeed it is. Of this I testify.

NOTES

1. Joseph Smith, *Teachings of the Prophet Joseph Smith*, sel. Joseph Fielding Smith (Salt Lake City: Deseret Book Co., 1938), p. 172.
2. Joseph Fielding Smith, *Doctrines of Salvation* (Salt Lake City: Bookcraft, 1955), 2:108–11.
3. Smith, *Doctrines of Salvation,* 2:108–10.
4. Smith, *Teachings of the Prophet Joseph Smith*, pp. 323, 337–38.
5. Smith, *Doctrines of Salvation,* 3:129–30.
6. Smith, *Doctrines of Salvation,* 2:117.
7. Boyd K. Packer, *The Holy Temple* (Salt Lake City: Bookcraft, 1980), p. 174; emphasis added.
8. Smith, *Doctrines of Salvation,* 2:127.
9. Spencer W. Kimball, devotional address given at the University of Utah LDS Institute of Religion, 10 Jan. 1975.
10. *Utah Genealogical and Historical Magazine,* Oct. 1934, p. 189.
11. Ezra Taft Benson, "What I Hope You Will Teach Your Children about the Temple," *Ensign,* Aug. 1985, p. 10.
12. Melvin R. Ballard, *Melvin J. Ballard, Crusader for Righteousness* (Salt Lake City: Bookcraft, 1977), p. 219.
13. In possession of the author.
14. Wilford Woodruff, in *Journal of Discourses* (London: Latter-day Saints' Book Depot, 1882), 22:334.
15. Neal A. Maxwell, in *Church News,* 1 Sept. 1990, p. 7.
16. In possession of the author.
17. *Church News,* 5 Jan. 1980, p. 12.

18. Melvin S. Tagg, *The Life of Edward James Wood: Church Patriot,* master's thesis, Brigham Young University, 1959, pp. 118–19.
19. Harold B. Lee, banquet speech delivered at the Eighth Annual Priesthood Genealogical Seminar, 3 Aug. 1973; printed in "Syllabus for the Ninth Annual Priesthood Genealogy Seminar," pp. 529–30. Typescript.
20. Benson, "What I Hope You Will Teach Your Children about the Temple," p. 10.
21. *Church News,* 26 Jan. 1986, p. 6.

CHAPTER SIX

"THE SPIRIT OF PROPHECY IS THE TESTIMONY OF JESUS"

D. KELLY OGDEN

Some Bible scholars claim that predictive prophecy does not exist. They say, for example, "So far as we can determine, when [the prophets' writings are] studied in their contexts apart from dogmatic preconviction, no prophet leaped across the centuries and foresaw the specific person Jesus of Nazareth. It is a plain violation of historical context to think that they did so and in practice those who interpret the prophets as predictors of Jesus obscure the settings in which the prophets functioned."[1]

The prophets themselves have unequivocably spoken contrary to that theory of men. Jacob, Nephi's brother, wrote that "we knew of Christ, and we had a hope of his glory many hundred years before his coming; and not only we ourselves had a hope of his glory, but also all the holy prophets which were before us" (Jacob 4:4). "None of the prophets have written, nor prophesied, save they have spoken concerning this Christ" (Jacob 7:11). Abinadi asked, "Did not Moses prophesy unto them concerning the coming of the Messiah, and that God should redeem his people? Yea, and even all the prophets who have prophesied ever since the world began—have they not spoken more or less concerning these things?" (Mosiah 13:33). Nephi, son of Helaman, later proclaimed that "there have been many prophets that have testified these things" (Helaman 8:19), and he listed examples: Moses, Abraham, Zenos, Zenock, Ezias, Isaiah, Jeremiah, Lehi, Nephi, "and also almost all of our fathers, even down to this time; yea, they have testified of the coming of Christ, and have looked forward, and have rejoiced in his day which is to come" (Helaman 8:22).

In the courtyard of the temple at Jerusalem, Peter boldly bore witness that "all the prophets from Samuel and those that follow after,

□ □ □ □ □

D. Kelly Ogden is associate professor of ancient scripture at Brigham Young University.

as many as have spoken, have likewise foretold of these days" (Acts 3:24). And even Jewish rabbinical writings affirm that "all of the prophets prophesied only concerning the days of the Messiah."[2]

The scriptures teach that one essential role of a prophet is to testify of the Lord Jesus Christ; in fact, John wrote, "The testimony of Jesus is the spirit of prophecy" (Revelation 19:10). In other words, testifying of Jesus is what prophecy is all about. There is no greater witness that the prophets could proclaim than that Jesus Christ is the Son of God and the Savior of the world. In fact, the Prophet Joseph Smith was asked, "What are the fundamental principles of your religion?" He answered, "The fundamental principles of our religion are *the testimony of the Apostles and Prophets, concerning Jesus Christ,* that He died, was buried, and rose again the third day, and ascended into heaven; and *all other things which pertain to our religion are only appendages to it.*"[3]

The testimony of Jesus is, of course, available to all the Saints—through the gift of the Holy Ghost. As Moses exclaimed, "Would God that all the Lord's people were prophets, and that the Lord would put his spirit upon them!" (Numbers 11:29). All members of God's kingdom can and should obtain a testimony of Jesus, which is the spirit of prophecy, yet our focus here is on the witness of those formally called and ordained as prophets to the Church of God and to the whole world. The testimony of Jesus is clearly evident in the extant writings of these prophets over the ages.

OLD TESTAMENT PROPHETS BEAR WITNESS OF CHRIST

Adam and Eve were expelled from the Garden of Eden and some time later learned the purpose of offering sacrifices unto the Lord: "This thing is a similitude of the sacrifice of the Only Begotten of the Father. . . . Wherefore, thou shalt do all that thou doest in the name of the Son, and thou shalt repent and call upon God in the name of the Son forevermore" (Moses 5:7–8). Adam and Eve also learned that they could be redeemed from their fall. Because of their transgression and subsequent fall into mortality, they could have children, know good and evil, and experience the "joy of our redemption" (Moses 5:11) and the potential of eternal life provided by the sacrifice of the Son of God (see Moses 5:9–11). Lehi later taught what Adam knew from the beginning: "Adam fell that men might be; and men are, that they might have joy. And the Messiah cometh in the fulness of time, that he may redeem the children of men from the fall" (2 Nephi 2:25–26).

Enoch was one of the privileged seers who saw the whole panorama of history from beginning to end. "I saw the Lord; and he stood before my face, and he talked with me, even as a man talketh one with another, face to face; and he said unto me: Look, and I will show unto thee the world for the space of many generations. . . . And behold, Enoch saw the day of the coming of the Son of Man, even in the flesh; and his soul rejoiced, saying: The Righteous is lifted up, and the Lamb is slain from the foundation of the world. . . . And he looked and beheld the Son of Man lifted up on the cross, after the manner of men. . . . And Enoch beheld the Son of Man ascend up unto the Father. . . . And it came to pass that Enoch saw the day of the coming of the Son of Man, in the last days, to dwell on the earth in righteousness for the space of a thousand years" (Moses 7:4, 47, 55, 59, 65). A New Testament writer recorded: "And Enoch also, the seventh from Adam, prophesied of these, saying, Behold, the Lord cometh with ten thousands of his saints" (Jude 1:14).

Noah preached the gospel of Jesus Christ to a corrupted world and warned that rejection would be answered with a cataclysm unparalleled in history: "Believe and repent of your sins and be baptized in the name of Jesus Christ, the Son of God, even as our fathers, and ye shall receive the Holy Ghost . . . and if ye do not this, the floods will come in upon you" (Moses 8:24). The people rejected more than Noah and his prediction of dramatic meteorological changes; they rejected Christ, their only hope for salvation.

Abraham is another of the prophets who learned directly from Jehovah: "I, Abraham, talked with the Lord, face to face, as one man talketh with another; and he told me of the works which his hands had made" (Abraham 3:11). Abraham was supremely tested when the Lord required him to take his promised son, Isaac, and offer him up as a sacrifice. Abraham responded. The patriarch came to understand that his trial was "a similitude of God and his Only Begotten Son" (Jacob 4:5). That eternal sacrifice was the most glorious message the world has ever heard. Jesus told the Jews in the inner court of the temple, "Your father Abraham rejoiced to see my day: and he saw it, and was glad" (John 8:56; see also Helaman 8:17).

Joseph was Abraham's great-grandson, and he perpetuated his ancestors' trust in the promises of the Lord concerning their seed. Joseph knew that the Messiah would come, as prophesied, in the meridian of time but also in the fulness of time: "And a branch shall be broken off, and shall be carried into a far country; nevertheless they shall be remembered in the covenants of the Lord, when the

Messiah cometh; for he shall be made manifest unto them in the latter days, in the Spirit of power; and shall bring them out of darkness into light" (JST Genesis 50:25; see also 2 Nephi 3:5).

Moses was a type of the Messiah, being a great law-giver and a great deliverer. After the Israelites' deliverance from the Egyptian armies at the Red Sea, Moses sang these words in a song of praise and triumph: "The Lord is my strength and song, and he is become my salvation: he is my God" (Exodus 15:2). The word *salvation* in Hebrew is *yeshua,* which is the very name by which the Messiah would be known in mortality. *Yeshua,* besides being translated into English as a common noun *salvation,* is also transliterated as the name *Jesus.*

Moses knew Christ personally. "When Moses was caught up into an exceedingly high mountain . . . he saw God face to face, and he talked with him, and the glory of God was upon Moses" (Moses 1:1–2). Moses recorded a prophecy of the Messiah to come: "The Lord thy God will raise up unto thee a Prophet from the midst of thee, of thy brethren, like unto me; unto him ye shall hearken" (Deuteronomy 18:15). Fulfillment of that prophecy, the coming of the Son of God in the flesh, is recorded in 3 Nephi 20:23–24 and in Acts 3:22–23.

Moses also raised up a type of the Savior in the wilderness, that whoever would look upon it—that is, whoever would believe in Him—would be healed and live (see Numbers 21:8–9). Moses knew that the Lord would be lifted up on the cross to draw all men to Him and offer them healing and life eternal. Nephi recorded and bore testimony of "the words which were spoken by this man, Moses, who had such great power given unto him, yea, the words which he hath spoken concerning the coming of the Messiah. Yea, did he not bear record that the Son of God should come? And as he lifted up the brazen serpent in the wilderness, even so shall he be lifted up who should come. And as many as should look upon that serpent should live, even so as many as should look upon the Son of God with faith, having a contrite spirit, might live, even unto that life which is eternal" (Helaman 8:13–15; see also Alma 33:19–20; 2 Nephi 25:20; John 3:14). Besides the serpent raised on a pole, the prophet Moses taught Israel by means of the Passover lamb, the manna from heaven, water from the rock, blood of the covenant, atonement sacrifice for the people, sacrificial offerings of animals without blemish, and the firstborn who were hallowed for divine service—all of which were types and shadows of the coming Messiah (cf. Hebrews 9; 10).

Isaiah's testimony of Christ was commended by Nephi to his brethren and to all those who want to come to a knowledge of their Redeemer: "I did read many things unto them which were written in the books of Moses; but that I might more fully persuade them to believe in the Lord their Redeemer I did read unto them that which was written by the prophet Isaiah" (1 Nephi 19:23). "And now I, Nephi, write more of the words of Isaiah, for my soul delighteth in his words. . . . For he verily saw my Redeemer, even as I have seen him" (2 Nephi 11:2).

Some of the most jubilant exclamations of prophecy in all of scripture about the coming of the Messiah are found in the writings of Isaiah: "Behold, a virgin shall conceive, and bear a son, and shall call his name Immanuel" (Isaiah 7:14). "For unto us a child is born, unto us a son is given: and the government shall be upon his shoulder: and his name shall be called Wonderful, Counsellor, The mighty God, The everlasting Father, The Prince of Peace. Of the increase of his government and peace there shall be no end" (Isaiah 9:6–7). Possibly the most articulate and poignant of all prophetic descriptions of the coming Messiah is recorded in Isaiah 53. We reverently ponder the combined meaning of all the adjectives Isaiah used to describe him: *stricken, smitten, afflicted, wounded, bruised,* and *oppressed.* The prophet defied the later popular expectation of a bigger-than-life political deliverer when he wrote that the Messiah would be "cut off out of the land of the living" (Isaiah 53:8).

BOOK OF MORMON PROPHETS BEAR WITNESS OF CHRIST

During the last centuries of the Old Testament record, prophets of God in the Western Hemisphere also bore fervent testimony of the Lord Jesus Christ.

Lehi followed a long line of Old Testament prophets who plainly testified that the Son of God was the promised Messiah. Lehi's son, Nephi, related his father's witness: "Yea, even six hundred years from the time that my father left Jerusalem, a prophet would the Lord God raise up among the Jews—even a Messiah, or, in other words, a Savior of the world. And he [Lehi] also spake concerning the prophets, how great a number had testified of these things, concerning this Messiah, of whom he had spoken, or this Redeemer of the world. Wherefore, all mankind were in a lost and in a fallen state, and ever would be save they should rely on this Redeemer" (1 Nephi 10:4–6). Nephi wrote that he, too, wanted to hear and see and understand the same vision and testified that "the Son of God was the Messiah who should come" (v. 17). Father Lehi's testimony was pure and unequivocal: "Redemption cometh in and through the Holy Messiah. . . . Wherefore, how great the importance to make these things known unto the inhabitants of the earth, that they may know that there is no flesh that can dwell in the presence of God, save it be through the merits, and mercy, and grace of the Holy Messiah, who layeth down his life according to the flesh, and taketh it again by the power of the Spirit, that he may bring to pass the resurrection of the dead" (2 Nephi 2:6, 8).

Nephi echoed the teachings of his father and bore his own testimony when he described the things in which he delighted: "Behold, my soul delighteth in proving unto my people the truth of the coming of Christ; . . . all things which have been given of God from the beginning of the world, unto man, are the typifying of him. . . . And my soul delighteth in proving unto my people that save Christ should come all men must perish" (2 Nephi 11:4, 6). "For according to the words of the prophets, the Messiah cometh in six hundred years from the time that my father left Jerusalem; and according to the words of the prophets, and also the word of the angel of God, his name shall be Jesus Christ, the Son of God. . . . And we talk of Christ, we rejoice in Christ, we preach of Christ, we prophesy of Christ, and we write according to our prophecies, that our children may know to what source they may look for a remission of their sins" (2 Nephi 25:19, 26).

One reason Nephi knew and loved the Savior was a vision he had seen of the virgin who conceived and bore a son, wherein his angelic guide said to him: "Behold the Lamb of God, yea, even the Son of the Eternal Father!" (1 Nephi 11:21). Nephi further saw that "the Son of the everlasting God was judged of the world" and "lifted up upon the cross and slain for the sins of the world" (vv. 32–33).

Jacob, son of Lehi and brother of Nephi, understood the doctrine of Christ and gave profound explanations of the Atonement: "For as death hath passed upon all men, to fulfil the merciful plan of the great Creator, there must needs be a power of resurrection, and the resurrection must needs come unto man by reason of the fall; and the fall came by reason of transgression; and because man became fallen they were cut off from the presence of the Lord. Wherefore, it must needs be an infinite atonement. . . . O how great the holiness of our God! . . . for behold, he suffereth the pains of all men, yea, the pains of every living creature, both men, women, and children, who belong to the family of Adam. And he suffereth this that the resurrection might pass upon all men, that all might stand before him at the great and judgment day" (2 Nephi 9:6–7, 20–22).

"Wherefore, beloved brethren, be reconciled unto him through the atonement of Christ, his Only Begotten Son, and ye may obtain a resurrection, according to the power of the resurrection which is in Christ. . . . And now, beloved, marvel not that I tell you these things; for why not speak of the atonement of Christ, and attain to a perfect knowledge of him" (Jacob 4:11–12).

The prophet Abinadi proclaimed that Moses and all the prophets have prophesied of the Messiah (see Mosiah 13:33). "Have they not said that God himself should come down among the children of men, and take upon him the form of man, and go forth in mighty power upon the face of the earth? Yea, and have they not said also that he should bring to pass the resurrection of the dead, and that he, himself, should be oppressed and afflicted?" (vv. 34–35). After quoting Isaiah (Isaiah 53), Abinadi added his own witness: "I would that ye should understand that God himself [meaning Jesus Christ] shall come down among the children of men, and shall redeem his people. And because he dwelleth in flesh he shall be called the Son of God" (Mosiah 15:1–2). Abinadi further encouraged his hearers to do what he was doing: "Teach them that redemption cometh through Christ the Lord" (Mosiah 16:15).

Alma heeded the words of Abinadi. He, too, boldly declared the most important part of his testimony: "I say unto you, that I know of myself that whatsoever I shall say unto you, concerning that which is to come, is true; and I say unto you, that I know that Jesus Christ shall come, yea, the Son, the Only Begotten of the Father, full of grace, and mercy, and truth. And behold, it is he that cometh to take away the sins of the world" (Alma 5:48). Having thus testified, Alma counseled others to "believe in the Son of God, that he will come to redeem his people, and that he shall suffer and die to atone for their sins; and that he shall rise again from the dead, which shall bring to pass the resurrection, that all men shall stand before him, to be judged at the last and judgment day" (Alma 33:22). Alma's missionary companion, Amulek, reaffirmed the same testimony: "My brethren, I think that it is impossible that ye should be ignorant of the things which have been spoken concerning the coming of Christ, who is taught by us to be the Son of God" (Alma 34:2).

NEW TESTAMENT PROPHETS BEAR WITNESS OF CHRIST

John the Baptist was heralded as a new prophet in the land of

Judah, after a long famine of hearing the word of the Lord. John testified that he was only a forerunner, the voice of one crying in the wilderness to prepare the way for the Holy One who was coming to fulfill His mission. Missing from the New Testament but recorded in modern scripture is the testimony of the Baptist regarding the Redeemer of the world: "I, John, bear record that I beheld his glory, as the glory of the Only Begotten of the Father, full of grace and truth, even the Spirit of truth, which came and dwelt in the flesh, and dwelt among us. . . . [And] he was called the Son of God" (D&C 93:11, 14; see also John 1:34).

Peter, the chief of the apostles, testified on several occasions that he knew who Jesus was. As Isaiah had prophesied (Isaiah 53:2), the Messiah would not come as a bigger-than-life political deliverer, as most of the Jews expected. His physical appearance was not so distinctive and overpowering that people would instantly recognize his divinity; he came as a mortal man. Even the apostles had to watch and pray and seek the Spirit to know who Jesus was. When the truth was revealed to Peter, he boldly declared his witness: "Thou art the Christ, the Son of the living God" (Matthew 16:16). And when many of the multitude in Galilee rejected him and stopped following him, Jesus asked the Twelve if they would also go away. "Then Simon Peter answered him, Lord, to whom shall we go? thou hast the words of eternal life. And we believe and are sure that thou art that Christ, the Son of the living God" (John 6:68–69).

Similarly, John the Beloved testified of Christ; it was still essential to hear the prophetic witness even when the Savior was on the earth. John wrote that Jesus performed many signs and wonders and "these are written, that ye might believe that Jesus is the Christ, the Son of God; and that believing ye might have life through his name" (John 20:31). John gave one of the simplest and most sublime explanations of the Lord's mortal mission: "For God so loved the world, that he gave his only begotten Son, that whosoever believeth in him should not perish, but have everlasting life" (John 3:16).

Paul, the apostle to the Gentiles, was brought to a knowledge of Christ in an abrupt and dramatic way while en route to Damascus. After his baptism and receipt of the Holy Ghost, Paul worshipped with the Saints in Damascus, and "straightway he preached Christ in the synagogues, that he is the Son of God" (Acts 9:20). With undaunted courage and indomitable energy, he spent the next thirty years preaching about the Lord Jesus. In Macedonia Paul "was pressed in the spirit, and testified to the Jews that Jesus was Christ"

(Acts 18:5). To the Romans Paul wrote of the gospel of Jesus Christ "(which he had promised afore by his prophets in the holy scriptures,) concerning his Son Jesus Christ our Lord, which was made of the seed of David according to the flesh; And declared to be the Son of God with power" (Romans 1:2–4). To the Hebrews Paul wrote that "God, who at sundry times and in divers manners spake in time past unto the fathers by the prophets, Hath in these last days spoken unto us by his Son, whom he hath appointed heir of all things, by whom also he made the worlds; Who . . . when he had by himself purged our sins, sat down on the right hand of the Majesty on high" (Hebrews 1:1–3).

LATTER-DAY PROPHETS BEAR WITNESS OF CHRIST

With a host of prophetic witnesses throughout the ages, one might suppose (and some do suppose) that there is no further need of witnesses to the great truth that Jesus Christ is the Son of God and the Savior of the world. Actually there can be no end to that testimony. As with all of God's work, the witness of Christ is one eternal round. In these latter days, the clear sound of the trump, the witness of Christ, is needed as much as in any previous period of the world. "I the Lord, knowing the calamity which should come upon the inhabitants of the earth, called upon my servant Joseph Smith, Jun., and spake unto him from heaven" (D&C 1:17). And the first words of God the Father from heaven were: *"This is My Beloved Son. Hear Him!"* (Joseph Smith–History 1:17).

Joseph Smith later wrote: "We, the elders of the church, have heard and bear witness to the words of the glorious Majesty on high. . . . By these things we know that there is a God in heaven. . . . Wherefore, the Almighty God gave his Only Begotten Son, as it is written in those scriptures which have been given of him. He suffered temptations but gave no heed unto them. He was crucified, died, and rose again the third day; And ascended into heaven, to sit down on the right hand of the Father" (D&C 20:16–17, 21–24). Before Joseph Smith sealed his witness in blood, he uttered this great capstone of prophetic testimony of Jesus: "And now, after the many testimonies which have been given of him, this is the testimony, last of all, which we give of him: That he lives! For we saw him, even on the right hand of God; and we heard the voice bearing record that he is the Only Begotten of the Father" (D&C 76:22–23).

The successors of Joseph Smith continue to testify of the life and mission of the Lord Jesus Christ and of the essential nature of his atoning sacrifice to the eternal hope of every human soul. The testimony of one more latter-day prophet represents all. President Harold B. Lee declared: "Fifty years ago or more, when I was a missionary, our greatest responsibility was to defend the great truth that the Prophet Joseph Smith was divinely called and inspired and that the Book of Mormon was indeed the word of God. But even at that time there were the unmistakable evidences that there was coming into the religious world actually a question about the Bible and about the divine calling of the Master, Himself. Now fifty years later, our greatest responsibility and anxiety is to defend the divine mission of our Lord and Master, Jesus Christ, for all about us[,] even among those who claim to be professors of the Christian faith, [there are those who] are not willing to stand squarely in defense of the great truth that our Lord and Master, Jesus Christ, was indeed the Son of God. So tonight it would seem to me that the most important thing I could say to you is to try to strengthen your faith and increase your courage and your understanding of the place of the Master in the great Plan of Salvation."[4]

The prophets in all ages and in all places have uttered a multitude of prophecies about the coming of the Son of God in the flesh; they have foreseen and recorded numerous details about events during his mortal life; they have foreshadowed and explained in marvelous clarity the meaning of his atoning sacrifice and resurrection from the dead; and they have predicted his imminent return to the earth to create a new world of peace and progress preparatory to its final change to celestial glory. From the beginning of the scripture we call the Old Testament right up to the most recent recorded witness of the latter-day prophets, we see that the prophets' subject of supreme interest and importance is the testimony of Jesus Christ.

NOTES

1. Norman K. Gottwald, *A Light to the Nations: An Introduction to the Old Testament* (New York: Harper and Row, 1959), p. 275.
2. Jacob Neusner, trans., *Tractate Sanhedrin, Chapters 9–11,* vol. 23c of *The Talmud of Babylonia: An American Translation* (Chico, Calif.: Scholars Press, 1985), p. 141.
3. Joseph Smith, *Teachings of the Prophet Joseph Smith,* sel. Joseph Fielding Smith (Salt Lake City: Deseret Book Co., 1938), p. 121; emphasis added.
4. Harold B. Lee, address delivered at LDSSA Fireside, Logan, Utah, 10 Oct. 1971.

CHAPTER SEVEN

SYMBOLIC ACTION AS PROPHECY IN THE OLD TESTAMENT

DONALD W. PARRY

Ancient Israelite religion featured groups and individuals who expressed themselves with symbolic actions. For example, Moses and Joshua removed their shoes while standing upon holy ground (Exodus 3:5; Joshua 5:15); Saul cut up two oxen and sent the pieces throughout Israel as a warning that individuals who failed to rally around the king would be similarly destroyed (1 Samuel 11:7); Solomon spread his hands toward heaven during the dedicatory prayer of the temple (1 Kings 8:22); Elijah divided the waters of the Jordan River by smiting them with his mantle (2 Kings 2:8); Elisha cast salt into a spring to heal its bitter waters (2 Kings 2:19–21); and Abraham took a heifer, a she-goat, and a ram and "divided them in the midst, and laid each piece one against another" (Gen. 15:10), after which he may have passed through the two parts (see Jeremiah 34:18). Several Old Testament prophets, including Abraham, Moses, Ahijah, Elijah, Isaiah, Jeremiah, and Ezekiel used such symbolic actions[1] to prophesy, without words, of future events. Their unconventional action, gesture, movement, or posture of itself may not have had an immediate practical purpose but had symbolic meaning or metaphoric application. The future action was the typological fulfillment of the first, original action.

Although the symbolic actions of prophetic characters of the Old Testament occurred during various gospel dispensations, within different geographic locations, and under varying circumstances and contexts, there are commonalities among them. First, a prophet played a major role in the symbolic actions as prophecy. On one

□ □ □ □ □

Donald W. Parry is visiting assistant professor of Hebrew at Brigham Young University.

hand, it was common for the prophet himself to dramatize the prophecy, as was the case with Melchizedek breaking the bread and blessing the wine (JST Genesis 14:17), Moses casting the tree into the bitter waters (Exodus 15:22–25), or Jeremiah breaking the clay vessel (Jeremiah 19). On the other hand, the prophet gave directions to or witnessed a second party who enacted the prophecy, as was the case with Jeremiah, who watched a potter create two vessels (Jeremiah 18:1–12) and who caused several nations to drink from the wine cup of fury (Jeremiah 25:15–29).

Second, the prophetic symbolic action originated from God. In most cases, the scriptural record sets forth in a straightforward manner that the prophets received direct revelation from God. Such a revelation was formulated in the texts with one of two common formulaic expressions or revelatory speech forms—the messenger formula and the revelation formula.[2] "Thus saith the Lord," "For thus saith the Lord God of Israel unto me," and "Thus saith the Lord God of Hosts" are variations of the messenger formula. The revelation formula features various expressions that indicate the prophet's reception of God's word, for example, "the word of the Lord came also unto me saying," "the Lord said unto the prophet . . . ," "God . . . said unto him," and so on. Generally recorded at the beginning of a new revelation, the formula introduces prophetic language; its primary purpose is to manifest the authority and origin of the revelation. Because the revelation originates with God and thus carries the authority of God through his prophet, the message (whether verbal or nonverbal) should therefore be accepted. Both the messenger and the revelation formulas "are indicative of prophetic authority and prerogative."[3] The formulas demonstrate that the symbolic actions conducted by the prophets originate from Deity and did not stem from the imaginations of the prophets.

Third, prophetic symbolic actions include either a ritualistic gesture, a movement, a posture, or a dramatized act. For example, Joshua stretched a spear toward the city of Ai (Joshua 8:18–19); Ahijah tore a new garment into twelve pieces (1 Kings 11:29–31); Isaiah wrote the name *Mahershalalhashbaz* upon a scroll and then united with his wife (Isaiah 8:1–4); Jeremiah placed stones in a brick kiln (Jeremiah 43:8–13); and Ezekiel ate a scroll (Ezekiel 2:8–3:6).

Fourth, the dramatized action represents something other than what is visible to onlookers or participants. For example, the Lord instructed Ezekiel to perform a certain action, which in turn became a nonverbal prophecy. On one occasion God told Ezekiel to shave his beard and to cut the hair of his head with a razor and a knife and divide the cut hair into three parts. Next God commanded, "Thou shalt burn with fire a third part [of the hair] in . . . the city . . . and thou shalt take a third part, and smite about it with a knife: and a third part thou shalt scatter in the wind" (Ezekiel 5:2). The Lord interpreted these strange acts by drawing direct parallels between the three portions of Ezekiel's cut hair and the inhabitants of Jerusalem: "a third part of [the inhabitants of Jerusalem] shall die with the pestilence, and with famine shall they be consumed in the midst of thee; and a third part shall fall by the sword round about thee; and I will scatter a third part into all the winds" (Ezekiel 5:12). Ezekiel's symbolic prophetic actions were fulfilled when the Jews were scattered or destroyed—some were consumed by famine, others by the sword, and still others were scattered upon the face of the earth.

Other scriptural objects serve as symbols and representations: Jeremiah's yoke signified bondage (Jeremiah 27–28); Ezekiel's journey from home symbolized an exile of Israel (Ezekiel 12:1–16); Hosea and his wife represented Jehovah and unfaithful Israel respectively (Hosea 1; 3:1–5); Ezekiel's two sticks referred to the Bible and the Book of Mormon (Ezekiel 37:15–28); Jeremiah's book of evil represented the destruction that would come upon Babylon (Jeremiah 51:58–64); and the serpent of brass pointed to Jesus Christ and his atonement (Numbers 21:6–9). On occasion, the prophet himself served as the symbol. Such was the case with Ezekiel, of whom the Lord explained, "for I have set thee for a sign unto the house of Israel" (Ezekiel 12:6). Similarly, Isaiah stated that "I and the children whom the Lord hath given me are for signs and for wonders in Israel from the Lord of hosts" (Isaiah 8:18). Many times the prophet's explanation of the symbolic action is included alongside prophecy (see 1 Kings 11:29–31; Isaiah 20:1–6; Jeremiah 18:1–12; Ezekiel 4:9–17).

Fifth, prophetic symbolic actions often required the participation of two or more individuals, or, if there were no actual participants, the symbolic action may have been conducted in the presence of an audience. In at least two instances in the Old Testament, the symbolic action included participation of the prophet and one or more other individuals—Elisha and Joash together shot an arrow (2 Kings 13:14–19), and Zechariah and others participated in a symbolic coronation ceremony (Zechariah 6:9–15). Other examples demonstrate audience observation. Ahijah ripped the garment as King Jeroboam looked on, and then Jeroboam received ten pieces of it (1 Kings 11:29–31); Ezekiel was not permitted to mourn the loss of his wife so that those who observed this act would inquire "wilt thou not tell us what these things are to us, that thou doest so?" (Ezekiel 24:19); Moses smote the rock from which water flowed "in the sight of the elders of Israel" (Exodus 17:6); Jeremiah was told to break a vessel "in the sight of the men that go with thee" (Jeremiah 19:10); he also hid stones in the clay of a brick kiln "in the sight of the men of Judah" (Jeremiah 43: 9).

Finally, because nonverbal prophecies originated with God, therefore they have been or will be fulfilled, according to the prophetic word. Yet false prophets imitated true prophets even in making nonverbal prophecies. Two false prophets[4]—Zedekiah and Hananiah—attempted to imitate the actions of the true prophets of God when they created dramatizations that did not originate with God. Zedekiah made horns of iron and then prophesied that kings Ahab and Jehoshaphat would push (like the horns of a ram) the Syrians "until they be consumed" (2 Chronicles 18:10). Hananiah removed and broke a yoke that was upon the neck of Jeremiah, prophesying that God would break the yoke (bondage) of the kings who were subject to the governance of the king of Babylon. In doing so, Hananiah contradicted an earlier prophecy made by Jeremiah (Jeremiah 27–28). Both of the false prophets, counterfeiting the true prophetic word, used revelatory language as they introduced their symbolic actions by uttering the formula "thus saith the Lord" (1 Kings 22:11; Jeremiah 28:11).

Of course, the "prophecies" of neither "prophet" were fulfilled. Very little is known of the end of Zedekiah (cf. 1 Kings 22:24–25). The fate of Hananiah, however, was prophesied by Jeremiah: "Hear now, Hananiah; The Lord hath not sent thee; but thou makest this people to trust in a lie. Therefore thus saith the Lord; Behold, I will cast thee from off the face of the earth: this year thou shalt die, because thou hast taught rebellion against the Lord. So Hananiah the prophet died the same year in the seventh month" (Jeremiah 28:15–17).

PROPHECIES OF JUDGMENT AND PROPHECIES OF CHRIST

Two themes constantly recur in the nonverbal prophecies—the theme of God's judgment against an individual, community, or nation and the theme of the mission, attributes, goals, or atoning sacrifice of Jesus Christ.

Prophecies of God's Judgment

A judgment of God or divine retribution is the "process of God's meting out merited requital—punishment for evil or reward for good."[5] For example, Isaiah was commanded by the Lord to "go and loose the sackcloth from off thy loins, and put off thy shoe from thy foot" (Isaiah 20:2). The prophet obeyed the Lord's command and walked for three years "naked and barefoot" (v. 2). The expression "naked and barefoot" may signify that Isaiah walked with no footgear nor clothing on the upper portion of his body. Such an action on the part of Isaiah gave him no practical or materialistic benefit; rather, the dramatization held a symbolic, prophetic message for those who beheld the prophet in such a state.

Isaiah explained his symbolic action. His walking "naked and barefoot three years" was for a "sign and wonder upon Egypt and upon Ethiopia; So shall the king of Assyria lead away the Egyptians prisoners, and the Ethiopians captives, young and old, naked and barefoot, even with their buttocks uncovered, to the shame of Egypt" (Isaiah 20:3–4). Isaiah's walking naked and barefoot was an unspoken prophecy, in the form of an action, that pointed to the time when the Egyptians and Ethiopians would be taken captive by the Assyrians, who would lead them away like slaves, without clothing or footgear. The prophecy was probably fulfilled in 667 B.C. when Ashurbanipal, king of Assyria, crushed an Egyptian rebellion and forced his captives to march like slaves to Nineveh.[6] Although God does not act directly in the judgment upon the Egyptians and Ethiopians, his role in the scene is understood.

The judgment upon the Egyptians and Ethiopians is but one of many prophecies connected with divine retribution. Joshua's stretching out of the spear toward the city of Ai spelled out an ominous judgment against the city, which was immediately fulfilled when the Israelites ambushed the city and "slew the men of Ai" (Joshua 8:21). An instance of judgment that was prophesied against a nation occurred when Jeremiah wrote in a book of the destruction that would come upon Babylon. Jeremiah afterwards tied the book to a rock and then tossed the book and the rock into the Euphrates River. His action signified impending judgment against Babylon, pointing to the time when Babylon would be destroyed (Jeremiah 51:58–64). Other instances of heaven-sent judgments against groups are common in the dramatized acts of Ezekiel. He drew a picture of Jerusalem upon a tile (Ezekiel 4:1–3); lay on his left and right side (4:4–8); baked bread that contained dung (4:9–17); trembled as he ate and drank (12:17–20); sighed, groaned, and beat his breast (21:6–7); and made sweeping movements with a sword (21:8–17).

All such actions prophesied of impending doom, destruction, and hardship upon various groups in the region.

Prophecies Regarding Jesus Christ

Many prophetic symbolic actions look forward to a future event that has greater significance than does the original symbolic action. For instance, the binding and offering up of Isaac by Abraham on Mount Moriah anticipated the atoning sacrifice of Jesus Christ. According to the book of Jacob, in this symbolic action Abraham represented Father in Heaven, and Isaac was an archetypal representation of Jesus. Abraham was "obedient unto the commands of God in offering up his son Isaac, which is a similitude of God and his Only Begotten Son" (Jacob 4:5). Abraham and Isaac were, of course, shadows when compared to the Heavenly Father and Son and their dramatized prophecy, a miniature model of the true and real moment when Jesus accomplished the Atonement.

In another example, Zechariah's actions connected with the making of the crowns are replete with Christ-centered symbolism (see Zechariah 6:9–15). The scripture begins with the formula "And the word of the Lord came unto me, saying" (Zechariah 6:9). Zechariah is commanded to "take silver and gold, and make crowns, and set [one] upon the head of Joshua the son of Josedech, the high priest; and speak unto him, saying, Thus speaketh the Lord of hosts, saying, Behold the man whose name is The BRANCH; and he shall grow up out of his place, and he shall build the temple of the Lord: even he shall build the temple of the Lord; and he shall bear the glory, and shall sit and rule upon his throne; and he shall be a priest upon his throne" (Zechariah 6:11–13). Several symbols in this passage have Jesus as their referent. The name *Joshua* is the Hebrew equivalent of the Greek *Jesus*.[7] Joshua, the high priest, has reference to Jesus, the "great high priest" (Hebrews 4:14; see also 3:1). The Branch identified in the passage is Jesus (see Jeremiah 23:5–6; Isaiah 11:1–5; Zechariah 3:8–10). The references to regalia—the crowns and the throne—and the statements regarding bearing the glory and sitting and ruling upon the throne point to Jesus as the "King of Zion" (Moses 7:53), "King of glory" (Psalm 24:7), and the "King of Kings, and Lord of Lords" (Revelation 19:16). In addition, the duplicated reference to the temple speaks of the crowned and enthroned Jesus Christ. It is evident, then, that Zechariah's participation in the coronation of Joshua, the high priest, prophesied of the future coronation of Jesus Christ.

PURPOSE OF NONVERBAL PROPHECIES

One obvious purpose of prophetic drama is that dramatic acts serve to pique the interest of the participants in the action, the audience of the action, or subsequent generations who would learn of the action. Drama is often much more interesting than the ordinary spoken word, for it appeals to both the ear and the eye. It is colorful, vivid, and three-dimensional. Dramatized action can be much more shocking than the spoken word—one prophet marries a harlot, and another one breaks a vessel while the public watches—causing the audience to pay great heed to the actions being performed. As with any theatrical production, symbolic actions tend to involve the audience, causing them to question the movements and postures and moving them to a higher plane of understanding. As with visual aids used in the classroom, the prophetic drama served to make the harsh message of judgment—or the sacred prophecy concerning Christ's atonement—both easier to understand and more memorable.

CONCLUSION

Understanding the environment and significance of symbolic actions in the Old Testament can aid Latter-day Saints in four ways. First, our religious tradition embraces a number of sacred ordinances, including baptism, the sacrament of the Lord's Supper, administrations on behalf of the sick, ordinations, confirmations, and temple ordinances. Within this system of ordinances are numerous movements, gestures, and actions (for example, the laying on of the hands, burial in water, the anointing with consecrated oil) that coincide in an approximate manner with the sacral movements of religious individuals of the Old Testament. As we study the symbolic actions of the Old Testament, both those conducted by the prophets and those performed by the community of Israel in the temple and in their religious festivals, we may learn of the meaning and symbolism of sacral movement in The Church of Jesus Christ of Latter-day Saints.

Second, a careful examination of the lesser-known dramatized actions of the Old Testament will increase our understanding of the more celebrated scriptures. For instance, we can now reread Ezekiel 37:15–28 (the sticks of Judah and Ephraim) and obtain new insights into why Ezekiel dramatized such an act, where he received his authority to do so, and in what manner the prophecy may be fulfilled.

Third, several of the nonverbal prophecies prefigure specific aspects of Jesus' atoning sacrifice. Consider the lifting of the serpent of brass by the prophet Moses. As he *lifted up* the brazen serpent in the wilderness on a pole, even so Jesus was *lifted up* on the cross. As Jesus was *lifted up* on the cross, those who look to Jesus on the cross will be *lifted up* into heaven. Again, as ancient Israel looked up at the serpent and were healed of the poison of the fiery serpents and thereby retained physical life, "even so as many as should look upon the Son of God with faith, having a contrite spirit, might live, even unto that life which is eternal" (Helaman 8:15).

Finally, the individual daily actions, movement, and posture of each member of the Church prophesy in a real sense what will become of that individual in the eternities. Righteous actions prophesy of the opportunity to dwell with Heavenly Father in the eternal world; wicked actions prophesy of the possibility of living outside of the realm of Heavenly Father, both in this sphere of existence and in the eternities.

TABLE 1

EXAMPLES OF NONVERBAL PROPHECIES

Source: JST Genesis 14:17 *Prophet: Melchizedek*
Prophetic Speech Formula: None
Object or Person Used as a Symbol: Bread and wine
Symbolic Action: Melchizedek breaks bread and blesses wine
Prophecy: Looks forward to Christ's atonement, his broken body, and blood sacrifice

Source: Genesis 22 *Prophet: Abraham*
Revelation Formula: "God . . . said unto him, Abraham" (Genesis 22:1)
Object or Person Used as a Symbol: Isaac
Symbolic Action: Abraham prepares to sacrifice Isaac
Prophecy: Looks forward to the atoning sacrifice of Jesus Christ (Jacob 4:5)

Source: Exodus 7:8–12 *Prophet: Aaron*
Revelation Formula: "And the Lord spake unto Moses and unto Aaron, saying" (Exodus 7:8)
Object or Person Used as a Symbol: Rod
Symbolic Action: Aaron casts down his rod, and it becomes a serpent
Prophecy: Points to the regal power and priesthood authority of Jesus

Source: Exodus 15:22–25 *Prophet: Moses*
Prophetic Speech Formula: None
Object or Person Used as a Symbol: Tree and waters
Symbolic Action: Moses throws a tree into waters of bitterness
Prophecy: The tree typifies and points forward to Jesus Christ, who is the Tree of Life

Source: Exodus 17:1–6; Numbers 20:1–11 *Prophet: Moses*
Revelation Formula: "And the Lord said unto Moses" (Exodus 17:5)
Object or Person Used as a Symbol: Water, rock, and rod
Symbolic Action: Moses smites a rock, and water gushes out
Prophecy: All three symbols—water, rock, and rod—point to Jesus

Source: Numbers 21:6–9 *Prophet: Moses*
Revelation Formula: "And the Lord said unto Moses" (Numbers 21:8)
Object or Person Used as a Symbol: Serpent of brass on a pole
Symbolic Action: Moses lifts a brazen serpent in sight of Israel
Prophecy: The future lifting of Christ on the cross and the subsequent healing of believers (John 3:14–15; Helaman 8:14–15; Alma 33:19)

Source: Joshua 8:18–19 *Prophet: Joshua*
Revelation Formula: "And the Lord said unto Joshua" (Joshua 8:18)
Object or Person Used as a Symbol: Spear
Symbolic Action: Joshua stretches the spear toward Ai
Prophecy: Joshua and his army will conquer the city

Source: 1 Kings 11:29–31 *Prophet: Ahijah*
Prophetic Speech Formula: None
Object or Person Used as a Symbol: New garment
Symbolic Action: Ahijah rips the new garment into twelve pieces and gives ten pieces to Jeroboam
Prophecy: Jeroboam will soon take possession of the ten tribes as king

Source: 1 Kings 19:19–21 *Prophet: Elijah*
Prophetic Speech Formula: None
Object or Person Used as a Symbol: Mantle
Symbolic Action: Elijah casts his mantle upon Elisha
Prophecy: Elisha will succeed Elijah as prophet and wear the prophetic mantle

Source: 2 Kings 13:14–19 *Prophet: Elisha*
Prophetic Speech Formula: None
Object or Person Used as a Symbol: Bow and arrow
Symbolic Action: Elisha and Joash shoot an arrow
Prophecy: Joash will receive deliverance from Syria

Source: Isaiah 8:1–4 *Prophet: Isaiah*
Revelation Formula: "The Lord said unto [Isaiah]" (Isaiah 8:1)
Object or Person Used as a Symbol: Mahershalalhashbaz
Symbolic Action: Isaiah writes the name *Mahershalalhashbaz* upon a scroll, unites with his wife (the prophetess), and she bears a son, whom they name Mahershalalhashbaz
Prophecy: With Isaiah 7:14–16, prophesies of the birth of Jesus Christ

Source: Isaiah 20:1–6 *Prophet: Isaiah*
Revelation Formula: "Spake the Lord by Isaiah the son of Amoz, saying" (Isaiah 20:2)
Object or Person Used as a Symbol: Isaiah
Symbolic Action: Isaiah removes his clothes and walks naked like a slave
Prophecy: The Assyrians will take the Egyptians and Ethiopians captive and cause them to walk naked

Source: Jeremiah 13:1–10 *Prophet: Jeremiah*
Messenger/Revelation Formula: "Thus saith the Lord unto me . . . And the word of the Lord came unto me the second time, saying" (Jeremiah 13:1, 3)
Object or Person Used as a Symbol: Linen girdle
Symbolic Action: Jeremiah clothes himself with a linen girdle, removes the girdle, and then hides it in the hole of a rock
Prophecy: Just as the people of Judah were once whole like the linen girdle, so will they become marred and rotten like the girdle that was placed in the rock

Source: Jeremiah 16:1–12 *Prophet: Jeremiah*
Revelation Formula: "The word of the Lord came also unto me, saying" (Jeremiah 16:1)
Object or Person Used as a Symbol: Jeremiah
Symbolic Action: Jeremiah was commanded to refrain from marrying and having children and from feasting in a joyous manner
Prophecy: Israel will be destroyed and not enjoy familial relations, and they, like Jeremiah, will be unable to mourn for the loss of family life

Source: Jeremiah 18:1–12 *Prophet: Jeremiah*
Revelation Formula: "The word which came to Jeremiah from the Lord, saying" (Jeremiah 18:1)
Object or Person Used as a Symbol: Potter and his clay
Symbolic Action: In the presence of Jeremiah, the potter creates two separate vessels—one marred and one pleasing in the eyes of the potter
Prophecy: God is the potter, and Israel is like clay in his hands. If they repent of their sins, they will become a good vessel; if they do not repent, they will become a marred vessel

Source: Jeremiah 19 *Prophet: Jeremiah*
Messenger Formula: "Thus saith the Lord" (Jeremiah 19:1)
Object or Person Used as a Symbol: Potter's vessel
Symbolic Action: Jeremiah breaks the vessel in the presence of men at Tophet, near the east gate of Jerusalem
Prophecy: "Thus saith the Lord of hosts; Even so will I break this people and this city, as one breaketh a potter's vessel, that cannot be made whole again: and they shall bury them in Tophet, till there be no place to bury" (v. 11)

Source: Jeremiah 25:15–29 *Prophet: Jeremiah*
Messenger Formula: "For thus saith the Lord God of Israel unto me" (Jeremiah 25:15)
Object or Person Used as a Symbol: Cup
Symbolic Action: God commands Jeremiah to cause many nations to drink from the wine cup of fury
Prophecy: Many nations will be destroyed by the sword

Source: Jeremiah 27–28 *Prophet: Jeremiah*
Revelation/Messenger Formula: "Came this word unto Jeremiah from the Lord, saying, Thus saith the Lord to me" (Jeremiah 1:1–2)
Object or Person Used as a Symbol: Yoke
Symbolic Action: Jeremiah makes yokes and bonds, places one around his neck (27:2; 28:10), and sends the remaining yokes and bonds to neighboring kings
Prophecy: The kings and kingdoms who do not submit to the governance of Nebuchadnezzar will be destroyed

Source: Jeremiah 32 *Prophet: Jeremiah*
Revelation Formula: "The word that came to Jeremiah from the Lord" (Jeremiah 32:1)
Object or Person Used as a Symbol: A field in Anathoth and an accompanying deed of land
Symbolic Action: Jeremiah buys a field in Anathoth and accepts the deed of land
Prophecy: Although Israel is experiencing calamity and destruction, the time will come when they will once again enjoy prosperity and peace, such as buying and selling land

Source: Jeremiah 35 *Prophet: Jeremiah*
Revelation Formula: "The word which came unto Jeremiah from the Lord" (Jeremiah 35:1)
Object or Person Used as a Symbol: Pots and cups of wine
Symbolic Action: Jeremiah accompanies the Rechabites into the temple and offers them wine
Prophecy: The obedient Rechabites will remain (symbolically) in the temple forever; on the other hand, the disobedient men of Judah and inhabitants of Jerusalem will be cursed

Source: Jeremiah 43:8–13 *Prophet: Jeremiah*
Revelation Formula: "Then came the word of the Lord unto Jeremiah in Tahpanhes, saying" (Jeremiah 43:8)
Object or Person Used as a Symbol: Great stones and brick kiln
Symbolic Action: Jeremiah hides stones in a brick kiln near the entry to Pharaoh's house
Prophecy: Nebuchadnezzer's throne will be set upon rocks and will burn the houses of the gods of Egypt

Source: Jeremiah 51:58–64 *Prophet: Jeremiah*
Messenger Formula: "Thus saith the Lord of hosts" (Jeremiah 51:58)
Object or Person Used as a Symbol: A book with a stone bound to it
Symbolic Action: Jeremiah writes in a book the evil that will come upon Babyon; the book is tied to a stone and thrown into the Euphrates
Prophecy: Evil and destruction will come upon Babylon, and it will sink and not rise again

Source: Ezekiel 2:8–3:6 *Prophet: Ezekiel*
Revelation Formula: "But thou, son of man, hear what I say unto thee" (Ezekiel 2:8)
Object or Person Used as a Symbol: Scroll
Symbolic Action: Ezekiel eats the scroll
Prophecy: As the eaten scroll contains lamentations, mourning, and woe, so Ezekiel's prophecies and revelations will consist of lamentations, mourning, and woe

Source: Ezekiel 4:1–3 *Prophet: Ezekiel*
Prophetic Speech Formula: None
Object or Person Used as a Symbol: Clay tile
Symbolic Action: Ezekiel places tile in front of him, draws a picture of Jerusalem on it, and creates details of a siege with mounds, a wall, battering rams, and camps
Prophecy: Jerusalem will be besieged by an army that will build mounds and use battering rams to break through the wall and take the city captive

Source: Ezekiel 4:4–8 *Prophet: Ezekiel*
Prophetic Speech Formula: None
Object or Person Used as a Symbol: Ezekiel
Symbolic Action: Ezekiel lies on his right and on his left side
Prophecy: Meaning uncertain

Source: Ezekiel 4:9–17 *Prophet: Ezekiel*
Prophetic Speech Formula: None
Object or Person Used as a Symbol: Bread, water, and dung
Symbolic Action: Ezekiel bakes bread with a mixture of dung, eats measured portions of it, and drinks measured portions of water
Prophecy: Israel will have to "eat bread by weight" and "drink water by measure" because God will make food and drink scarce. Also, Israel will "eat defiled bread among the Gentiles, whither [the Lord] will drive them" (vv. 10–11, 13)

Source: Ezekiel 5 *Prophet: Ezekiel*
Prophetic Speech Formula: None
Object or Person Used as a Symbol: Hair
Symbolic Action: Ezekiel shaves the hair of his head and his beard, divides it into three parts, and then burns one-third, strikes one-third, and scatters one-third
Prophecy: One-third of Jerusalem's inhabitants will be burned with fire and destroyed with pestilence, one-third will be smitten with the sword, and one-third will be scattered to the four winds

Source: Ezekiel 12:1–16 *Prophet: Ezekiel*
Revelation Formula: "The word of the Lord also came unto me, saying" (Ezekiel 12:1)
Object or Person Used as a Symbol: Personal belongings of Ezekiel
Symbolic Action: Ezekiel packs his bags and goes forth from his home
Prophecy: The children of Israel will pack their personal effects and be led away captive to Babylonia

Source: Ezekiel 12:17–20 *Prophet: Ezekiel*
Revelation Formula: "Moreover the word of the Lord came to me, saying" (Ezekiel 12:17)
Object or Person Used as a Symbol: Food and drink
Symbolic Action: Ezekiel trembles as he eats his food and drinks his drink
Prophecy: Israel's land will be stripped of its produce, and the inhabitants of Israel will eat and drink with great trembling because of their fearful hearts

Source: Ezekiel 21:6–7 *Prophet: Ezekiel*
Prophetic Speech Formula: None
Object or Person Used as a Symbol: Ezekiel
Symbolic Action: Ezekiel sighs, groans, and beats his breast
Prophecy: Bad news is coming that will cause hearts to melt, hands to become feeble, spirits to faint, and knees to become weak as water

Source: Ezekiel 21:8–17 *Prophet: Ezekiel*
Revelation Formula: "Again the word of the Lord came unto me, saying" (Ezekiel 21:8)
Object or Person Used as a Symbol: Sword
Symbolic Action: Ezekiel strikes his hands together (around the sword?) and then makes several movements with the sword, moving it to the right and left and so on
Prophecy: In every direction that Ezekiel points and slashes with the sword, so will the Lord cause slaughter and destruction upon the people

Source: Ezekiel 21:18–24 *Prophet: Ezekiel*
Revelation Formula: "The word of the Lord came unto me again, saying" (Ezekiel 21:18)
Object or Person Used as a Symbol: Two roads
Symbolic Action: Ezekiel marks out two roads and places a signpost where the two roads branch out
Prophecy: The king of Babylon will stand at the head of the two roads with his sword and choose through divination one of the two roads

Source: Ezekiel 24:15–24 *Prophet: Ezekiel*
Revelation Formula: "Also the word of the Lord came unto me, saying" (Ezekiel 24:15)
Object or Person Used as a Symbol: Wife of Ezekiel
Symbolic Action: Ezekiel's wife dies, and he does not mourn for her
Prophecy: Just as Ezekiel does not mourn the loss of his wife, even so the children of Israel will not be permitted to mourn the loss of their spouses and children whom they will lose during wars and tribulations

Source: Ezekiel 37:15–28 *Prophet: Ezekiel*
Revelation Formula: "The word of the Lord came again unto me, saying" (Ezekiel 37:15)
Object or Person Used as a Symbol: Two sticks or two pieces of wood
Symbolic Action: Ezekiel takes two sticks, writes upon them, and then joins them together in one hand
Prophecy: The Bible and the Book of Mormon will come forth together for the use of humanity; the two scriptures will result in the union of the twelve tribes of Israel with Jesus Christ as their king

Source: Hosea 1:2–11 *Prophet: Hosea*
Revelation Formula: "The beginning of the word of the Lord by Hosea. And the Lord said to Hosea" (Hosea 1:2)
Object or Person Used as a Symbol: Hosea and Gomer, his wife of whoredoms, and their children
Symbolic Action: Hosea marries Gomer, and they have three children
Prophecy: A prophecy that Israel (Jehovah's wife) will commit whoredoms by departing from Jehovah (Hosea) and chasing after false deities (spiritual adultery). The children represent different aspects of the Lord's relationship with Israel

Source: Hosea 3 *Prophet: Hosea*
Revelation Formula: "Then said the Lord unto me" (Hosea 3:1)
Object or Person Used as a Symbol: Hosea and Gomer
Symbolic Action: Hosea is once more commanded to demonstrate love to his wife, the adulteress
Prophecy: As Hosea once more shows love for his wife, so the Lord will once more show love to Israel

Source: Zechariah 6:9–15 *Prophet: Zechariah*
Revelation Formula: "And the word of the Lord came unto me, saying" (Zechariah 6:9)
Object or Person Used as a Symbol: Gold and silver crowns
Symbolic Action: Zechariah makes crowns of silver and gold and sets them upon Joshua the high priest and others
Prophecy: The coronation of the Branch, who is Jesus Christ

TABLE 2

EXAMPLES OF FALSE PROPHETS' NONVERBAL PROPHECIES

Source: 1 Kings 22:11; 2 Chronicles 18:10 *False Prophet: Zedekiah*
Messenger Formula: "Thus saith the Lord" (1 Kings 22:11)
Object or Person Used as a Symbol: Iron horns
Symbolic Action: Zedekiah makes iron horns
Prophecy: Prophesies (falsely) that kings Ahab and Jehoshaphat will conquer the Syrians

Source: Jeremiah 28:10–11 *False Prophet: Hananiah*
Messenger Formula: "Thus saith the Lord" (Jeremiah 28:11)
Object or Person Used as a Symbol: Yoke
Symbolic Action: Hananiah removes the yoke from the neck of Jeremiah and breaks it
Prophecy: Prophesies (falsely) that God will break the yoke of the kings from the captivity of King Nebuchadnezzer

NOTES

1. Symbolic action as prophecy is but one legitimate type of prophecy in the scriptures. Other types of prophecy include single fulfillment (the prophecy has but one legitimate fulfillment or accomplishment), multiple fulfillment (the prophecy has more than one legitimate fulfillment or accomplishment), conditional (the prophecy is not absolute but contains a condition or stipulation), unconditional (no conditions are attached to the prophecy), and type (a symbol that looks forward in time and is attached to a typological meaning).

2. See my article, "'Thus Saith the Lord': Prophetic Language in Samuel's Speech," *Journal of Book of Mormon Studies* 1 (Fall 1992): 181–83.
3. Parry, "'Thus Saith the Lord,'" p. 183.
4. Beyond the world of the Old Testament, wherein both true prophets of God and false prophets acted out prophecies, David E. Aune, in *Prophecy in Early Christianity and the Ancient Mediterranean World* (Grand Rapids, Mich.: Eerdmans Publishing Co., 1983), p. 100, claims that pagans of the Greco-Roman world also possessed similar types of prophecy.
5. Trent C. Butler, ed., *Holman Bible Dictionary* (Nashville, Tenn.: Holman Publishers, 1991), p. 373.
6. John D. W. Watts, *Word Biblical Commentary, Isaiah 1–33* (Waco, Tex.: Word Books, 1985), p. 265.
7. O. Odelain and R. Seguineau, *Dictionary of Proper Names and Places in the Bible* (Garden City, N.Y.: Doubleday, 1981), p. 222.

CHAPTER EIGHT

SEALS AND SEALING AMONG ANCIENT AND LATTER-DAY ISRAELITES

DANA M. PIKE

When a Latter-day Saint encounters the terms *seal* and *sealing,* thoughts of temples and eternal marriage come immediately to mind. In a more secular context, we may look for the "Good Housekeeping Seal of Approval" when purchasing certain products, and we obtain a notary's seal on important documents. What we may not realize is that our use of secular seals and our religious concepts of sealing have a history that can be traced back several thousands of years to the ancient Near East.[1] Knowledge of the history of seals and sealing helps us to understand the figurative use of these terms in many passages of scripture and also to appreciate our own use of words and concepts that draw on millennia-old practices.

WHAT IS A SEAL?

A seal is a small object into which a design and/or words have been cut.[2] Most seals in the ancient Near East were made from stone of various types, including semiprecious ones, but some few were made from ivory, bone, or metal. Because a seal was made to be pressed into a soft substance—generally damp clay but sometimes wax—the words and/or design were cut into the seal in mirror image to produce a readable impression. That necessity, plus the small size of seals—most of which were about one inch long—required a great deal of skill on the part of the artisans who produced them. Ancient seals have rightly been described as "Art in Miniature."[3]

The cylinder seal and the stamp seal were the two basic types of seals used in the ancient Near East. Cylinder seals were small, engraved cylinders that were rolled in clay or wax to create a

□ □ □ □ □

Dana M. Pike is assistant professor of ancient scripture at Brigham Young University.

continually repeating impression. They were the common type of seal used in Mesopotamia. (This area, between and around the Tigris and the Euphrates rivers, was home to the Sumerians, Assyrians, and Babylonians.) A hole was drilled through the length of the cylinder, allowing the insertion of a metal or wooden pin that had an eyelet at one end and often had an endcap at the other. Alternatively, a small handle was sometimes attached to metal endcaps. The pin or handle increased the ease of rolling the seal, and the eyelet or handle allowed the seal to be worn on a cord around the neck or the wrist.

The stamp seal appears to have been the earliest type used, and it became the standard in Israel and the other small kingdoms in the east Mediterranean area (Aram, Ammon, Moab, Edom, Phoenicia). Stamp seals were also common in Egypt, where they were generally shaped like the scarab beetle. Stamping stones were usually conical or scaraboid in shape, and the engraved end was most often circular or oval. Stamp seals were often worn around the neck or the wrist by means of a cord threaded through a hole drilled laterally through the unengraved end or through a metal clasp that was attached to the seal. The practice of wearing seals is alluded to in the Song of Solomon, in which the woman requests of her lover that he "set me as a seal upon thine heart, as a seal upon thine arm" (Song 8:6).[4] Some stamp seals were set in rings that were worn on cords around the neck or the wrist or directly on a finger. Seals worn on a finger are called *signets.*

Whether an Israelite stamp seal contained a pictorial design or not—and many did not—the words on Israelite seals were usually *l-,* the Hebrew preposition translated in this context as *belonging to,* and the owner's name, which was often followed by a patronymic and/or a title.[5] For example, seals have been found inscribed as "belonging to Shema, servant of Jereboam,"[6] "belonging to Ya'azanyahu, servant of the king,"[7] "belonging to Ma'adanah, daughter of the king,"[8] "belonging to Berekyahu, son of Neriyahu, the scribe,"[9] and "mayor of the city."[10]

THE USE OF SEALS

Seals and the process of sealing had several important functions in all ancient Near Eastern societies, Israel included. Because the name, title, and/or design carved into a seal were intended to be unique to the owner of the seal, seals and seal impressions functioned to identify an individual. Not everyone owned a seal, however. In Israel, as in most countries in the ancient Near East, the ownership and the use of seals was restricted to those who needed or could afford them. So although many of those in the upper and middle classes owned seals, it appears that the vast majority of citizens—the farmers, shepherds, and others of the lower classes of Israelite society—did not possess personal seals.

SEALS IN THE OLD TESTAMENT

The following six passages illustrate the use of seals in Old Testament times:

1. As recorded in 1 Kings 21, Ahab, king of the Northern Kingdom of Israel (874–853 B.C.) and a contemporary of the prophet Elijah, wanted to buy the family vineyard of Naboth, a Jezreelite. Naboth, however, refused to sell to the king. "Jezebel his wife said unto him, Dost thou now govern the kingdom of Israel? arise, and eat bread, and let thine heart be merry: I will give thee the vineyard of Naboth the Jezreelite. So she wrote letters in Ahab's name, and *sealed* them with his *seal,* and sent the letters unto the elders and to the nobles" (1 Kings 21:7–8; emphasis added).

The letters sent by Queen Jezebel, and thousands of others like them, were written on sheets of papyrus, which were folded and then secured with a string. A lump of damp clay was placed on the string's knot, and this clay lump was then "sealed," that is, impressed with the sender's seal. The document or letter was suspect if the clay lump with the impression of the sender's seal (*bulla*) was missing on delivery.[11] The episode recorded in 1 Kings 21 thus illustrates two of the best attested uses of ancient seals and seal impressions: to indicate authorization from a superior to subordinates and to create a situation in which tampering with important documents would be immediately obvious. The bullae were in this respect the ancient equivalent of the tamper-resistant wrapping now found on many products. Many of these bullae, or clay lumps containing seal impressions, have been found, some even with the impression of the string that secured the document.

2. In Daniel 6, we read of how jealous administrators attempted to frame and then to eliminate Daniel, who lived during and after the Babylonian exile of the Jews, by persuading the Persian King Darius (ca. 500 B.C.) to make it illegal for thirty days to pray to anyone other than the king himself. Daniel's failure to comply was reported to the king. "Then the king commanded, and they brought Daniel, and cast him into the den of lions. . . . And a stone was brought, and laid upon the mouth of the den; and the king *sealed* it with his own

signet, and with the *signet* of his lords; that the purpose might not be changed concerning Daniel" (Daniel 6:16–17; emphasis added).[12] From this description it appears that a wad of clay (or perhaps wax) was pressed along a portion of the juncture of the stone cover and the mouth of the lions' den. This clay wad was then impressed with signets to certify the authority of the act and to indicate whether or not the stone cover remained intact. Although a document was not involved in this instance, the use of the signets of the king and his officials in this manner illustrates again how seals were used to indicate the authority of an action and render that act tamper-resistant.

3. Queen Esther, like Daniel, did not live in Israel. Following Esther's elevation to the position of queen of Persia and her subsequent exposure of Haman's plan to destroy the Jews living in that area (ca. 475 B.C.), King Ahasuerus instructed Mordecai to reverse the orders of Haman. The king said, "Write ye also for the Jews, as it liketh you, in the king's name, and *seal it* with the king's ring: for the writing which is written in the king's name, and *sealed* with the king's ring, may no man reverse. Then were the king's scribes called . . . and it was written . . . unto every province according to the writing thereof, and unto every people after their language, and to the Jews according to their writing, and according to their language. And he [Mordecai] wrote in the king Ahasuerus' name, and *sealed it* with the king's ring, and sent letters" (Esther 8:8–10; emphasis added).[13]

Once again, we see a ruler's signet used to authoritatively seal a document to ensure its validity and enforce its acceptance.

4. The prophet Jeremiah lived in Jerusalem around 600 B.C., and thus was a contemporary of Lehi, Mulek, and others of that era whose journeys to the Americas are recounted in the Book of Mormon. Among the glimpses into the personal experiences of the prophet Jeremiah preserved in the book of Jeremiah is one in which his cousin Hanamel approached him and requested that Jeremiah buy his (Hanamel's) land in their ancestral hometown of Anathoth (see Jeremiah 32). Significantly, the major elements involved in that transaction are preserved for us. Jeremiah states: "I subscribed the evidence [lit., "I wrote the deed"], and *sealed it,* and took witnesses, and weighed him the money in the balances. So I took the evidence [deed] of the purchase, both that which was *sealed* according to the law and custom, and that which was open: And I gave the evidence [deed] of the purchase unto Baruch the son of Neriah, . . . in the presence of the witnesses that subscribed [Heb., *hakkōthîm*] the book [deed] of the purchase, . . . And I charged Baruch before them,

saying, Thus saith the Lord of hosts, the God of Israel; Take these evidences [deeds], this evidence [deed] of the purchase, both which is *sealed,* and this evidence [deed] which is open; and put them in an earthen vessel, that they may continue many days" (Jeremiah 32:10–14; emphasis added).

As related in this episode, a legal transaction involving property was conducted in the presence of witnesses. Two deeds were prepared, one which was folded, tied, and sealed and one which was left open, or unsealed, so as to be accessible. These were both stored in a pottery container for safekeeping. The scroll that was not sealed could be easily consulted, but if a dispute arose and there was any question that the unsealed deed had been tampered with, then the sealed deed could be consulted with appropriate legal supervision. We thus see the status of a sealed document in a properly witnessed private transaction. Furthermore, it appears that the witnesses, as well as Jeremiah, were required to use their seals.

5. Another example, of a more infamous nature, involves the use of a person's seal as a sure means of identification. As recounted in Genesis 38, Judah, the son of Jacob, gave his "signet" and "bracelets" and "staff" to a woman he thought was a prostitute as a pledge, or guarantee, of future payment for the sexual relations he had with her. (The word translated *bracelets* in the KJV [Gen. 38:18, 25], *pātîl,* actually means "cord, string." That word is used to mean the string of a bow in Judges 16:9, and in this context it undoubtedly refers to the cord on which the seal was worn.[14]) The woman was Judah's widowed daughter-in-law, Tamar, in disguise. Tamar conceived twins from this encounter with Judah. Her subterfuge was motivated by Judah's failure to comply with an earlier promise involving levirate marriage customs. When news of Tamar's pregnancy reached Judah, who still did not know the true identity of the woman, he indignantly demanded that she be condemned and burned for having had sexual relations with someone other than one of his sons. At this point, Tamar said, "By the man, whose these are, am I with child: and she said, Discern, I pray thee, whose are these, the signet, and bracelets [or "cord"], and staff. And Judah acknowledged them, and said, She hath been more righteous than I; because that I gave her not to Shelah my son. And he knew her again no more" (Genesis 38:25–26). It is unusual that Judah would part with his personal seal not only for such a selfish, unrighteous reason but with what seems to be so little concern. His seal did, however, identify him and, thus, what he had done.

6. Some of Ezra's efforts to rejuvenate the spirituality of the Jews living in Judah in the middle of the fifth century (ca. 450 B.C.) are recorded in the book of Nehemiah, chapters 8 through 10. Chapters 9 and 10 relate a covenant renewal ceremony in which political, religious, and family leaders swore to adhere to the law of Moses in a community effort to live in but not be part of the world. We read: "We make a sure covenant, and write it; and our princes, Levites, priests, *seal* unto it. Now those that *sealed* were, Nehemiah, the Tirshatha, the son of Hachaliah, and Zidkijah" (Nehemiah 9:38–10:1; emphasis added). In this episode, the leaders used their stamp seals to seal, or in effect sign, the document recording the covenant into which they were entering. The act of sealing attested to the commitment of the individuals. It publicly indicated the serious, binding nature of their vow.

To summarize, these passages illustrate the actual use of seals in ancient Israel. We have observed that in addition to providing a means of *identification* (Genesis 38), seals and their impressions were used to indicate the *authoritative origins and approval of* the contents of a document (1 Kings 21; Esther 8) or an action (Daniel 6). Seals were also used to indicate the *consent* of those involved in or witnessing binding activities, such as a legal transaction (Jeremiah 32) or a religious covenant (Nehemiah 9; 10).

A Secondary Use of the Term Seal *in the Old Testament*

Developing from the use of seals in Israelite society, the Hebrew verb meaning "to seal" (*ḥātam*) was sometimes employed with the sense of "to shut securely, to close up" but without the connotation of being officially sealed with an impressed bulla, like a papyrus document or a stone over a lions' den.[15] The following four passages illustrate this extended usage:

1. Among the laws relating to ritual purity is the stricture that "when any man hath a running issue out of his flesh, because of his issue he is unclean. And this shall be his uncleanness in his issue: whether his flesh run with his issue, or his flesh be stopped [or, *"sealed"*; Heb., *heḥtîm*] from his issue, it is his uncleanness" (Leviticus 15:2–3).

2. In the Song of Solomon, the male describes his female lover who cannot be with him as "a spring shut up, a fountain *sealed*" (Song 4:12; emphasis added).

3. Job comments to the Lord that "my transgression is *sealed* up in

a bag, and thou sewest up mine iniquity" (Job 14:17; emphasis added).

4. Job observes that the Lord "commandeth the sun, and it riseth not; and *sealeth* up the stars," so that their light does not appear at night (Job 9:7; emphasis added).

Seal *and* Sealed *As Metaphors*

Three passages from the Old Testament illustrate that forms of the term *seal* are used in that ancient record in a religious context. In the first passage, the verb *seal* does not appear to have been meant narrowly, in its primary sense, but more broadly, in its secondary sense of "securely closed up." In the second and third passages, it is clear that the terms *seal* and *signet* are metaphors based on the real-world practice of sealing.

1. Isaiah 29 is familiar to many Latter-day Saints because it contains a prophecy of "a book that is *sealed,* which men deliver to one that is learned, saying, Read this, I pray thee: and he saith, I cannot; for it *is sealed:* And the book is delivered to him that is not learned, saying, Read this, I pray thee: and he saith, I am not learned" (Isaiah 29:11–12; emphasis added; cf. 2 Nephi 27:15–20). The Hebrew word *sēper,* which is here translated *book,* was broadly used to indicate any written text, from letters and deeds (see Jeremiah 32) to larger royal and religious documents. Most written records in Israel were sheets of papyrus or parchment scrolls, so it is understandable that some Bible scholars, having no belief in the Book of Mormon as a fulfillment of this prophecy, would suggest that this passage in Isaiah 29 refers to a document that was rolled or folded, tied with a string, and sealed with a stamped bulla.[16] Accordingly, such a "book" could not be read, for it was "sealed" with a seal and was not available for inspection except as presided over by the appropriate official under certain circumstances. Latter-day Saints, however, understand the "book" in Isaiah 29 to mean Mormon's plates, which Moroni hid and later, as a resurrected being, delivered to Joseph Smith. The passage in Isaiah 29 refers to Martin Harris's experience with Professor Charles Anthon of Columbia University.[17]

Concerning the set of plates he received from Moroni, the Prophet Joseph commented that "the volume was something near six inches in thickness, a part of which was *sealed.*"[18] George Q. Cannon stated that "all the sheets were bound together by three golden rings that passed through one edge, and three smaller rings fastened the other edge of about one-third, so that this part was *sealed.*"[19] The sealed portion of the plates seems to be the reason that Martin Harris, and subsequently Charles Anthon, referred to the plates as a sealed book, as prophesied by Isaiah (see 2 Nephi 27:10, 17).

In conjunction with Isaiah's prophecy of a sealed book, it should be noted that some prophets who have received visions and revelations about the last days have been commanded to "seal" their records to make them unavailable to the wicked so that the records may be brought forth to the righteous by the Lord at the appropriate time. Moroni wrote of the vision of the brother of Jared, which is recorded in the yet-sealed portion of the plates of Mormon, "And the Lord said unto him: Write these things and *seal* them up; and I will show them in mine own due time unto the children of men" (Ether 3:27; emphasis added). The prophet Daniel, after recounting at least part of a great apocalyptic vision, was commanded by the Lord to "shut up the words, and *seal* the book, even to the time of the end" (Daniel 12:4; emphasis added). That instruction was then followed by a brief vision of the time of the fulfillment of the events related in the preceding vision. Daniel commented that "I understood not: then said I, O my Lord, what shall be the end of these things? And he said, Go thy way, Daniel: for the words are closed up and *sealed* till the time of the end" (Daniel 12:8–9; emphasis added).[20]

If such language in these passages in Ether and Daniel is not meant to suggest that the written records of these visions were securely bound and bore some type of seal impression, it certainly alludes metaphorically to such practice in that these records (or their interpretation) were to be secured and unavailable for public scrutiny until the Lord declared otherwise. In addition, the concept of a sealed record suggests that the text would not be tampered with. Therefore, the visions seen by Daniel and the brother of Jared will come forth according to the will of the Lord in a pure, unadulterated form, not having lost any of their "plain and precious" passages.[21]

Also in relation to sealed religious records, consider the clear allusion to the ancient Near Eastern practice of sealing documents that is found in the book of Revelation. The apostle John wrote: "I saw in the right hand of him that sat on the throne a book written within and on the backside, *sealed* with seven *seals* [or seal impressions]. And I saw a strong angel proclaiming with a loud voice, Who is worthy to open the book, and to loose the *seals* thereof? And no man in heaven, nor in earth, neither under the earth, was able to open the book, neither to look thereon. . . . And one of the elders saith unto me, Weep not: behold, the Lion of the tribe of Juda, the Root of

David [the Messiah], hath prevailed to open the book, and to loose the seven *seals* thereof" (Revelation 5:1–5; emphasis added). In latter-day revelation the Lord stated that this great book, or scroll, which was bound and secured with seven seal impressions (*bullae*), contained "the revealed will, mysteries, and the works of God; the hidden things of his economy concerning this earth during the seven thousand years of its continuance, or its temporal existence" and that each seal represented a thousand years of that existence (D&C 77:6). John learned in his vision that the only one who could open this sealed scroll was the Messiah. No one else had the authority to open it, nor the power to bring to pass the "hidden things" of God of which it contained a record. When the allotted time has passed and all these figurative seals have been broken, then and only then—at the end of the world's "temporal existence"—will this scroll be opened and its contents, the "mysteries and the works of God," be made manifest to all.[22]

2. About 733 B.C., a military and political crisis loomed over the kingdom of Judah. The Lord, through the prophet Isaiah, taught that He, Jehovah, could be "a sanctuary" to His people if they trusted in Him, but that because of unfaithfulness, He and His doctrines would be like "a stone of stumbling and for a rock of offence to both the houses of Israel, for a gin and for a snare to the inhabitants of Jerusalem. And many among them shall stumble, and fall, and be broken, and be snared, and be taken" (Isaiah 8:14–15). The Lord then instructed Isaiah to "bind up the testimony, *seal* the law among my disciples" (Isaiah 8:16; emphasis added). In this last phrase, the Hebrew word *tôrâ,* translated in the King James Version of the Bible as *law,* is better rendered as *teaching* or *instruction.* It is possible that the Lord was here commanding Isaiah to create a written record of his teachings and then to bind and seal it, but that is unlikely because sealing the document would make it inaccessible. Isaiah was instructed to "seal" this teaching, whether written or oral, "among" or "with" (Hebrew *bĕ-*) the Lord's disciples. It seems that the Lord wanted the prophet Isaiah to deliver His message by the authority of his calling and with the power of the Holy Spirit, so that those who embraced his message could receive it knowing that it came from the Lord, that it represented His will, and that it had not been tampered with in any way (Isaiah 8:20). The Lord's Spirit would *seal,* or confirm, Isaiah's preaching in their hearts. This view is corroborated by the Lord's use of this expression in latter-day revelation: "Therefore, tarry ye, and labor diligently, that you may be perfected in your

ministry to go forth among the Gentiles for the last time, as many as the mouth of the Lord shall name, to bind up the law and *seal* up the testimony, and to prepare the saints for the hour of judgment which is to come; that their souls may escape the wrath of God" (D&C 88:84–85; emphasis added; see also 109:46).

3. The prophet Haggai, who lived in Jerusalem during the last part of the sixth century B.C. among the Jews who had returned from the Babylonian captivity, was commanded thus by the Lord: "Speak to Zerubbabel, governor of Judah, saying, I will shake the heavens and the earth; And I will overthrow the throne of kingdoms, and I will destroy the strength of the kingdoms of the heathen. . . . In that day, saith the Lord of hosts, will I take thee, O Zerubbabel, my servant, the son of Shealtiel, saith the Lord, and will make thee as a *signet:* for I have chosen thee, saith the Lord of hosts" (Haggai 2:21–23; emphasis added).

This prophetic passage alludes to the practice of ancient Near Eastern kings wearing signets on their fingers. Zerubbabel, typifying the Davidic royal line (and perhaps the Messiah himself), would be accepted by Jehovah, the heavenly king, and be as close to Him as a ring on His finger. More significantly, just as the use of a king's signet represented that a document or an action was royal in origin and thus authoritatively binding, so Zerubbabel would represent the person and the power of the Lord. The significance of this concept is made clear by comparing the promise to Zerubbabel with the invective uttered by the Lord through Jeremiah against Coniah (also known as Jehoiachin or Jeconiah), who was the next-to-last king of Judah, ruling for only three months (598–597 B.C.) before being exiled to Babylon: "As I live, saith the Lord, though [Heb., *'im,* meaning "if"] Coniah the son of Jehoiakim king of Judah were the *signet* upon my right hand, yet would I pluck thee thence; and I will give thee into the hand of them that seek thy life" (Jeremiah 22:24–25; emphasis added).

Coniah, or Jehoiachin, like so many other kings of Israel and Judah before him, failed to exemplify the attributes of Israel's divine ruler, Jehovah, thus producing serious consequences for himself and his nation. Jehoiachin's position as ruler of the Lord's people is likened to being a signet on the hand of the Lord; the Lord's dissatisfaction with Jehoiachin meant that he would be forcefully removed from his position of privilege and from the blessings of the Lord, as a ring is stripped from a finger.

SEALS, SEALING, AND LATTER-DAY ISRAELITES

The concepts represented in ancient Israelite sealing practices are very much a part of our latter-day terminology and should therefore be familiar to modern, covenant Israelites. The term *seal* is used in the language of the restored gospel in at least three ways that are also found in ancient scripture.

1. A sobering use of the term *seal* occurs in descriptions of those prophets and other Saints who, in all ages of the world, have become martyrs for the cause of the Lord. Their innocent blood, shed by adversaries, acts as a seal of their testimonies. For example, Abinadi was brought before King Noah and his priests for interrogation and accusation, but the prophet testified of the central importance of the Lord and His redeeming sacrifice. When he refused to retract his testimony, Abinadi was killed by fire. Mormon observed that Abinadi was "put to death because he would not deny the commandments of God, having *sealed* the truth of his words by his death" (Mosiah 17:20; emphasis added). In our own dispensation, an eyewitness to the deaths of Joseph Smith and his brother Hyrum, included that same concept in a eulogy of those martyrs. John Taylor's description is part of our latter-day scripture: "Joseph Smith, the Prophet and Seer of the Lord . . . lived great, and he died great in the eyes of God and his people; and like most of the Lord's anointed in ancient times, has *sealed* his mission and his works with his own blood; and so has his brother Hyrum. In life they were not divided, and in death they were not separated!" (D&C 135:3; emphasis added; cf. 135:1, 7). The Lord revealed through the prophet Brigham Young three and a half years after Joseph's death: "Many have marveled because of his death; but it was needful that he should *seal* his testimony with his blood, that he might be honored and the wicked might be condemned" (D&C 136:39; emphasis added).

Just as an ancient seal impression on a document identified the person with whom it had originated and also authenticated its contents, so the innocent blood of prophets and other martyrs acts as a seal, to identify their faith and courage, to indicate the completion of their earthly missions, and to authenticate the veracity of their testimonies of the divinity of Jesus Christ.

2. Given the significance of temples and the ordinances performed therein, it is easy to understand why most Latter-day Saints think of the keys of sealing in connection with the terms *seal* and *sealing*. The term *keys* signifies the right to preside over and direct Church affairs

and ordinances. The keys to seal are the authority to use priesthood power to bind or seal actions, ordinances, and relationships in heaven as well as on earth. By the authority and keys of the priesthood that he held, Elijah "sealed," or closed, the heavens so that no rain fell for three years (see 1 Kings 17–18). Curiously, the Hebrew verb meaning "to seal" does not occur in the description of the prophet Elijah's activity in ancient Israel, as recounted in the Hebrew Bible. Nevertheless, Elijah's authority was like that of Nephi, son of Helaman, to whom the Lord said: "Behold, I declare . . . that ye shall have power over this people, and shall smite the earth with famine, and with pestilence, and destruction, according to the wickedness of this people. Behold, I give unto you power, that whatsoever ye shall *seal* on earth shall be *sealed* in heaven; and whatsoever ye shall loose on earth shall be loosed in heaven; and thus shall ye have power among this people. And thus, if ye shall say unto this temple it shall be rent in twain, it shall be done. And if ye shall say unto this mountain, Be thou cast down and become smooth, it shall be done" (Helaman 10:6–9; emphasis added; see also Jesus' comment to Peter as recorded in Matthew 16:19).

The sealing keys, on the earth in various ages past but lost through apostasy, were restored in 1836 by the resurrected prophet Elijah in the Kirtland Temple (see D&C 110:13–16). Thus, the Lord has taught that in these latter days when priesthood keys are properly employed, "whatsoever you *seal* on earth shall be *sealed* in heaven; and whatsoever you bind on earth, in my name and by my word, saith the Lord, it shall be eternally bound in the heavens" (D&C 132:46; emphasis added).

Just as an ancient king would allow his chief steward to act in his name by sealing proclamations and documents with his signet (see Genesis 41:41–43; Esther 3:10; 8:8–10), so the Lord, our heavenly King, has allowed his authorized servants to act with his power, in his name. Ordinances performed with sealing keys can thus be authoritatively binding throughout the eternities.

3. Latter-day Saints realize that just because they participate in an ordinance in which the sealing keys are employed, the desired outcome, which is exaltation, is not automatically guaranteed but is conditional. The Lord has taught that for our ordinances to be binding in heaven as well as on earth, we must prove ourselves faithful and true to Him in all things. Thus, proving ourselves faithful results in our being sealed by the Holy Spirit of Promise. The title "Holy Spirit of Promise" designates a function of the Holy Ghost, who is empowered

to approve of and attest to the veracity of our ordinances, actions, and convictions. He thus figuratively places His stamp of approval on our lives, just as an ancient king used his personal seal to certify the validity of a document or an action.

Actually, the seal of the Holy Spirit of Promise is involved in the *process* of our progression as well as the *outcome*. Elder Bruce R. McConkie taught: "When the Holy Spirit of Promise places his ratifying seal upon a baptism, or a marriage, or any covenant, except that of having one's calling and election made sure, the seal is a conditional approval or ratification; it is binding in eternity only in the event of subsequent obedience to the terms and conditions of whatever covenant is involved. But when the ratifying seal of approval is placed upon someone whose calling and election is thereby made sure—because there are no more conditions to be met by the obedient person—this act of being sealed up unto eternal life is of such transcendent import that of itself it is called being sealed by the Holy Spirit of Promise, which means that in this crowning sense, being so sealed is the same as having one's calling and election made sure. Thus, to be sealed by the Holy Spirit of Promise is to be sealed up unto eternal life."[23]

The Lord has clearly indicated in scripture that to achieve exaltation in the celestial kingdom, one must obtain this seal of the Holy Spirit of Promise on one's life. In modern revelation the Lord has taught that "all covenants, contracts, bonds, obligations, oaths, vows, performances, connections, associations, or expectations, that are not made and entered into and *sealed* by the Holy Spirit of promise, of him who is anointed, both as well for time and for all eternity . . . are of no efficacy, virtue, or force in and after the resurrection from the dead; for all contracts that are not made unto this end have an end when men are dead" (D&C 132:7; emphasis added).

The Prophet Joseph Smith stated: "Peter exhorts us to make our calling and election sure [2 Peter 1:10]. This is the sealing power spoken of by Paul in other places.

"'13. In whom ye also trusted, that after ye heard the word of truth, the Gospel of your salvation: in whom also after that ye believed, ye were *sealed* with that Holy Spirit of promise,

"'14. Which is the earnest of our inheritance until the redemption of the purchased possession, unto the praise of His glory, that we may be *sealed* up unto the day of redemption.'—Ephesians, 1st chapter.

"This principle ought (in its proper place) to be taught, for God hath not revealed anything to Joseph, but what He will make known unto the Twelve, and even the least Saint may know all things as fast as he is able to bear them, for the day must come when no man need say to his neighbor, Know ye the Lord; for all shall know Him (who remain) from the least to the greatest. How is this to be done? It is to be done by this *sealing* power, and the other [i.e., second] Comforter spoken of, which will be manifest by revelation."[24]

CONCLUSION

Just as the many seals used by ancient Israelites were used to create impressions in thousands of clay bullae, so may we impress the significant concepts that employ the terminology of ancient sealing practices into our minds and hearts. Although it is interesting and beneficial to understand seals and sealing as an aspect of Israelite culture, it is obviously more important to understand the doctrines of eternity that are represented by that cultural practice. The Persian King Ahasuerus told Mordecai that "the writing which is written in the king's name, and *sealed* with the king's ring, may no man reverse" (Esther 8:8; emphasis added). As we reverently recall the martyred Saints of the near and distant past, as we participate in the sacred ordinances provided in the holy houses of the Lord, and as we strive to be true to the Lord in all things, let us liken the words of King Ahasuerus to our own, Latter-day Saint context: although Satan will surely extend his tampering and disruptive influence, no adversary, mortal or otherwise, has power to reverse or undo those ordinances that are sealed with the Lord's authentic priesthood keys nor keep from eternal glory those Saints whose lives have received the essential seal of the Lord's Holy Spirit of Promise.[25]

Let us keep before us the two-thousand-year-old expression of King Benjamin's desire for his people: "Therefore, I would that ye should be steadfast and immovable, always abounding in good works, that Christ, the Lord God Omnipotent, may *seal* you his, that you may be brought to heaven, that ye may have everlasting salvation and eternal life, through the wisdom, and power, and justice, and mercy of him who created all things, in heaven and in earth, who is God above all. Amen" (Mosiah 5:15; emphasis added).

NOTES

1. The term *Near East* is used in ancient studies to refer to roughly the same geographic area that is called the *Middle East* in modern times.
2. D. Collon, *Near Eastern Seals* (Los Angeles: University of California Press/ British Museum, 1990), p. 11, notes that whereas the vast majority of seal carvings were recessed, or *intaglio,* producing a raised impression, a relatively few

seals were carved as cameos so that a depression was made when the seal was used.

3. E. Porada, in *Sumerian Art in Miniature,* ed. D. Schmandt-Besserat (Malibu, Calif.: Undena, 1976), p. 107, as quoted in *Ancient Seals and the Bible,* ed. L. Gorelick and E. Williams-Forte (Malibu, Calif.: Undena, 1983), p. 5. For general information about seals and their use in the ancient Near East, see D. Collon, *First Impressions: Cylinder Seals in the Ancient Near East* (London: British Museum Publications, 1987); Collon, *Near Eastern Seals;* Gorelick and Williams-Forte, *Ancient Seals and the Bible;* R. Hestrin and M. Dayagi-Mendels, *Inscribed Seals* (Jerusalem: Israel Museum, 1979); N. Avigad, *Hebrew Bullae from the Time of Jeremiah* (Jerusalem: Israel Exploration Society, 1986); O. Keel and C. Uehlinger, *Altorientalische Miniaturkunst* (Mainz: Philipp von Zabern, 1990); W. A. Ward, *Studies on Scarab Seals,* 2 vols. (Warminster, England: Aris and Phillips, 1978–1984); M. Gibson and R. D. Biggs, eds., *Seals and Sealing in the Ancient Near East* (Malibu, Calif.: Undena, 1977), as well as entries in Bible dictionaries.
4. In addition to the commentaries, see the discussion of W. W. Hallo, "'As the Seal upon Thine Arm': Glyptic Metaphors in the Biblical World," in Gorelick and Williams-Forte, *Ancient Seals and the Bible,* pp. 10–12.
5. Because relatively few inscriptions have survived from ancient Israel, the information gleaned from seals and impressed bullae is of enhanced value. Both the titles of government officials and the personal names contained on seals provide many important, if not dramatic, insights into Israelite society. For further discussion, see, for example, Hestrin and Dayagi-Mendels, *Inscribed Seals,* pp. 11–15; and D. M. Pike, "Names," in *Harper's Bible Dictionary,* ed. P. J. Achtemeier (San Francisco: Harper and Row, 1985), pp. 682–84.
6. Since this seal dates to the first half of the eighth century and was found at Megiddo, it is assumed that Shema was a servant of King Jeroboam II of Israel, who ruled 793–753 B.C. See Hestrin and Dayagi-Mendels, *Inscribed Seals,* p. 18.
7. See Hestrin and Dayagi-Mendels, *Inscribed Seals,* p. 20.
8. See P. J. King, "The Marzeah Amos Denounces," *Biblical Archaeology Review,* July/Aug. 1988, p. 42.
9. See Avigad, *Hebrew Bullae,* pp. 28–29.
10. See Avigad, *Hebrew Bullae,* pp. 30–33.
11. Compare the passage in the Book of Mormon in which Giddianhi declared in a letter he wrote to Lachoneus that "I have written this epistle, sealing it with my own hand" (3 Nephi 3:5). It is not clear whether Giddianhi's action involved sealing as one would sign a letter or an action analogous to the external tying and sealing just described.
12. This passage in the Hebrew Bible, Daniel 6:17–18, is from that portion of the book of Daniel that is written in Aramaic, not Hebrew. The English verb *sealed* renders the Aramaic *ḥătam,* whereas *signet* renders Aramaic *ʿizqâ.* Note the analogy between the action in this passage and that in Matthew

27:66, in which the soldiers, following Pilate's order, "went, and made the sepulchre [of Jesus] sure, sealing the stone, and setting a watch."

13. See also Esther 3:10, 12; 8:2. The Hebrew word translated as *ring* in these passages in Esther is not *ḥôtām,* the Hebrew noun usually rendered as *seal* or *signet,* but *ṭabbaᶜat*. This latter noun also occurs in Genesis 41, in which Joseph's rise to power in Egypt is recounted and which probably also refers to a signet ring: "And Pharaoh said unto Joseph, See, I have set thee over all the land of Egypt. And Pharaoh took off his ring [*ṭabbaᶜat*] from his hand, and put it upon Joseph's hand, and arrayed him in vestures of fine linen, and put a gold chain about his neck; . . . and he made him ruler over all the land of Egypt" (Genesis 41:41–43). Elsewhere, *ṭabbaᶜat* occurs in passages where it is not possible to determine whether the ring was a signet or merely an ornamental finger ring, although the latter is more likely (see, for example, Numbers 31:50; Isaiah 3:21). It occurs about thirty-five times in the book of Exodus, usually designating the gold rings attached to the outside of the ark of the covenant (see, for example, Exodus 25:26–27).
14. This is the way this word and this passage have been understood for a century or more. It is unlikely, as Hallo suggests (" 'As the Seal upon Thine Arm': Glyptic Metaphors in the Biblical World," p. 14), that the *staff* in this passage refers to a seal pin. Neither is it clear, given what we now know about stamp seals, why the seal "must therefore have been a cylinder seal," as Hallo and others have contended.
15. Although it is not certain, it is often assumed that the Hebrew noun *ḥôtām,* "a seal," represents a borrowing of the Egyptian *ḫtm* (as do, similarly, other West and South Semitic attestations), in which case the Hebrew verb *ḥātam,* "to seal," is a denominative. For a more complete discussion of the primary and derived meanings of this verb and noun, see *Theological Dictionary of the Old Testament,* ed. G. J. Botterweck and H. Ringgren (Grand Rapids, Mich.: Eerdmans Publishing Co., 1986), 5:263–69, s.v. "*ḥātam.*"
16. See, for example, Avigad, *Hebrew Bullae,* p. 123.
17. For an account of Martin Harris's experience, see Joseph Smith–History 1:59–65. For a more complete discussion of the contents of Isaiah 29, see V. Ludlow, *Isaiah: Prophet, Seer, and Poet* (Salt Lake City: Deseret Book Co., 1982), pp. 268–77.
18. Joseph Smith, *History of The Church of Jesus Christ of Latter-day Saints,* 2d ed. rev., edited by B. H. Roberts (Salt Lake City: Deseret Book Co., 1974), 4:537; emphasis added.
19. George Q. Cannon, *A History of the Prophet Joseph Smith for Young People* (Salt Lake City: Deseret Book Co., 1957), p. 27; emphasis added. An inversion of these proportions is found in Orson Pratt's statement that "when the Book of Mormon was translated from the plates, about two-thirds were sealed up, and Joseph was commanded not to break the seal." *Journal of Discourses* (London: Latter-day Saints' Book Depot, 1856), 3:347.
20. Since some of "the words" are recorded and preserved in the book of Daniel, it seems likely that this verse at least partially implies that the interpretation of the words will be unavailable until the future.

21. Similarly, note the Lord's comment to Nephi in 1 Nephi 14:24–26.
22. For a more complete discussion of this passage, see Richard D. Draper, *Opening the Seven Seals* (Salt Lake City: Deseret Book Co., 1991), pp. 52–60.
23. Bruce R. McConkie, *Doctrinal New Testament Commentary* (Salt Lake City: Bookcraft, 1973), 3:335–36. As Elder McConkie indicates (pp. 342–47), even if one makes one's calling and election sure in mortality and is thus sealed by the Holy Spirit of Promise, it is still possible to forfeit one's exaltation. The sins of denying the Holy Ghost, committing murder in which innocent blood is shed, and committing adultery all have the effect of *unsealing* the Lord's promise of exaltation to any Saint.
24. Joseph Smith, *Teachings of the Prophet Joseph Smith,* sel. Joseph Fielding Smith (Salt Lake City: Deseret Book Co., 1938), p. 149; emphasis added.
25. Unless, of course, one breaks the seal by committing certain sins. See note 23.

CHAPTER NINE

AARON'S CONSECRATION: ITS NATURE, PURPOSE, AND MEANING

J. LYMAN REDD

In the twenty-ninth chapter of Exodus, we read God's prescriptive (administrative) instructions concerning the consecration of Aaron preparatory to his performing ministerial duties as the high priest of Israel. He was to be washed, clothed with sacred vestments, anointed, and then sanctified by means of sacrifices. In the eighth chapter of Leviticus, we read the descriptive (procedural) order of how his consecration was actually carried out. The prescriptions in the book of Exodus for Aaron's consecration may be perplexing, and a casual reading of the complex process in Leviticus often creates more questions than it answers, but an examination of Aaron's consecration in light of other well-documented ceremonies and phenomena of the ancient Near East may clarify the meaning that consecration had for ancient Israel and that it could have for covenant Israel today. Because of differences in time, culture, and geography, it is possible that a completely accurate interpretation of Aaron's consecration is beyond our understanding. The methodology used here to engender insights, understanding, and meaning at best might be labeled as seeing through a glass, darkly (see KJV 1 Corinthians 13:12).[1] Nonetheless, I believe it is better to "see through a glass, darkly" than to see nothing at all, particularly if the initial images seen darkly can be made clear and validated by prophetic statements, revealed truth, and personal inspiration. And thus, using a perspective from the ancient Near East, I attempt here to augment our understanding of the nature, the purpose, and the possible meanings of Aaron's consecration.

□ □ □ □ □

J. Lyman Redd is an instructor in ancient scripture at Brigham Young University.

AARON'S CONSECRATION

The Hebrew verb *qadas,* often translated *to consecrate,* conveys the following meanings: "to separate or set apart from the common and the profane" (see Exodus 3:5; Leviticus 8:10–12; Numbers 3:13; 16:37–38; Deuteronomy 15:19; Judges 17:3); "to be holy or clean" (see Exodus 13:2; 19:10, 14, 22–23); "to dedicate or devote" (see Leviticus 21:12; Numbers 6:9, 18–19; Hosea 9:10); or "to be sanctified" (see John 10:36; 17:19; 1 Corinthians 7:14; 2 Timothy 2:21). The process by which Aaron and those who served with him were to become clean, set apart, dedicated, holy, and sanctified for their service in the tabernacle is thus "being consecrated."

Aaron's consecration begins with this injunction: "*The Lord said* to Moses, 'Bring Aaron and his sons, their garments, the anointing oil, the bull for the sin offering, the two rams and the basket containing bread made without yeast, and gather the entire assembly at the entrance to the Tent of Meeting.' Moses did as the *Lord commanded him,* and the assembly gathered at the entrance to the Tent of Meeting. Moses said to the assembly, 'This is what the *Lord has commanded* to be done'" (NIV Leviticus 8:1–5; emphasis added).

It is important to note that three different times in the course of five verses, Moses makes it clear that God is the author of these injunctions, not Moses himself. In other words, Aaron has been divinely appointed.

The element of divine appointment is commonly attested in the ancient Near East. Prophets, priests, and kings were appointed by God or in some way received a manifestation of their divine appointment. Mesopotamian kings in the second millennium B.C. derived their authority from divine election. During the Old, Middle, and New Kingdoms in Egypt, the inflexible rule of divine appointment became operative at the death of Pharaoh. In Assyria, the king inquired of the gods whether they wanted one of his sons to succeed him. If they answered favorably, the heir was installed. The Assyrian crown prince was not necessarily the eldest son but was the one chosen by deity, as in the case of Esarhaddon (671 B.C.): "I was the younger brother of my adult brothers. (Yet) my father who begat me exalted me in the assembly of my brothers at the command of Assur, Shamash, Marduk, Nebo, Ishtar of Nineveh, and Ishtar of Arbela, saying: 'This one is my successor.' He questioned Shamash and Adad through oracles. They replied to him in the affirmative: 'It is he who should be thy successor.'"[2]

This element of election was manifested most clearly in Israel in the hereditary transfer of authority from one leader to the next. David's dynasty was set in motion by God; therefore, one could say that all who succeeded David were also divinely appointed. The Bible makes clear that Saul (see 1 Samuel 9:1–10), David (see 1 Samuel 16:1–13), and Solomon (see 1 Kings 1:30–35) were each selected by means of divine affirmation. That principle of divine choice in the Northern Kingdom may account for the frequent changes of dynasty.[3]

In Aaron's situation, the element of divine appointment is significant for several reasons. It was an obvious manifestation of God's divine approval of the newly appointed leader. It also ratified and placed a stamp of approval on the transfer of authority from one leader to the next. Finally, it established Aaron as a type and foreshadowing of Jesus Christ, in that both had God's unequivocal authority to preside. Perhaps it was this divine appointment, and all that it meant to ancient Israel, that allowed Aaron to assume his position of authority and to be recognized by Israel from this point until the end of his life, when that authority was then passed to someone else as designated by God.

Another significant element of Aaron's consecration is the location, specified several times as "the entrance to the Tent of Meeting" (NIV Leviticus 8:5; see also Exodus 29:10). The tent of meeting, or the tabernacle, was Israel's portable temple. The expression in biblical Hebrew that specifies the building Solomon erected in Jerusalem, as well as other buildings of the same category, was "house of Yahweh" *(bet Yahweh)*, or "house of God" *(bet Elohim)*. That name arises from the concept of divine residence and describes the intrinsic nature of the structure, which was considered by ancient Israel to be God's dwelling place. To enter the tabernacle, in a very real sense, was to enter the presence of God.[4]

The entrance to the tent of meeting refers to the area just outside the door of the tabernacle proper but inside the courtyard in the same area as the altar and laver.[5] Ancient Israel considered this courtyard sacred, and it was not open to the public. Hence, Aaron's consecration took place in one of the areas deemed most sacred by Israel during their sojourn in the Sinai.

The element of sacred space was commonly found among most civilizations in the ancient Near East. Israel, Egypt, Sumeria, Assyria, and Persia were emphatic that sacred ceremonies be performed in either a temple or an area designated as sacred space.[6] That concept and practice are also attested in Babylon and ancient Greece.[7]

The sacredness of the location also implies an element of exclusiveness and restricted access, making such ceremonies inaccessible to the general public. From a twentieth-century perspective and particularly in a society where absolute equality seems to be the ultimate goal, the "secrecy" of such ceremonies may seem, at best, antisocial. From the perspective of ancient Israel, however, the message of such a practice was clearly that those who had been called of God, all those who were to be consecrated to God, and all those who desired to enter his presence had to separate themselves, or set themselves apart, from the common and the profane.

After Aaron and his sons had been presented at the door of the tabernacle, "Moses brought Aaron and his sons forward and *washed* them with water" (NIV Leviticus 8:6; emphasis added). An obvious purpose for this washing seems to be the achievement of purity and cleanliness of the initiate in preparation for the rituals to come. This was necessary in ancient Israel both before and after contact with holy things.[8] Both the Bible and the Book of Mormon make it clear that the ancients understood the necessity of attaining a state of purity, for no unclean thing could enter God's presence. The ritual washings seem to be the primary metaphors for the necessary cleansing process. The washing of the hands was emblematic of the need for works of righteousness. The washing of the feet characterized the necessity of walking in paths of righteousness.[9]

Ritual washings were virtually universal to other religions of the ancient Near East. Water was the most common element used for attaining ritual purity. Such is clearly attested among the Mandaeans in the sixth century after Christ: "He washes his hands in order to be freed from all the prohibited things to which he has stretched his hands before; he rinses his mouth in order to cleanse it from all falsehood and fault that may have issued from it; he rinses his nose to cleanse it from whatever forbidden things he has smelt; he washes his face in order to be absolved from every shameful thing; his feet in order to be cleansed from every instance of having walked in rebellious and mistaken paths; while he wipes his head and ears he wishes to be absolved from every unreasonable thing which is counter to the religious law, and further, while wiping his face from all the acts of disobedience which he has committed."[10] This ablution differed from other ordinary ablutions insofar as it was effective forever. The meaning is quite clear: it is the complete removal of all that is sinful and unclean that belongs to his former life.

In Aaron's situation, God's mandate was that anyone approaching the Lord or rendering service in his name "shall wash their hands and their feet . . . that they die not" (KJV Exodus 30:19–20), clearly teaching the absolute necessity of being clean before entering the service or the presence of the Lord. In addition to purification and cleansing, the washing may have also represented the symbolic bestowal of other attributes and blessings as well. In the ancient Near East, ceremonial washings, or ablutions, were believed to purify the initiate, avert evil, give life and strength, and at times, symbolize a rebirth.[11]

After the ritual washing, Moses was commanded to clothe Aaron with six sacred vestments: described in Exodus and Leviticus are (1) the white linen tunic, or "coat," which was worn next to the body; (2) the blue robe, woven without seam; (3) the ephod; (4) the waistband, sash, or girdle; (5) the breastpiece; and finally (6) the headdress, or miter, with the sacred diadem, or "golden plate," set at the front of the miter. These sacred vestments, by heavenly design, were both functional and richly symbolic. They were to be distinguished from "other garments" (KJV Ezekiel 42:14; see also 44:17–18; Leviticus 16:4), were to be made only by special craftsmen "filled with the spirit of wisdom" (KJV Exodus 28:3), were to be used only for temple service (see Exodus 28:43), and were to be handed down from father to son (see Exodus 29:29–30).

The first, and innermost, garment of the six vestments was a white tunic, or "coat": "And thou shalt embroider the coat of fine linen" (KJV Exodus 28:39). The Hebrew word for "coat" *(kuttoneth)* used in Exodus is derived from the same root as the word used to describe the coat or garment given by God to Adam and Eve in the Garden of Eden (see Genesis 3:21) and the coat given to Joseph who was sold into Egypt. The word refers to a "linen cloth" or "skin" that was meant "to cover or to hide." White linen in ancient times had several symbolic meanings and various functions. The color white symbolized innocence, virtue, and light—all qualities of God himself and his anointed.[12] Egyptian royalty, for example, attired themselves in clean, white linen for ceremonial washings and other rituals because wool was considered unclean and was not to be worn in the temples.[13] In the scriptures, linen garments represent the robes of righteousness, washed pure and white through the blood of the Lamb (see Alma 5:21–24; Ether 13:10–11; D&C 109:76), in which we must be clothed to stand without shame in the presence of the Lord. As in the case of Adam and Eve, the linen tunic may also represent the protection we find only through the great sacrifice made by the Son of God. Aaron's tunic, in contrast to the coats prescribed for the other priests, was a coat of checkerwork or a "broidered coat" of *oreg* workmanship, which was a distinguishing factor in the gradation of holiness and importance (KJV Exodus 28:4; see also v. 39). Hence, Aaron's tunic seems to be a special garment with an explicit emphasis on its sacred nature, purity, and protection.

The next vestment, which was worn over the white tunic, was the blue robe: "'Make the robe of the ephod entirely of blue cloth, with an opening for the head in its center. There shall be a woven edge like a collar around this opening, so that it will not tear. Make pomegranates of blue, purple and scarlet yarn around the hem of the robe, with gold bells between them. The gold bells and the pomegranates are to alternate around the hem of the robe'" (NIV Exodus 28:31–34). The robe was made entirely of blue colored woolen threads woven into one piece, hem to hem, without a seam. It was made with a bound opening in the middle, similar to a modern poncho.

There is some controversy concerning the etymology of the word *me'il,* translated *robe.* Most scholars ascribe the origin of the word to a Hebrew root, *'ly,* which means something "over." Görg, however, traces the word to Egyptian origins. He believes the Egyptian word *m'r* is phonetically equivalent to the Hebrew *me'il* and more closely defines it. The word *m'r,* found in rituals of the New Kingdom and in Ptolemaic times, referred to "divine clothing" of "extraordinary flawlessness."[14]

Josephus tells us that the lower edge of the robe had bells of gold and tassels shaped and colored like pomegranates, stitched so that between each pair of bells there hung a pomegranate.[15] Anciently, the hem of a garment made an important social statement. The more important the individual, the more elaborate and the more ornate was the embroidery on the hem, of which tassels were an extension. Extrabiblical texts teach us that an ornate hem was a symbolic extension of the owner himself and, more specifically, of his rank and authority. When the hem was cut off, a part of the person's personality, rank, and authority was also removed. In essence, an ornate hem "was worn by those who counted; it was the 'I.D.' of nobility."[16]

In addition to the symbolism of the hem, the robe's color was also important. Colored robes often represented royalty. The symbolism of a colored robe may have been not so much the intrinsic meaning or symbolism of the color itself as much as it was the extraordinary cost of coloring the material. Blue dye, for example, was obtained from the hypobranchial gland of the murex snail. The snails were plentiful, but the amount of dye each yielded was infinitesimal, requiring twelve thousand snails to provide 1.4 grams of dye. Milgrom fixes the cost of one pound of dye in 200 B.C. at $36,660.[17] Thus, the garment described in the Pentateuch would not only have had a "royal price tag" but would also have commanded respect; certainly it could have been afforded only by the affluent or those in positions of power and authority.

The blue color of the high priest's robe not only points to the heavenly origin and the royal nature of Aaron's authority but also directs our minds to the source of Aaron's authority: the great High Priest, even Jesus Christ. The ornate hem had distinct allusions to His power and authority. The seamless robe represented the perfect wholeness, completeness, and unity of His life (see John 19:23). The embroidered pomegranates symbolized the refreshing nature of Jehovah's word in a dry, barren, and desolate world. The bells signaled the high priest's entrance and exit of the holy place "that he die not" (KJV Exodus 28:35). The bells may also have enabled those outside the tabernacle to participate vicariously in Aaron's activities by listening to his movements toward each of the sacred items inside the tabernacle.

Over the blue robe, Aaron was to place the *ephod:* "'Make the ephod of *gold,* and of blue, purple and scarlet *yarn,* and of finely twisted *linen*—the work of a skilled craftsman. It is to have two shoulder pieces attached to two of its corners. . . . Take two onyx stones and engrave on them the names of the sons of Israel . . . and fasten them on the shoulder pieces . . . as memorial stones for the sons of Israel. Aaron is to *bear the names* on his shoulders as a memorial before the Lord'" (NIV Exodus 28:6–7, 9, 12; emphasis added). To make the ephod, a strand of gold (carefully cut from thin sheets of gold) was woven with a strand of blue, a strand of purple, or a strand of scarlet dyed wool and linen, constituting threads that were each half gold. This combination of gold, fine linen, and dyed wool was a mixture prohibited in other garments because it was considered holy. Gold was obviously the main element in this garment, producing its dominant color and constituting the principal part of its weight.[18]

Despite the distinctiveness of the ephod and the detailed description of it in the biblical text, essential aspects of the ephod's design and fashion are still the source of much scholastic controversy. The ephod has been described as a sleeveless garment extending from the armpits down to the heels; as a garment with sleeves like a modern bathrobe;

as an "enclosure" of the body from waist to feet; and as a Greek robe for gods, priests, and kings.[19] Although the Hebrew language may not offer any clues to the ephod's design, the Egyptian language and culture may. Friedrich asserts that the word *ephod* is derived etymologically from Egyptian, not Hebrew. He explains *ephod* as coming from the Egyptian word *ifd,* which denotes "a type of material woven with four threads." Friedrich concludes that the Israelite ephod may have been similar to the Egyptian linen apron.[20] This apron, often an indicator of Egyptian royalty and a representation of its wearer's authority, was called the *shen'ot,* or "royal skirt." It was generally of precious cloth, of gold and gilded leather, until the Nineteenth Dynasty, when it was changed to a pleated and decorated apron.[21] If this etymology is correct, the ephod of the Israelites would have been much more like the royal *shen'ot* than a waistcoat, surcoat, or sleeveless garment.

The concept of the ephod as an apron of some sort also fits well with the description given in Exodus[22] of an outer vestment worn over the blue robe and bound to the body with the curious girdle, sash, or belt. The "curious girdle of the ephod" (KJV Exodus 28:8) was of the same workmanship and material—gold, linen, and dyed wool—as the ephod. Josephus describes it as four fingers in breadth, embroidered or loosely woven so that the open texture gave it the appearance of a serpent's skin.[23]

The two shoulder pieces had an onyx stone set in gold, upon which were engraved the names of the tribes of Israel. Symbolic of the Great High Priest, who was Jesus Christ, Aaron carried Israel on his shoulders, supported by and "girded" with an ephod, which represented (if the Egyptian etymology is accurate) the power and authority to preside.

Attached to the ephod by means of two shoulder straps was the *breastpiece:* "'Fashion a breastpiece . . . like the ephod: of gold, and of blue, purple and scarlet yarn, and of finely twisted linen. It is to be square—a span long and a span wide—and folded double. Then mount four rows of precious stones on it. . . . There are to be twelve stones, one for each of the names of the sons of Israel. . . . Whenever Aaron enters the Holy Place, he will *bear the names of the sons of Israel* over his heart on the breastpiece of decision as a continuing memorial before the Lord. Also *put the Urim and the Thummim in the breastpiece,* so they may be over Aaron's heart whenever he enters the presence of the Lord. Thus Aaron will always bear *the means of making decisions for the Israelites* over his heart before the Lord'" (NIV Exodus 28:15–17, 21, 29–30; emphasis added).

The breastplate was woven in the same manner and of the same materials as the ephod. Of skillful workmanship, it measured approximately nine inches square, "a span long and a span wide" (NIV Exodus 28:16*a*). The etymology of the term *hfoshen* also engenders a particular insight concerning its function and meaning. Görg alludes to the possibility that the word is not Semitic but Egyptian, like many other terms for priestly clothing. His concluding suggestion is that *hfoshen* might be a combination of two Egyptian words: *hfw,* meaning a covering for the breast, and *s~n,* meaning "cartouche," on which was inscribed the king's sacred name given to him in the temple.[24] Breastpieces, or pectorals, were a common accoutrement in the ancient Near East. Thus, in Israel, the high priest could appropriately wear a pectoral bearing sacred names.

The aim of Aaron's consecration (washing, anointing, and donning of sacred vestments) was to engender a fruition of divine qualities necessary for him to preside effectively in his position, and he was provided with additional means to assist him in his responsibility of rendering divine judgment. Inside the breastpiece was placed the Urim and Thummim (see Exodus 28:30).[25] In a way, the possession of the Urim and Thummim reflects not only the kingly quality of divine approval, authority, and appointment but also the capability of divine judgment. Just as ancient leaders were endowed in their coronations with the ability to do justice and make covenants of kingship, so also was Aaron given an instrument (the Urim and Thummim) that enabled him to make decisions for the Israelites and thereby to keep his "covenant of leadership." Thus Aaron would bear the names of the children of Israel "upon his heart" during his ministerial duties, symbolizing the similar action of the Savior during His ministry.[26]

The final two sacred vestments were the *turban* and the sacred *diadem* that adorned Aaron's head: "'And make the turban of fine linen'" (NIV Exodus 28:39), "'make a plate of pure gold and engrave on it as on a seal: HOLY TO THE LORD. . . . It will be on Aaron's forehead continually so that they will be acceptable to the Lord'" (NIV Exodus 28:36, 38). For the other priests, "decorated turbans" are prescribed, whereas Aaron's is a miter. The decorated turban of the other priests was considered an accoutrement of beauty and distinction, but the more imposing miter is considered a synonym for a crown.[27] The band, or plate on the miter, which is made of pure gold and has the words "Holiness to the Lord" *(qodesh le-YHWH)* engraved on it, hangs on a blue thread in front of the miter.

Crowns are mentioned in the literature of different civilizations in the ancient Near East, each crown having a slightly different form and meaning. In Egypt, the king was presented with the two crowns of Upper and Lower Egypt. The red crown of Lower Egypt was a "flat cap, with a spiral at the front and a tall projection at the rear," which symbolized physical life; the white crown of Upper Egypt was "tall and conical with a knob at the top," symbolizing the continuation of eternal life.[28] Some crowns were cloth or cowhide caps, such as those used by Persian and Hittite kings in the sixth century B.C. The Persian king's crown is described in detail: "The cap was made of stiffer material, and was higher than that worn by any of the (his) subjects. It assumed a broader circular shape, as it reached the flat top, and a blue fillet (or band), spotted with white, encircled it at the bottom."[29] Anciently, ceremonial crowns seem to have been used for symbolic purposes as a means of conveying a message to its bearer rather than for vain or practical purposes. The use of crowns was associated at first with temple service, and only later did they find their way into social and political realms. Widengren speculates that for the participant in the temple service, the earthly crown was a type of the heavenly crown—the crown of glory to be awarded in some future day to the obedient, or those who lived up to the quality inscribed on the headband, that is, "holiness." The participants were to become not only kings and queens but gods and goddesses.[30]

The phrase "Holiness to the Lord," engraved on Aaron's headband, is a powerful statement that indeed could have been the insignia of all Israel. It dictates the essential characteristic of Israel's lifestyle and, at the same time, reminds them of their status in the Lord's eyes, that is, holy.

After Aaron had been attired with the sacred vestments, he was ready for the next phase of his consecration ceremony: "Then Moses took the anointing oil. . . . He poured some of the anointing oil on Aaron's head and anointed him to consecrate him" (NIV Leviticus 8:10, 12). The purpose of the anointing is made clear in Exodus 29:9: to establish in perpetuity the right and obligation of this priestly service. The anointing with holy oil was the divinely appointed process for the inauguration of prophets, priests, and kings. Symbolically, it represented an elevation in status (from profane to sacred) as well as a confirmation of authority or an appointment to an office.[31] Great respect was afforded to those so endowed as the "Lord's anointed" (1 Samuel 26:9). The anointing also seems to have been symbolic of an outpouring of the Spirit of God *(ru'ah YHWH)*, the Holy Ghost and all other blessings that come with such an endowment—that is, the Lord's support (see 1 Samuel 16:13–14; 18:12), strength (see Psalm 89:21–25), and wisdom (see Isaiah 11:1–4). Saul, at his anointing, was promised that "the Spirit of the Lord will come upon thee, and thou . . . shalt be turned into another man" (KJV 1 Samuel 10:6). At David's anointing, the scriptures say, "the Spirit of the Lord came upon David from that day forward" (KJV 1 Samuel 16:13). Peter wrote, "God anointed Jesus of Nazareth with the Holy Ghost and with power" (KJV Acts 10:38).

A closely related benefit of the anointing was to symbolically sanctify Aaron for his duties in the tabernacle. The interrelationship between the presence of the Spirit and the process of sanctification in the scriptures is well attested (see Alma 13:12; 3 Nephi 27:20). One final representation of the anointing is paramount. The Hebrew word meaning "anointed," when translated into Greek, becomes *Christ*. Here again we find messianic forecasts.

After the anointing, God commanded Moses to make three offerings to complete Aaron's consecration: one was the sin offering of the bullock (Leviticus 8:14), the other was the burnt offering of the ram (Leviticus 8:18), and finally the ordination offering (Leviticus 8:22–23). "He then presented the other ram, the ram for the ordination. . . . Moses slaughtered the ram and took some of its blood and put it on the lobe of Aaron's right ear, on the thumb of his right hand and on the big toe of his right foot" (NIV Leviticus 8:22–23).

The word *sacrifice,* from the Latin *sacrificium* (*sacer,* "holy"; *facere,* "to make"), carries the connotation of an act that sanctifies or consecrates an object. In all ages of the earth's history, blood has been the symbol of life and its shedding the symbol of the offering of one's life. Sacrifices have also been equated with expressions of gratitude and acts associated with securing a continuance of God's favor and mercy.[32]

Aaron's sacrifices imply that his consecration involved the whole man—all his actions—and circumscribed the entirety of his behavior. He was to be God's man, a representative of God to the people, portraying holy separation from ceremonial impurity and sin. As a representative of the people, he was to offer the sacrifices on their behalf and to officiate in the prescribed services. Thus, Aaron functioned as the official mediator between God and man—another exact parallel to the relationship and position that Jesus Christ holds between God the Father and humanity.

The first two sacrifices were to be followed with the ordination offering and a feast: "Moses then said to Aaron and his sons, 'Cook the meat at the entrance to the Tent of Meeting and eat it there with the bread from the basket of ordination offerings, as I commanded'" (NIV Leviticus 8:31; see also v. 23). This sacral meal was the final element of what God prescribed as Aaron's consecration ceremony.

THE NATURE OF AARON'S CONSECRATION

The nature of Aaron's consecration, from a holistic view of the process, seems to have been a series of divinely appointed activities that teach symbolically the requirements for entering the presence of God and offer instruction about the process of so doing.

THE MEANING OF AARON'S CONSECRATION

Every component of Aaron's consecration points to and is symbolic of the Great High Priest, Jesus Christ. And yet, if we couch Aaron's consecration in the cultural context of the ancient Near East, we find other dimensions of the symbolism as well. In nearly every ancient and medieval society, kingship is a well-attested and important phenomenon. The central ritual of kingship was the coronation ceremony. That important initiation and transitional ceremony set the individual apart from the "commonalty" and endowed him with power, authority, and other qualities considered necessary to govern a society.

Most ancient societies of the Near East have coronation ceremonies whose structure and components bear remarkable similarities to each other, despite vast differences in time and geography. It must be pointed out that no one culture manifests every single element, nor do any two cultures match perfectly with each other, and there are differences in meaning that each of the ritual acts may have in its own context. Nevertheless, remarkable similarities have been found among numerous and often widely separated cultures, making it feasible to compile a coronation typology representative of the ancient Near East. The seventeen most widely attested features of coronation ceremonies are divine appointment, sacred space, secrecy, ablutions, special garments, kingship covenants, crowns, royal regalia, anointings, sacrifices, sacred feasts, thrones, jubilation, reverence, rehearsal of a creation motif, humiliation, and processions.[33] Aaron's consecration clearly reflects eleven of these seventeen elements (divine appointment, sacred space, secrecy, ablutions, special garments, kingship covenants, the crown, royal regalia, anointings, sacrifices, and sacred feasts) and is similar to several others. I do not believe that Aaron saw himself as a king, nor do I suggest that ancient Israel viewed him as their anointed monarch. I do propose that Aaron may have been viewed by the ancients as a representation of the supreme king of Israel, the King of Kings, even Jesus Christ.

THE PURPOSE OF AARON'S CONSECRATION

The Lord told Enoch that "all things have their likeness" and that "all things" were created and made to bear record of Jesus Christ. That, he said, was true of things both temporal and spiritual, "things which are in the heavens above, and things which are on the earth, and things which are in the earth, and things which are under the earth, both above and beneath: all things bear record of me" (Moses 6:63). Amulek explained that the whole meaning of the law of Moses, of which Aaron's consecration was a part, was to point to Christ: "every whit pointing to that great and last sacrifice; and that great and last sacrifice will be the Son of God, yea, infinite and eternal" (Alma 34:14).

The consecration of Aaron is a beautiful example of just how accurate and profound these statements are. By studying the consecration prescriptions, we learn, in a very profound way, first, what Jesus Christ has done for us and second, what we must do to regain his holy presence. We learn of his divine appointment and that, through his blood, our robes will become white. We gain a sense of the protection he offers us and a feeling for his heavenly origin, regal nature, power, and authority. We gain a tender glimpse of his love and the concern he has for Israel and an indication of his duty as the divine judge. Finally, we cannot help but recognize his sacred roles as our Redeemer and our Mediator with the Father.

Concerning what we must do to regain his presence, we sense how important it is to separate ourselves from sin and "the world." We learn how important it is to be clean in both the things we do and in the paths we walk. We are impelled to contemplate the protection that can be found through his great and last sacrifice, as well as the importance and function of the Holy Ghost in achieving that protection. We are motivated by the thought of that crown of glory that awaits the obedient and are brought to ponder the import of being sanctified. We learn the importance of consecrating our entire being to his service and the bounteous blessings—sweet to the taste, refreshing to the spirit, and soothing to the soul—that are promised those who, with all their heart, "come unto him" (2 Nephi 26:33).

NOTES

1. In addition to the King James Version, I have used *The NIV Study Bible: New International Version* (Grand Rapids, Mich.: Zondervan, 1985) because of its particularly good translation of the words describing the sacred vestments worn by Aaron. Direct quotations are cited to the KJV or the NIV parenthetically within the text.
2. Henri Frankfort, *Kingship and the Gods* (Chicago: University of Chicago Press, 1978), pp. 243–48. Several different procedures of reenthronement are analyzed, from the Mesopotamian ad hoc solution to the smooth-flowing system employed by the ancient Egyptians.
3. "King, Kingship," *Encyclopedia Judaica,* 17 vols. (Jerusalem: Keter Publishing, 1973), 10:1012–22.
4. Menahem Haran, *Temples and Temple-Service in Ancient Israel* (Oxford: Clarendon Press, 1978), p. 206.
5. "All the ritual acts, both those performed inside the tabernacle and those performed in the court, are sometimes referred to . . . by the all-embracing formula: 'when they go into the tent of meeting, or when they come near the altar to minister . . .' (Exod. 28:43; 30:20; cf. 40:32; in Lev. 10:9 the phrase is undoubtedly truncated, with the second half, 'or when you come near the altar', omitted). This formula makes it clear that there are two areas of ritual activity—the tent of meeting (i.e. the tabernacle) and the altar." Haran, *Temples and Temple-Service,* p. 206.
6. We know that Joash's consecration took place in the temple (2 Kings 11:4–14; 2 Chronicles 23:3–12). In *Ancient Israel* (New York: McGraw-Hill, 1961), 1:102, Roland de Vaux postulates that "the consecration of the other kings of Judah after Solomon took place" there. According to Alan H. Gardiner, "The Coronation of King Haremhab," *Journal of Egyptian Archaeology* 39 (1953): 13–31, the coronation of certain Egyptian kings, such as Haremhab, took place in the temple. Further, as Frankfort notes in *Kingship and the Gods,* pp. 245–47, both Sumerian and Assyrian texts describe coronation ceremonies performed in the temples of Erech and Assur. So, also, in ancient Persia the enthronement rites of the king generally took place in a temple at the ancient capital of Pasargadae; see P. N. Dhalla, *Zoroastrian Civilization* (New York: Oxford University Press, 1922), p. 227.
7. A. M. Hocart, *Kingship* (London: Oxford University Press, 1927), p. 78; Samuel H. Hooke, *Babylonian and Assyrian Religion* (Norman: University of Oklahoma Press, 1963), p. 47; Thorkild Jacobsen, *The Treasures of Darkness: A History of Mesopotamian Religion* (New Haven, Conn.: Yale University Press, 1976), p. 16. Each verifies that temple rites were jealously guarded secrets among the Mesopotamians. The concept of secrecy has also been verified as an Egyptian practice in H. W. Fairman, "Worship and Festivals in an Egyptian Temple," *Bulletin of the John Rylands Library* 37 (1954–55): 174, 187, 201; and M. V. Setton-Williams, *Ptolemaic Temples* (Cambridge: Setton-Williams, 1978), p. 38. The same holds true for secrecy surrounding the rituals performed in sanctuaries of ancient Greece. See C. Kerényi, *Eleusis: Archetypal Image of Mother and Daughter,* trans. Ralph Manheim (New York: Bollingen

Foundation, 1967), p. 118; George Mylonas, *Eleusis and the Eleusinian Mysteries* (Princeton, N.J.: Princeton University Press, 1961), p. 225.

8. De Vaux, *Ancient Israel,* 1:460–61.
9. Joseph Fielding McConkie, *Gospel Symbolism* (Salt Lake City: Bookcraft, 1992), pp. 104–5, 200–201.
10. E. S. Drower, *The Mandaeans of Iraq and Iran* (Oxford: Clarendon Press, 1937), p. 104.
11. Samuel A. B. Mercer, *The Pyramid Texts* (New York: Longmans, Green, and Co., 1952), 4:55; cf. Aylward M. Blackman, "An Ancient Egyptian Foretaste of the Doctrine of Baptismal Regeneration," *Theology* 1 (July 1920): 140–41.
12. Ad de Vries, *Dictionary of Symbols and Imagery* (Amsterdam: North-Holland Publishing, 1974), p. 388.
13. Bob Brier, *Ancient Egyptian Magic* (New York: William Morrow and Co., 1980), p. 38. As we study the ceremonial vestments, we find that they all have one thing in common: they each have a garment which is white in color. Why? Because white means innocence or virtue. DeVries, *Dictionary of Symbols and Imagery,* p. 388.

    Throughout the scriptures, white is also symbolic of light. Plato, Plutarch, and Hesiod express the idea that the only color which will take all others is white. It is also the only color in which all colors are, all the colors of the spectrum. That is why white is the only perfect color. Linen may have been used because it does not decay, smell, and attract bugs to the degree that leather and wool, being animal products, do. Linen remains white and clean. With extreme age it may yellow, but we have thousands of pieces of linen of great antiquity from Egypt in beautiful condition. Linen beautifully made, the equal, as Drioton says, to any linen that could be made in France today.
14. Susan Rattray, review of *Zum Sogenannten Priesterlichen Obergewand,* by Manfred Görg, *Biblische Zeitschrift* 20 (1976): 242–46.
15. See Flavius Josephus, *Antiquities of the Jews* 3.7.4, trans. William Whiston (Peabody, Mass.: Hendrickson, 1987), p. 89.
16. Jacob Milgrom, "Of Hems and Tassels," *Biblical Archaeology Review* 9 (May/June 1983), pp. 61–62.
17. Milgrom, "Of Hems and Tassels," p. 62.
18. Haran, *Temples and Temple-Service,* p. 167. "According to the Talmud, each thread of the ephod consisted of six blue strands, six of purple, six of scarlet, and six of fine twisted linen, with a thread of gold in each twist of six strands, making a total of twenty-eight strands." "Ephod," *Encyclopedia Judaica,* 6:805.

    Haran explains that the wool strands were dyed three different colors: blue-purple, red-purple, or red, extracted from the *murex truncillus,* the *murex brandaris* (shellfish indigenous to the eastern Mediterranean), and the insect *kermocuccus vermilio,* respectively. The fabric as a whole, rather than each single thread, was a wool-linen mixture, and the proportion of gold actually amounted to about half of the fabric. The inclusion of gold cords in a woven fabric should not surprise us. Something akin to this may be referred to in Psalm 45:9 (cf. LXX) and v. 14; Song of Solomon 3:10.

Examples of this sort of workmanship containing a large proportion of gold or silver threads in the weave are known at least from the Hellenistic period.

19. "Ephod," *Encyclopedia Judaica,* 6:804–6. According to Rashi's commentary on Exodus 28:6, the ephod was a square, sleeveless garment, falling from just below the armpits to the heels, "like a sort of horsewoman's surcoat," thus enveloping the entire body. R. Samuel ben Meir has the ephod enclosing the body from the waist downward, with the upper part of the body being covered by the breastpiece. Josephus, in *Antiquities* 3.7.5 and *Wars* 5.5.7, states that the ephod had sleeves and resembled a type of waistcoat. Another form of the Hebrew word *ephod,* mentioned in Exodus 28:8, 39:5 and Isaiah 30:22, is related to a verb that has the meaning "to gird" or "to adorn." This root may be connected with the Akkadian *epattu* (plural, *epadatu*), which signifies a garment in the Cappadocian tablets. The word also appears in the Ugaritic tablets as *ipd,* with possibly the same meaning. It may also be analogous to the Greek overgarment, which, similar to the ephod, served as an outer garment for gods, priests, and kings.
20. Ingolf Friedrich, *Ephod und Choschen im Lichte des Alten Orients* (Wein: Varlag Merder, 1968), reviewed by David Wright, in *Wiener Beitraege zur Theologie,* vol. 20.
21. See Millia Davenport, *The Book of Costume* (New York: Crown, 1964), vol. 1.
22. Haran, *Temples and Temple-Service,* p. 166. The apron was kept in position by means of the two shoulder pieces, as well as the curious girdle by which the apron is "girdled to the loins" (see Exodus 29:5; Leviticus 8:7). It is difficult to say whether the passage "girdled to the loins" has reference to a fastening device or the two apron strings simply being tied. According to Haran, the assumption is that when the priest wishes to remove the ephod from his waist, he can simply untie the 'joining' at his back and take it off from the front, rather than lifting it over his head.

The ephod, along with the other three garments worn only by Aaron, correlate perfectly with the quality, materials, and workmanship of the hangings and curtains of the court. Both are of the sacred mixture wool and linen, and both are designated as *hoseb* workmanship. Nevertheless, Haran points to several important differences. First, although the ephod corresponds to the veil of the temple, there is no mention of cherubim being woven into its designs. Second, the fabric of the ephod contains strands of gold, something missing from the prescriptions of the veil (see Exodus 26:31). But what is more interesting, gold becomes the dominant ingredient, both in color and in weight. In explaining how the fabric is to be woven, the text goes into great detail explaining that the gold wires were worked "in the blue and in the purple and in the scarlet and in the fine linen" (Exodus 39:3). Haran explains: "The repetition of the preposition 'into' (*betok*), seems to indicate that the gold cords are not assumed to be worked into a ready-made fabric, but woven together with every individual thread of wool or linen from the very beginning, the ephod thus being prepared from these partly golden threads. There is neither hammered-out work nor gold overlay involved here, nor even golden embroidery. And yet the gold becomes the main element in this garment, producing its dominant color and constituting the principal part of its weight."

The word *ephod* usually applies to the ornamented vestment which was worn by the high priest over the blue robe (*me'il*), but as time progressed, its meaning seemed also to include the breastplate, which was fastened to the ephod by the two "wreathen" shoulder chains. Thus the ephod, the breastplate, and the Urim and Thummim became synonymously known as the principal vehicle for inquiring of God—even though we are actually referring to three separate articles.

23. Josephus, *Antiquities* 3.7.2.
24. Susan Rattray, review of *Der Brustschmuch des Hohenpristers,* by M. Görg, *Biblische Notizen* 15 (1981): 32–34.
25. I. Mendelsohn, "Urim and Thummim," *Interpreter's Dictionary of the Bible* (Nashville, Tenn.: Abingdon Press, 1962), pp. 739–40. The exact function of the Urim and Thummim, and the technique employed by the priest in handling them, is not known. The same uncertainty exists concerning the material from which they were made. We do know from various biblical passages, however, that the initiator of the process was the priest who laid before God a question couched in precise words. According to Numbers 27:21, Joshua was commanded to direct his questions to the priest Eleazar, who in turn "shall inquire for him by the judgment of the Urim before the Lord; at his word they shall go out, and at his word they shall come in, both he and all the people of Israel with him, the whole congregation." The expected answer was most often given in the form of a yes or no. Consequently, it was to the high priest that the leaders and kings turned when decisions of both national and personal importance were to be made. Examples of the process include David's petitions to Abiathar in 1 Samuel 23:9–12 and 30:7–8 and Saul's inquiries in 1 Samuel 14:36–37; 18; 41; and Judges 20:27.

The process itself constituted another means of seeking the counsel of God and of obtaining a revelation of his will. There were many Israelite prohibitions against soothsaying and divination by means of auguries; subsequently, along with prophecy, this provided a second channel by which the Israelites could obtain revelation from God on a wide variety of needs. This procedure of divine communication is technically termed "to come before the Lord" or to inquire of the Lord (Exodus 28:30; Numbers 27:21).

There seems to have been a decrease in the use of this method of communication at the end of the first temple period, and there are indications of a total abandonment of it by the beginning of the second temple period. The Urim and Thummim are not mentioned in the Bible after the period of David, while Josephus indicates that the "oracle" had been silent for two hundred years before his time. Although some believe that the increasing influence of the prophets contributed to the eclipse of its use, Ezra 2:63 and Nehemiah 7:65 hint at an overabundance of "pollutions" and a lack of qualified priesthood servants as the cause. Hosea 3:4 goes even further and directly links Israel's violation of the covenant and her gross disobedience to the disappearance of the ephod, as well as other aspects considered sacred in their religious life.

26. Milgrom, *Leviticus 1–16,* in *The Anchor Bible* (Garden City, N.Y.: Doubleday, 1964), pp. 601–4. A note on the purpose these oracles may have served: the Dead Sea Scrolls have disclosed a new Hebrew word, *'wrtwm,* which, according to the context, means "perfect illumination." It is highly probable that it was formed by combining the singulars of *'wr(m),* "light," and *twm(m),* "perfect." It would explain why these words were chosen for the Aleph and Taw. God created *'or,* "light," first (see Genesis 1:3), and *tamim* means "complete, finished." That corresponds with the rabbinic interpretation: "Urim, because it illuminates their (the inquirers') words; Thummim because it completes (fulfills) their words."
27. "Priestly Vestments," *Encyclopedia Judaica,* 13:1063–69. Also see allusions to the crown in Ezekiel 21:31 and Isaiah 62:3.
28. Thomas Milton Stewart, *The Symbolism of the Gods of the Egyptians* (London: Bakerville Press, 1927), p. 118.
29. Dhalla, *Zoroastrian Civilization,* p. 259.
30. Geo Widengren, *Religionsphänomenologie* (Berlin: Walter de Gruyter and Co., 1969), pp. 50–51.
31. "King, Kingship," *Encyclopedia Judaica,* 10:1012–22.
32. Theo Baaren, "Theoretical Speculations on Sacrifice" *Numen* 11 (January 1964): 1–12.
33. Civilizations and societies used as a basis to establish common elements in coronation rituals of the ancient world are Fiji, India, England, Siam, Africa, Japan, Egypt, Israel, and several societies in ancient Mesopotamia. See Hocart, *Kingship, pp.* 1–5, 70–71; Frankfort, *Kingship and the Gods,* pp. 231–48; Stephen D. Ricks and John A. Sroka, "King, Coronation, and Temple: Enthronement Ceremonies in History," Brigham Young University, unpublished paper. For other summations of attested evidence of these common features, see M. Eliade, *Patterns in Comparative Religion,* trans. Rosemary Sheed (Cleveland, Ohio: World, Meridian, 1963), pp. 188–89; Geo Widengren, "Royal Ideology and the Testament of the Twelve Patriarchs," in F. F. Bruce, ed., *Promise and Fulfilment* (Edinburgh: T. and T. Clark, 1963), p. 207; and "Kings, Kingship," *Encyclopedia Judaica,* 10:1012–22.

CHAPTER TEN

JACOB IN THE PRESENCE OF GOD

ANDREW C. SKINNER

Few prophets in the Old Testament teach us more about covenant making and personal revelation than Jacob, the father of the twelve tribes. Jacob was a son of promise and of *the* promise. His own father was the meek and obedient Isaac, whose willingness to be offered as a sacrifice in the presence of God forever stands as a similitude of the atonement of God's Only Begotten Son (see Genesis 22; Jacob 4:5). Indeed, the apostle Paul refers to Isaac as Abraham's "only begotten son" (Hebrews 11:17). As a consequence of obedience, the promises God had established with Abraham were handed down to the patriarch's posterity—from Abraham to Isaac, from Isaac to Jacob (see Genesis 22:16–18; 26:1–5), and so on.

It is not difficult to imagine that as children Jacob and Esau were taught or, at the very least, heard about their father's and grandfather's supreme faithfulness. As the brothers matured, however, they took different paths. Esau became a cunning hunter; Jacob is described in the Hebrew text as an *'ish tam,* a man "whole, complete, perfect" (Genesis 25:27*b*). The implication is that Esau was concerned about one pursuit to the exclusion of other important considerations.

As a younger man, Esau seems to have possessed little sensitivity to spiritual matters. Certainly, he thought more about immediate physical concerns than either the covenants of God or those turning points in life which go on to determine the future. Thus, Esau sold the birthright (see Genesis 25:29–34). And, like some of us, he valued what was lost only after it was gone (see Genesis 27:38).

Esau added to his own misery and that of his parents by vowing to kill Jacob because of the lost birthright and blessing, even though he

□ □ □ □ □

Andrew C. Skinner is assistant professor of ancient scripture at Brigham Young University.

himself was responsible for the loss and Isaac did give him a blessing in the end (Genesis 27:39–42). Moreover, Esau married outside the covenant, which caused great grief to Isaac and Rebekah (see Genesis 26:34–35). Without doubt, Esau's behavior was on his mother's mind when she exclaimed: "I am weary of my life because of the daughters of Heth: if Jacob [also] take a wife of the daughters of Heth . . . what good shall my life do me?" (Genesis 27:46). In other words, Rebekah saw all her life's work, all her planning and teaching about the importance of the Abrahamic covenant, all her care in guarding and guiding its perpetuation according to divine desires, as worthless and wasted if Jacob were to follow in Esau's footsteps.

Here we see the Old Testament at its best, for the recurring problems of the ages are laid bare in an ancient context. Is there anything so heart-wrenching for a pure-hearted parent as a child of hope choosing to devalue covenants of the eternal family bond or so depressing as a loved one who esteems lightly matters of the Spirit? Do faithful parents of any gospel dispensation ever *not* worry about their Esaus?

After Esau saw "that the daughters of Canaan pleased not Isaac his father," he took another wife from the lineage of Ishmael, Abraham's posterity (Genesis 28:8–9). But again he missed the point. It was not simply a matter of marrying someone from a proper family; it was a matter of understanding and appreciating the significance of the covenant, of one's whole attitude toward sacred things.

By contrast, Jacob trifled not with sacred things (cf. D&C 6:12). He chose to obey his mother and father in many things and ultimately set out on a journey to seek a wife from among a known and acceptable branch of the covenant family. That was of paramount importance to his mother, for she was ever conscious of God's promises regarding her twin boys, especially the promise of Jacob's ascendancy over nations, though he was the younger (Genesis 25:23). Perhaps Jacob's foretold soberness and obedience were qualities that had been developed, nurtured, and proven over and over throughout the long eons of a premortal existence and lay at the heart of Jehovah's promise to Rebekah of Jacob's future greatness (see Genesis 25:23–26).

Before Jacob left his home to go to Padan-aram, his father, Isaac, blessed him in accordance with patriarchal privileges and reconfirmed to him the opportunity of receiving the blessings and covenant of Abraham: "Arise, go to Padan-aram, to the house of Bethuel thy mother's father; and take thee a wife from thence of the daughters of Laban thy mother's brother. And God Almighty bless thee, and make thee fruitful, and multiply thee, that thou mayest be a multitude of people; And give thee the blessings of Abraham, to thee, and to thy seed with thee; that thou mayest inherit the land wherein thou art a stranger, which God gave unto Abraham. And Isaac sent away Jacob" (Genesis 28:2–5).

With this blessing fresh on his mind, Jacob left Beer-sheba on what would prove to be a journey of many years. What Jacob thought about on this first leg of his travels we do not know, but one supposes it was about the covenants of the Lord and promises of obedience. When he got to the place he would later name Bethel, he settled down to spend the night and, while asleep, a marvelous vision was opened to him (see Genesis 28:11–15).

Jacob saw a ladder on the earth, which reached to heaven. Ascending and descending on the ladder were the angels of God, sentinels to the portals of heaven. Above the ladder was the Lord himself, whom Jacob heard and with whom he would make the very same covenant that his grandfather Abraham had made—the same covenant his father, Isaac, had prepared him to receive. "And, behold, the Lord stood above it, and said, I am the Lord God of Abraham thy father, and the God of Isaac: the land whereon thou liest, to thee will I give it, and to thy seed; and thy seed shall be as the dust of the earth, and thou shalt spread abroad to the west, and to the east, and to the north, and to the south: and in thee and in thy seed shall all the families of the earth be blessed. And, behold, I am with thee, and will keep thee in all places whither thou goest, and will bring thee again into this land; for I will not leave thee, until I have done that which I have spoken to thee of" (Genesis 28:13–15).

When Jacob arose in the morning, he sanctified the site of his vision with anointing oil and vowed, or covenanted, to live in complete harmony with God's will. He concluded his affirmation with a promise to tithe all that he would come to possess (see Genesis 28:18–22).

The significance of Jacob's first vision was at least sixfold. First, as the Prophet Joseph Smith indicated, this vision was Jacob's opportunity to begin to comprehend for himself "the mysteries of Godliness."[1] From this comment we also know that Jacob was a righteous Melchizedek Priesthood holder, because the Doctrine and Covenants teaches that "this greater priesthood administereth the gospel and holdeth the key of the mysteries of the kingdom, even the key of the knowledge of God" (D&C 84:19). Jacob would later use that key to unlock a spiritual door.

Second, Jacob's status as a prophet was confirmed. He heard the voice of the Lord Jehovah, the premortal Christ, and, as the apostle John later taught, "the testimony of Jesus is the spirit of prophecy" (Revelation 19:10).

Third, Jacob learned that in his seed, or through his own lineage, all the other families of the earth would be blessed (see Genesis 28:14). That promise was literally fulfilled in the mortal advent of the Savior, Jesus Christ (Galatians 3:16), and it is not impossible that Jacob glimpsed that fulfillment. Moreover, this promise has also been fulfilled as Jacob's seed have become Melchizedek Priesthood ministers and missionaries of the name and gospel of God, which gospel will ultimately bring salvation, even eternal life, to everyone who receives it (Abraham 2:10–11).

Fourth, Jacob learned that if he kept the covenant, God would be with him everywhere he went, that God would fulfill everything He promised to do for Jacob, and that God would bring him back to the land of his inheritance.

Fifth, Jacob learned that sanctity and place can be, and often are, linked together. "Surely, the Lord is in this place; and I knew it not . . . this is none other but the house of God," said Jacob (Genesis 28:16–17).

Sixth—and this point ties the other five points together—Jacob received his endowment at Bethel on the occasion of his first vision. President Marion G. Romney said: "When Jacob traveled from Beersheba toward Haran, he had a dream in which he saw himself on the earth at the foot of a ladder that reached to heaven where the Lord stood above it. He beheld angels ascending and descending thereon, and Jacob realized that the covenants he made with the Lord there were the rungs on the ladder that he himself would have to climb in order to obtain the promised blessings—blessings that would entitle him to enter heaven and associate with the Lord. . . . Temples are to us all what Bethel was to Jacob. Even more, they are also the gates to heaven for all of our unendowed kindred dead. We should all do our duty in bringing our loved ones through them."[2]

The great promises and blessings proffered to Jacob on this occasion were conditional rather than absolute. Nowhere does the text say that they were sealed or ratified with surety at this point, as is sometimes supposed. Jacob would have a long time to prove his loyalty and secure for himself the unconditional guarantee of all the terms of the covenant. Neither does the text say that Jacob's dealings with the Lord constituted the ultimate theophany, or revelation of God, which the scriptures promise to the faithful. Such would come later, after years of righteousness. From Bethel, Jacob undoubtedly came away understanding the order of heaven, the possibilities for exaltation, and the promises of the Abrahamic covenant if he proved faithful.

Other great prophets have left us accounts of their Jacob-like experiences, especially the apostle Paul and the Prophet Joseph Smith. Joseph Smith said, apparently to help us understand his own visions: "Paul ascended into the third heavens, and he could understand the three principal rounds of Jacob's ladder—the telestial, the terrestrial, and the celestial glories or kingdoms, where Paul saw and heard things which were not lawful for him to utter. I could explain a hundred fold more than I ever have of the glories of the kingdoms manifested to me in the vision, were I permitted, and were the people prepared to receive them."[3]

Jacob's life after the vision at Bethel (see Genesis 29–31) is one of the best-known biblical love stories, set as it is against the background of a manipulative uncle turned father-in-law. It need not concern us here, except as it points out Jacob's patience and loyalty to God in the face of frustrations, challenges, and manipulations. After more than twenty years of labor under the household rule of the scheming and jealous Laban (Genesis 31:1–15, 38), Jacob finally left Padan-aram to return to the land of his covenantal inheritance. But his departure was not without a final confrontation with the father of his two wives, who hotly pursued Jacob's caravan. Ultimately, Jacob and Laban came to a respectful parting of the ways and established a boundary covenant which would long divide the territory of the Israelites from the northern Aramaeans (see Genesis 31:44–45). But, the point is, Jacob's life was never one of ease or devoid of challenges and conflicts. Indeed, Jacob says, in effect, to Laban at a moment of intense frustration during their last confrontation: "Why are you chasing me? Why won't you let me go home in peace? What is my sin against you? I have served you in the day when drought consumed me and at night in frost and sleep departed from my eyes . . . You have changed my wages ten times . . . and except the fear of God had been with me, surely you would have sent me away destitute" (Genesis 31:36–42).

Perhaps that last statement is one we should focus on when we think of Jacob. God was with him as had been promised. In the face of every trial, Jacob remained faithful and retained the companionship of the Lord who watched over him. It was, after all, the Lord who commanded Jacob to leave Laban's land and return to the land of Canaan. The vision of God's instruction to leave Padan-aram bears a significant similarity to one given to Abraham, in which he also was told to leave a country and go to Canaan (see Genesis 1:11–13; cf. Abraham 1:16–18).

Jacob's journey home was remarkable for its continuing theophany. En route, the patriarch was met by "God's host," angels of the Lord, who undoubtedly blessed him. It is also likely these angels reminded Jacob of his powerful and life-changing vision of the ascending ladder at Bethel when he was leaving the promised land twenty years before. Now, Jacob was returning and carrying with him those troubles incident to the brotherly conflict with Esau, which had been partially responsible for his flight from Canaan in the first place. The angelic ministration during Jacob's return trip appears to have been a sign and a reminder of divine protection and assistance in what surely must have seemed to Jacob an inevitable and intense confrontation with Esau.

That the looming conflict weighed heavily on Jacob's mind seems beyond question, because immediately after his encounter with the angels, Jacob sent messengers to Esau's territory in hopes of laying the groundwork for a peaceful reunion with his brother (see Genesis 32:3–5). The messengers returned with gravely distressing news: Esau was coming to meet him with four hundred men. Jacob became exceedingly fearful and divided his entourage into two groups intending to preserve at least part of his covenantal family should Esau attack. The threat of a vengeful brother probably cannot be overestimated, for it was a life crisis of staggering proportion. In Jacob's mind, his family, as well as the covenant itself, faced annihilation. Just as important, the promises of God were on trial. Perhaps for a moment or two they looked like empty words and hollow phrases. But this life crisis set the stage for two events that would confirm forever the course of Jacob's future. First, Jacob yearningly prayed to God for safety; second, he wrestled that night for a desperately needed blessing at the hand of Deity (see Genesis 32:9–13, 24–30).

We do not know how long Jacob prayed that day at the river Jabbok, but surely his prayer was intense. In it, Jacob acknowledged the Lord's goodness as well as his own sincerely felt unworthiness before God. He pleaded for deliverance from the impending catastrophe, reminding God that He had told Jacob to leave Padan-aram and that He had also promised Jacob that his posterity would be as innumerable as the sands of the sea. How could this promise come to pass if Jacob and his family were annihilated? (see Genesis 32:9–12).

That night, as Jacob was settling down, inspiration came. He selected a large herd of animals as a gift to be given to Esau and instructed his servants how to offer the present when Esau approached (see Genesis 32:13–21). Jacob's gift of 580 animals indicates how much wealth he had accumulated while in the land of Laban and how much he had prospered through the Lord's guidance.

Next, Jacob sent his wives and eleven sons away from the main camp, across the Jabbok River on the east side of the Jordan, so they could have an extra measure of protection. Then, with the provisions set in order, Jacob was left alone—alone in terms of mortal company—to ponder, pray, and prepare.

Night is a horrible time for those who face trials. How much more difficult the night must be in the face of a test of a lifetime, an Abrahamic test of complexity and contradiction. Nighttime seems to magnify challenges; at night problems seem to weigh particularly heavy on the mind. Night is the time when the Prince of Darkness does his best work.

At some point, Jacob was joined by a being who would wrestle with him for the rest of the night. The details of Jacob's wrestle are not made clear in the biblical record, but we have enough information that we can see profound truths and patterns in this episode of the patriarch's life.

It seems reasonable to conclude that Jacob's wrestle was physical as well as spiritual, because the text is emphatic in its description of Jacob's dislocated hip (see Genesis 32:25, 31–32). Perhaps that detail is mentioned precisely to show that his wrestle was a literal as well as a metaphoric occurrence. It is also reasonable to suppose that Jacob's opponent that night was a being from the unseen world of heavenly messengers, a divine minister possessing a tangible but translated body, because he was able to wrestle all night and throw Jacob's hip out of joint (see Genesis 32:24–25).

That the personage was merely a mortal seems unlikely, first of all, because the text takes care to point out that Jacob was left completely alone, with no other humans close by (see Genesis 32:22–24). Second, the nature of Jacob's encounter was of special and profound consequence. The Hebrew word used to describe Jacob's visitor is simply *'ish,* meaning "man," without overt reference to divine status.[4] Nevertheless, the same word is used elsewhere to denote divine messengers in several Old Testament passages that deal with angels or heavenly beings who are sent to convey revelation. When used in this way, the word also often connotes the operation of the principle of divine investiture of authority—the authorization that God grants to others to speak in his name and even sometimes as though they were God himself. "Thus, the angel of Yahweh ([Hebrew] *mal'akh*) often appears in the form of an *'ish,* 'a man.' Either both terms are used interchangeably for an angel . . . or angels who appear at first only as men afterwards speak with divine authority (Gen. 19:12ff.; Jgs 13:3ff.; Josh. 5:15) or even as God himself (Gen. 18:9ff.), or they act in the place of God (19:10f.; Jgs 13:20). . . Also in the prophets, the angel of God appears in the form of an *'ish*."[5]

As implied in Doctrine and Covenants 129:4–7, divine messengers of Jacob's day (or any dispensation, for that matter) who had physical contact with earthly beings had to possess physical bodies themselves. The Prophet Joseph Smith "explained the difference between an angel and a ministering spirit; the one a resurrected or translated body, with its spirit ministering to embodied spirits—the other a disembodied spirit, visiting and ministering to disembodied spirits."[6] Furthermore, Elder Joseph Fielding Smith indicated that whenever divine messengers had a mission to perform among mortals, those messengers "had to have tangible bodies" and, thus, were translated beings.[7]

The Prophet Joseph Smith taught that translated beings are coworkers with God to bring to pass His great plan of salvation. "Their place of habitation is that of the terrestrial order, and a place prepared for such characters He held in reserve to be ministering angels unto many planets."[8] Of Enoch, the preeminent translated personage, the Prophet said: "He is a ministering Angel to minister to those who shall be heirs of Salvation."[9]

Thus, it seems very unlikely that the being involved with Jacob was Jehovah himself, because the Lord did not yet possess a physical body. And the being could not have been a resurrected being, because Christ was the "firstfruits" of the resurrection (1 Corinthians 15:20).

Though encounters with translated beings in Jacob's day are not explicitly recorded, those beings certainly existed. Enoch and his entire city had been translated and taken up into heaven as a result of their righteousness (see Moses 7:18–24). Melchizedek possessed that same kind of great faith. He "and his people wrought righteousness, and obtained heaven, and sought for the city of Enoch which God had before taken" (JST Genesis 14:34). In fact, other men with that same faith and possessing the same priesthood as Melchizedek and Enoch had also been translated and taken up into heaven (see JST Genesis 14:32).

At Jabbok, Jacob faced a crossroads. He was brought to the brink of his faith and understanding. He stood in the place his grandfather Abraham had stood when God asked for the life of Isaac and Abraham could not see how the promises of the covenant (specifically the promise of a great posterity) would be fulfilled. But Abraham was obedient in the face of a test that shook him to his very core. The Prophet Joseph Smith said: "The sacrifice required of Abraham in the offering up of Isaac, shows that if a man would attain to the keys of the kingdom of an endless life; he must sacrifice all things."[10] Furthermore, in an 1833 revelation, the Prophet wrote, "Therefore, [the Saints] must needs be chastened and tried, even as Abraham" (D&C 101:4).

Jacob likewise was obedient in the face of his ordeal and desired a blessing to strengthen his resolve and faith. He wanted and needed greater light and knowledge. Despite his intimate contact with Deity and his temple experience twenty years earlier, the threatening situation with Esau was more than he could comprehend. How could the covenant continue if the bearers of the covenant were destroyed? In faith he wrestled for a blessing with a divine sentinel, one appointed to guard the portals of heaven (perhaps like those in Jacob's vision of the ladder) and now sent to test Jacob's resolve and his request. They wrestled all night, and Jacob would not let the celestial sentinel go until he gave Jacob the requested blessing. Jacob's resolve was great, and his fortitude enduring.

Other men and women in every dispensation have had to wrestle at some point in their lives for blessings, greater truth, and light from God. Sometimes, spiritual wrestles or struggles of tremendous magnitude become intensely physical. Enos said at the beginning of his record that he wanted to tell us "of the wrestle which [he] had before God" (Enos 1:2). The story of his wrestle has become a classic account of persistent, powerful faith exercised to receive a blessing at the hand of God.

Likewise, Alma "labored much in the Spirit, *wrestling* with God in mighty prayer" that others would be blessed (Alma 8:10; emphasis added). Though it was to no avail, for the people hardened their hearts and rejected the Spirit, the wrestle was a great blessing in Alma's own life as the Lord revealed himself to the prophet (see Alma 8:15).

Joseph Smith applied the concept of "wrestling for a blessing" to Zacharias, whose situation, at least in principle, parallels that of Jacob. Zacharias had no children. He "knew that the promise of God must fail, consequently he went into the Temple to *wrestle* with God according to the order of the priesthood to obtain a promise of a son."[11]

President Brigham Young said that all of us are situated "upon the same ground," in that we must "struggle, *wrestle,* and strive, until the Lord bursts the veil and suffers us to behold His glory, or a portion of it."[12] And so it was with Jacob on that lonely night near the River Jabbok, when he began to wrestle with a divine visitor for a blessing—a blessing that would, in President Young's words, "burst the veil" and shower down on him greater light and glory from God.

The biblical text at this point is most instructive: "And he [the messenger] said, Let me go, for the day breaketh. And he [Jacob] said, I will not let thee go, except thou bless me. And he [the messenger] said unto him, What is thy name? And he said, Jacob. And he [the messenger] said, Thy name shall be called no more Jacob, but Israel: for as a prince hast thou power with God and with men, and hast prevailed. And Jacob asked him, and said, Tell me, I pray thee, thy name. And he [the messenger] said, Wherefore is it that thou dost ask after my name? And he [the messenger] blessed him there. And Jacob called the name of the place Peniel: for I have seen God face to face, and my life is preserved" (Genesis 32:26–30).

That passage discloses some specific concepts that illuminate Jacob's experience. Jacob's spiritual tenacity, aided by his great physical strength, achieved for him his desired result. After intense persistence and endurance, Jacob was rewarded with an endowment of power as the divine minister said, "for as a prince hast thou power with God and with men" (Genesis 32:28). This great endowment came in accordance with the principle described in Ether 12:6: "for ye receive no witness until after the trial of your faith." As President Young might have said, after the wrestle comes the bursting of the veil.

The bestowal upon Jacob of that rich gift, or endowment, of power followed a familiar pattern. Jacob was asked first to disclose his given name, and then he was given a new name, Israel, which symbolized his struggle before God and men for a blessing. Jacob's blessing that night seems to have been bestowed in two stages. After the divine minister announced that Jacob had been given a new name and great power (which was the first stage of the blessing), Jacob then turned the tables and asked the name of the minister: "Tell me, I pray thee, thy name" (Genesis 32:29). Perhaps he was really asking what name or personage the messenger represented and by whose authority the messenger bestowed the new name and new power. Numerous passages of scripture show that the Hebrews attached great importance to the meaning and possession of names. A name of power was a symbol of authority. In some respects, even to know a name was regarded as giving one power or control over the object or being in question.

The messenger answered Jacob's question with another question: "Wherefore is it that thou dost ask after my name?" (Genesis 32:29). The messenger wanted to know why Jacob was asking. But the biblical text at this juncture records no response from Jacob, and yet some exchange must have taken place, for the messenger was satisfied enough that he gave Jacob something more, something beyond a new name and new power. "He blessed him there" (Genesis 32:29).

The sequence of events up to this point is clear:

1. Jacob wrestled all night for a blessing in the face of great trial, in which he, his family, and the fulfillment of the covenant all faced annihilation.
2. Jacob was asked for his name, and he disclosed his own given name to a divine messenger or minister.
3. Jacob was then presented with a new name.
4. Jacob was next given an endowment of power, which would be recognized in the eyes of both God and men.
5. Jacob was finally given an additional blessing, and the divine minister was not heard from again.

The text is silent about the nature of the additional blessing. We get only Jacob's response to the blessing bestowed upon him at that moment. But what an arresting response it was, for it tells us what we may read into the narrative. The text says, "And he [the divine being] blessed him there. . . . And Jacob called the name of the place Peniel: for I have seen God face to face, and my life is preserved" (Genesis 32:29–30). Let there be no misunderstanding; the text says Jacob was blessed, and then the very next words out of his mouth which are (or, perhaps, can be) reported to us are, "I have seen God face to face, and my life is preserved" (Genesis 32:30). Thus, the event occurring between verses 29 and 30, though only implied, was no less than the ultimate theophany of Jacob's life—his being ushered into the presence of God to have every promise of past years sealed and confirmed upon him.

CONCLUSION

The events described in chapter 32 of Genesis may be seen as the culmination of a process begun twenty years before at Bethel, when Jacob first encountered God and became a candidate for exaltation by vowing to live according to the Abrahamic covenant. At Bethel, Jacob had his first temple experience, according to President Romney. For twenty years thereafter, Jacob proved himself at every hazard and under every circumstance. The Prophet Joseph Smith said: "When the Lord has thoroughly proved [someone], and finds that the man is determined to serve Him at all hazards, then the man will find his calling and his election made sure, then it will be his privilege to receive the other Comforter. . . . Now what is this other Comforter? It is no more nor less than the Lord Jesus Christ Himself . . . that when any man obtains this last Comforter, he will have the personage of Jesus Christ to attend him, or appear unto him from time to time, and even He will manifest the Father unto him, and they will take up their abode with him . . . and the Lord will teach him face to face, and he may have a perfect knowledge of the mysteries of the Kingdom of God; and this is the state and place the ancient Saints arrived at."[13]

That describes Jacob. The crisis of Jacob's life at the River Jabbok pushed him to the brink of his understanding—it pushed him to the limits of his faith. Life seemed to hang in the balance. Perhaps just as important to Jacob was the possibility that God's promises to fulfill the Abrahamic covenant through him were all empty words, that God was not omnipotent and omniscient, that He was, after all, just like the gods of the Canaanites.

Events on the eve of that life crisis caused Jacob to wrestle for a blessing, just as Enos and Alma would do. His wrestle resulted in, to use President Brigham Young's poignant words, "the Lord burst[ing] the veil . . . to behold [reveal] His glory."[14] Indeed, the story of Jacob's wrestle discloses tokens and promises with which all his posterity, literal or adopted, may become familiar. At the River Jabbok, Jacob was given the ultimate blessing and guarantee that can be given in mortality. Years later, as he was blessing the sons of Joseph, the aged patriarch referred to events on the night of his wrestle when he mentioned "the Angel which redeemed me from all evil" (Genesis 48:16).

Thus we see a pattern and are able to recognize consistency in the great plan of happiness given to all people by a loving Heavenly Father. Joseph Smith taught that "all that were ever saved, were saved through the power of this great plan of redemption, as much so before the coming of Christ as since; if not, God has had different plans in operation, (if we may so express it,) to bring men back to dwell with himself; and this we cannot believe."[15]

Abraham, Isaac, and Jacob desired, sought for, wrestled for, and craved the literal presence of God. They prayed for it, worked for it, and lived for it. Abraham, Isaac, and Jacob were successful in their quest, and the Old Testament is a powerful, personal record of their success. The Doctrine and Covenants tells us that these patriarchs "have entered into their exaltation, according to the promises, and sit upon thrones, and are not angels but are gods" (D&C 132:37).

We are the seed of Abraham, Isaac, and Jacob and the inheritors of the Abrahamic covenant. What is the Abrahamic covenant to us? Is it not candidacy for exaltation? As with Jacob, the task of turning candidacy into reality is up to us.

Let us wrestle for this blessing as we continue to worship in the temples of our God.

NOTES

1. Joseph Smith, *History of The Church of Jesus Christ of Latter-day Saints,* 2d ed. rev., edited by B. H. Roberts (Salt Lake City: The Church of Jesus Christ of Latter-day Saints, 1932–51), 1:283.
2. Marion G. Romney, "Temples—The Gates to Heaven," *Ensign,* Mar. 1971, p. 16.
3. Joseph Smith, *Teachings of the Prophet Joseph Smith,* sel. Joseph Fielding Smith (Salt Lake City: Deseret Book Co., 1938), pp. 304–5.
4. Joseph Fielding Smith thought it "more than likely" that the visitor was a messenger but not an angel. Joseph Fielding Smith, *Doctrines of Salvation,* comp. Bruce R. McConkie (Salt Lake City: Bookcraft, 1970), 1:17.
5. G. Johannes Botterweck and Helmer Ringgren, eds., *Theological Dictionary of the Old Testament,* rev. ed. (Grand Rapids, Mich.: Eerdmans Publishing Co., 1983), 1:233.
6. Smith, *Teachings of the Prophet Joseph Smith,* p. 191.
7. Smith, *Doctrines of Salvation,* 2:110–11.
8. Smith, *Teachings of the Prophet Joseph Smith,* p. 170.
9. Andrew F. Ehat and Lyndon W. Cook, comps. and eds., *The Words of Joseph Smith* (Orem, Utah: Grandin Book Co., 1991), p. 41.
10. Smith, *Teachings of the Prophet Joseph Smith,* p. 322.
11. Ehat and Cook, *Words of Joseph Smith,* p. 235; emphasis added.

12. Brigham Young, in *Journal of Discourses* (London: Latter-day Saints' Book Depot, 1856), 3:192; emphasis added.
13. Smith, *Teachings of the Prophet Joseph Smith,* pp. 150–51.
14. Young, in *Journal of Discourses,* 3:192.
15. *The Evening and the Morning Star,* Mar. 1834, p. 143.

CHAPTER ELEVEN

THE WIFE/SISTER EXPERIENCE: PHARAOH'S INTRODUCTION TO JEHOVAH

GAYE STRATHEARN

A most important aspect of the ministry of Abraham was his concept of the nature of deity. Throughout the ancient world, nations worshipped a pantheon of gods that were responsible for particular geographical areas. The ancient Babylonians, Assyrians, and Egyptians were henotheistic, that is, they were quite willing to allow that other gods existed outside their pantheon. Nevertheless, each nation believed that the power of its gods was superior to that of the gods of the other nations, and this belief was determined, to a large extent, on the battlefields. If the Egyptians won a battle against the Assyrians, then that showed the Egyptian gods were more powerful than the Assyrian gods. In contrast, the book of Abraham makes it clear that as Abraham traveled throughout the Levant, he did not shift his divine allegiance as he crossed a new political border. Instead, he worshipped a god who knew no geographical boundaries, and Abraham taught those he encountered about that god. Abraham's God, Jehovah, was the same whether Abraham was in Ur of the Chaldees (see Abraham 1:1–16), Haran (see Abraham 2:5–14), Bethel (see Abraham 2:20), or Egypt. But that was not all: not only was Jehovah unencumbered by geographical boundaries but his power knew no equal. Although the power of Jehovah was manifested dramatically in Egypt and in the various Israelite battles, during the life of Abraham, Jehovah's power was manifested in more subtle ways. One important manifestation of Jehovah's influence and power occurred in the confrontation between Abraham and Pharaoh in Egypt in which Pharaoh took Sarah into his harem. That event

□ □ □ □ □

Gaye Strathearn is a Ph.D. student in New Testament studies at Claremont Graduate School.

ultimately led to Pharaoh's seeking a blessing at the hands of Abraham—an interesting demonstration of humility for someone of Pharaoh's power and prestige.

THE WIFE/SISTER MOTIF

The book of Genesis contains a trilogy of incidents in which the wife/sister motif was used by either Abraham or Isaac. The first account describes Abraham's journey into Egypt after a famine enveloped the land of Canaan (see Genesis 12:10–13:4). Similar situations arose later when both Abraham and Isaac dwelt in the city of Gerar (see Genesis 20:1–2; 26:7–8). Although in each instance the patriarch identified his wife as his sister to avert a potentially dangerous situation, these accounts have puzzled many readers and scholars because of the apparent deception involved. Why did the patriarchs resort to such action? That is a difficult theological issue. In attempting to justify the patriarchs' actions, writers have proposed a number of different explanations that offer some significant insights into the three episodes; however, we can gain a still greater understanding, especially of the episode of Abraham's sojourn in Egypt, if we take into account the insights provided by the book of Abraham and the Genesis Apocryphon (1QapGen), one of the scrolls from the Dead Sea corpus. By doing so, we see the hand of God in Abraham's request of Sarah, for Abraham's actions initiated a confrontation between himself and Pharaoh. Because of Abraham's obedience, God was able to introduce himself to the Egyptian Pharaoh in power and glory. Even though it was only the first of a series of such encounters, it is clear that the God of Abraham was announcing his jurisdiction over all the families of the earth and not just over Abraham and his descendants. That concept is fundamental to our understanding of all of Jehovah's subsequent dealings with humankind throughout the Old Testament.

The biblical account introduces the episode in the following manner: "And there was a famine in the land: and Abram went down into Egypt to sojourn there; for the famine *was* grievous in the land. And it came to pass, when he was come near to enter into Egypt, that he said unto Sarai his wife, Behold now, I know that thou *art* a fair woman to look upon: Therefore it shall come to pass, when the Egyptians shall see thee, that they shall say, This *is* his wife: and they will kill me, but they will save thee alive. Say, I pray thee, thou *art* my sister: that it may be well with me for thy sake; and my soul shall live because of thee" (Genesis 12:10–13).

From these verses it appears that Abraham's major motivation for asking Sarah to say she was his sister was the beauty of Sarah, which would put his life in danger. Certainly that situation was not unique to Abraham and Sarah. Israel's great king David was willing to kill Uriah for his wife Bathsheba (see 2 Samuel 11:14–17), and we see similar incidents in the Egyptian literature. One example, which is found in the Pyramid Texts, records a king boasting of his virility by declaring, "I am the owner of seed who takes women from their husbands whenever he wishes, according to his desire."[1] Similarly, the Papyrus D'Orbiney recounts the "Tale of Two Brothers," in which the Pharaoh, on the advice of his wise men, sent envoys in search of the daughter of Ra-Harmachis. The text describes her as "more beautiful . . . than any woman in the whole land." Unfortunately for the Pharaoh, she was married to Bata, who was willing to slay anyone who tried to take her from him. When Bata killed his envoys, the Pharaoh sent soldiers and a woman who lured the daughter of Ra-Harmachis away from her husband with "all kinds of beautiful ladies' jewelry." The story then explains that, having been given the "rank of Great Lady,"[2] the woman advised the Pharaoh to dispose of Bata, which he promptly did. Although in this instance the Pharaoh acted at the behest of the wife, it is clear that he had no compunction in terminating Bata's life so that he could have an uncontested claim to a beautiful woman.

Historical Interpretations

Though these records seem to validate Abraham's concern for his life, both ancient and modern authors have been concerned about the method Abraham used. Did Abraham ask Sarah to lie just to protect himself? The question of whether there was indeed any blood relationship between Abraham and Sarah has been a constant source of dispute. The ancient Jewish historian, Josephus, approached the incident by merely saying that Abraham "pretended to be her [Sarah's] brother."[3] A number of scholars believe that there is at least some basis for the identification and thus have attempted to justify the action. Appealing to the Bible, we find only two passages that address this issue. In Genesis 11:27–29 we read: "Now these are the generations of Terah: Terah begat Abram, Nahor, and Haran; and Haran begat Lot. And Haran died before his father Terah in the land of his nativity, in Ur of the Chaldees. And Abram and Nahor took them wives: the name of Abram's wife was Sarai; and the name of

Nahor's wife, Milcah, the daughter of Haran, the father of Milcah, and the father of Iscah."

In the past, some have argued that the Iscah mentioned in verse 29 is Sarah.[4] Unfortunately, the book of Abraham does not shed any light on the matter. In Abraham 2:2, in the Pearl of Great Price, we read merely that Abraham's brother, Nehor, married his niece, Milcah, but the author says nothing about Sarah's family line. Since the turn of the century, scholars have dismissed the attempt to equate Iscah with Sarah,[5] but it is clear that Jewish and Muslim writings in antiquity assumed that Sarah was Abraham's niece through Haran.[6] In discussing this problem, it is important to realize that in the ancient Near East the nuclear family, as we now know it, did not exist. Rather, a family unit encompassed grandparents, aunts, uncles, and cousins. This state is reflected in ancient Semitic languages, including biblical Hebrew, in which there is no definite linguistic separation between siblings and their offspring. We find one example of this in the passage that tells of the five Canaanite kings capturing Sodom and Gomorrah. When Abraham is advised of Lot's capture, twice he refers to Lot as his brother (see Genesis 14:14, 16) even though, by western standards, he is clearly Abraham's "nephew" (see Genesis 11:27). So it is at least possible that Sarah belonged to Abraham's extended family and was thus considered to be his "sister" in the sense of a near blood relative. Even allowing for that possibility, however, those who write about this biblical incident generally feel uncomfortable relying solely on such an explanation.[7] Therefore, the search for understanding continues.

The second biblical passage relating to Sarah's and Abraham's nonmarital relationship is found in Genesis 20:12. Here Abraham justified identifying Sarah as his sister to Abimelech by saying that "indeed *she* is my sister; she *is* the daughter of my father, but not the daughter of my mother" (Genesis 20:12). In other words, Abraham claimed that Sarah was his half-sister. Two later Christian documents clearly based their understanding of the wife/sister motif by appealing to that claim. The author of *The Book of the Cave of Treasures,* dating from the sixth century A.D., indicated that Sarah was Terah's daughter by another wife. Hence we read, "Now Sârâ was the sister of Abraham on the father's side, because Terah took two women to wife. When Yâwnû, the mother of Abraham, died, Terah took to wife a woman whose name was "Naharyath" (or Shalmath, or Tona, or Taḥdif), and of her Sârâ was born."[8] Similarly, the *Book of the Bee,* another Syriac text (thirteenth century A.D.), states that Terah's two wives were Yônâ and Shelmath.[9] There are obvious similarities between these two names and the ones in the *Cave of Treasures*.

Those interpretations were the prevailing arguments up until the late 1960s. In 1963, E. A. Speiser proposed another theory. By a legal process found in the Nuzi documents, artifacts of a Near Eastern Bronze Age city-state Speiser asserted, under Hurrian law a woman could legally be adopted by her husband to give her greater privileges and social status.[10] Speiser's argument initially received wide support in the academic arena, but in recent years a number of scholars have questioned his conclusions. Van Seters acknowledges that the documents do describe an adoptive process, but he argues that this practice was for commercial purposes. By adopting the woman, a man would become her legal guardian and could then benefit from a marriage dowry; however, Van Seters argues, "this did not necessarily create a variety of different marriage types or place women on varying levels of social status."[11] Therefore, it is difficult to understand Abraham's request by an appeal to a linguistic or cultural understanding of the term *sister.*

Another Look at a Complex Situation

So, where does that leave us? Although these hypotheses have some merit in adding to our understanding of a difficult passage of scripture, they fail to take into account the insights provided by the book of Abraham and the Genesis Apocryphon. Both of these texts demonstrate that Abraham acted not merely out of an interest in self-preservation but in obedience to a divine command. Thus we read in Abraham 2:22–25: "And it came to pass when I was come near to enter into Egypt, the Lord said unto me: Behold, Sarai, thy wife, is a very fair woman to look upon; Therefore it shall come to pass, when the Egyptians shall see her, they will say She is his wife; and they will kill you, but they will save her alive; therefore see that ye do on this wise: Let her say unto the Egyptians, she is thy sister, and thy soul shall live. And it came to pass that I, Abraham, told Sarai, my wife, all that the Lord had said unto me—Therefore say unto them, I pray thee, thou art my sister, that it may be well with me for thy sake, and my soul shall live because of thee."

Similarly, the author of the Genesis Apocryphon, which differs slightly in detail from the book of Abraham, explains the nature of Abraham's request at great length. When Abraham traveled to Egypt, he was given instructions in a dream. It is not explicitly stated, but the implication is that the dream came from God. "And I, Abram, had a dream in the night of my entering into the land of Egypt and I saw in my dream [that there wa]s a cedar, and a date-palm (which was) [very beautif]ul; and some men came intending to cut down and uproot the cedar, but leave the date-palm by itself. Now the date-palm cried out and said, 'Do not cut down the cedar, for cursed (?) is he who fells (?) the [cedar].' So the cedar was spared with the help of the date-palm, and [it was] not [cut down]" (1QapGen XIX:14–17).[12]

When Abraham awoke, he described the dream to Sarah. Although the text is somewhat damaged at this point, it is clear that Abraham identified himself with the cedar and Sarah with the date-palm. Therefore, he asked Sarah to identify herself as his sister.

But why did God require Abraham to make such a request? In discussing this question, Stephen Ricks shows that though this commandment might seem strange, obedience is the primary concern.[13] There are numerous passages throughout the scriptures in which God commands people to perform "strange" acts. God's commandment to Nephi to slay Laban was obviously difficult for Nephi, who wrote: "I was constrained by the Spirit that I should kill Laban; but I said in my heart: Never at any time have I shed the blood of a man. And I shrunk and would that I might not slay him" (1 Nephi 4:10).[14] Also, when Abraham returned to the land of Canaan he was given another difficult commandment—to sacrifice his son Isaac (see Genesis 22:1–2). Given the circumstances in Abraham's own life, in which Abraham faced a sacrificial death himself (see Abraham 1:12–15), this commandment must certainly have appeared contradictory to him. On another occasion, God commanded the apostle Peter in a dream to eat meat that was unclean under the law of Moses (see Acts 10:9–18). Each of those commandments seems to violate one of God's laws. Each one placed the individual in a position where he had either to follow a preexisting law or follow God's current command. The Prophet Joseph Smith taught us: "That which is wrong under one circumstance, may be, and often is, right under another. God said, 'Thou shalt not kill;' at another time He said, 'Thou shalt utterly destroy.' This is the principle on which the government of heaven is conducted by revelation adapted to the circumstances in which the children of the kingdom are placed. Whatever God requires is right, no matter what it is, although we may not see the reason thereof till long after the events transpire."[15]

As we read of the commandments given to Nephi, Abraham, and Peter, in each case the scriptures go on to show us the reason for

God's actions. For Nephi, it was so that his people would have the scriptures to remind them of their covenants (in contrast to the people of Zarahemla, who had no records). The scriptures also tell us that Abraham was asked to sacrifice Isaac as a test of his obedience and as a foreshadowing of the eventual sacrifice of God's Only Begotten Son. And the commandment given to Peter was to let him know that God was opening the way for the Gentiles to hear the gospel. But the scriptural account is silent about God's instruction concerning Sarah. We must turn instead to the Genesis Apocryphon to provide us with some insight concerning God's possible motivation.

THE INTERCHANGE BETWEEN ABRAHAM AND PHARAOH

The very fact that Abraham went down into Egypt sets up an important contrast between himself and Pharaoh. Bowie observes: "How insignificant Abraham and all he represented appeared to be as compared with Egypt! On the one hand, an unimportant wanderer; on the other hand, a proud civilization, ancient and deep-rooted. At the time when Abraham . . . came within its borders the history of its life already went back more than two thousand years. From the rich valley of the Nile and from their conquests beyond it the Pharaohs drew the wealth to build the magnificence of Memphis and Thebes and the colossal temples at Karnak; and the pyramids were even then centuries old. What did it matter to Egypt or to history that this Hebrew should exist? To Egypt, nothing: to history, more than Egypt itself would ultimately mean. Egypt represented material pride and power and possessions, and all these would crumble. Abraham represented a new spiritual impulse, and this would be creative long after Egypt should have ceased to count."[16]

Why did Abraham, even though he was insignificant in comparison to the mightiest man of his time, have such a profound influence on the history of the world? It seems that Jehovah was setting the scene to make a statement not only to Pharaoh but also to all of Egypt and to all who read of this event that He wanted them to understand His power and sphere of influence. Therefore, He orchestrated the circumstances around Abraham's introduction to the Egyptian Pharaoh. As Abraham's sister, Sarah provided that introduction, but that was only the first step in a powerful set of events. To appreciate the whole saga, we must delve deeper into the social and religious implications of the confrontation between the apparently insignificant Abraham and the mighty Egyptian Pharaoh.

As a result of the Pharaoh's reaction to Sarah's beauty, the Genesis account tells us that "the Lord plagued Pharaoh and his house with great plagues" (Genesis 12:17). As we turn again to the Genesis Apocryphon we find a similar reaction: "In that night the Most High God sent a pestilential spirit to afflict him and every man of his house, an evil spirit that kept afflicting him and every man in his house" (1QapGen. XX:16b-17a). As a result of these plagues, the Pharaoh called in all his wise men, both the religious advisers *('spy')* and the physicians *(aśy)*. This division of the wise men into religious and medical groups reflects the dualistic approach the ancient Egyptians had to the healing of sickness. They acknowledged the limitations of their considerable scientific knowledge and recognized the need for divine intervention from deity. To fully appreciate the significance of these divisions in the Egyptians' attitudes toward healing and their effect on the Genesis account, we must first explore the nature of ancient Egyptian medical practices. We can only appreciate the nature of the contest if we understand the power of the Pharaoh.

Egyptian Medical Practices

In antiquity, other nations considered Egypt the center of medical science. The fame of Egyptian physicians commanded international respect. Homer wrote in the Odyssey that "there [in Egypt] every man is a physician, wise above human kind."[17] There are similar statements in other ancient writings. Herodotus commented that the two Persian emperors, Cyrus and Darius, were impressed by their Egyptian physicians and that "each physician is a healer of one disease and no more. All the country is full of physicians, some of the eye, some of the teeth, some of what pertains to the belly, and some of the hidden diseases."[18] Stead explains that "by trial and error the Egyptians learnt the use of many natural drugs and realised the importance of rest and care of the patient, as well as basic hygiene as a means of preventing the onset of certain problems."[19]

Two important medical documents dating from the sixteenth century B.C. are the Edwin Smith Papyrus and the Ebers Papyrus. The Edwin Smith Papyrus is a surgical textbook, which "differentiates with utter strictness between the examination method, diagnosis, therapy or prescription, and prognosis."[20] Even today those aspects are an integral part of modern medical practice. Indeed, Wiseman comments that the "level of knowledge" the Edwin Smith Papyrus demonstrates "was not otherwise attained until later classical Greek times or in England in the sixteenth century A.D."[21] The inclusion in the Ebers Papyrus of religious formulas, along with the medical discussions, indicates that the art of healing during this time was not a pure science but was used in conjunction with religious rituals. It began with an appeal for the gods *Rê* and *Thot* to aid the physicians in their healings.[22]

Thus we find two types of physicians mentioned in the ancient writings of Egypt: the *ḫry-ḥᵉb,* "carrier of the ritual book," a religious adviser, and the *synw,* "physician."[23] Wiseman believes that "both probably underwent a formal training based on traditions passed down from father to son."[24] It was the *synw* who held the governmental positions, however. In the account in the Genesis Apocryphon, it appears that Pharaoh summoned both groups to his aid, yet both of them failed. Egypt, with all of its medical knowledge and religious powers, was not able to provide any relief for its Pharaoh. With no other recourse available to them, Pharaoh's servant, Hirqanos, came and "begged . . . [Abraham] to pray over the king" and to "lay *(sămak̲)* . . . [his] hands upon him that he might live" (1QapGen. XX:22). Fitzmyer notes that this line is the first time in a Jewish source that the rite of the laying on of hands is used for healing.[25] The author's word choice and its significance in this instance is important in helping us understand the nature of Abraham's action. Why did the author choose the verb *sămak̲* to describe the nature of laying on of hands? In the Old Testament the word *sămak̲* has some very specific connotations that are important for an understanding of our passage.

The Old Testament Practice of Laying on of Hands

In the King James Version of the Bible, the translators consistently use the verb *lay* to describe the action of placing hands upon something during priesthood activities. That is true, regardless of the ritual being performed. But in the Hebrew text two different verbs are used: *šît̲* and *sămak̲*.[26] To distinguish between these two verbs is important because the author of the Genesis Apocryphon specifically used the latter to describe Abraham's blessing of Pharaoh. Generally *šît̲* was the verb of preference when the laying on of hands was associated with a blessing. That was certainly the case when Jacob blessed each of his sons: "and Israel [Jacob] stretched out his right hand, and laid *(šît̲)* it upon Ephraim's head, who was the younger, and his left hand upon Manasseh's head, guiding his hands wittingly; for Manasseh was the firstborn" (Genesis 48:14). This usage contrasts with the specialized usage of *sămak̲*. Daube argues that the difference between *šît̲* and *sămak* can be distinguished by the amount of pressure used by the officiator. He prefers to translate *šît* as "place," and *sămak* as "lean." The difference was that when a person "leans" *(sămak)* during the rite of the laying on of hands, there was a symbolic transference of something from the officiator to the recipient.[27]

The matter can be clarified further when we examine the occasions when *sămak* was the verb of choice in describing the rituals of the laying on of hands. As Réne Péter demonstrates, its use is categorized in one of two ways—it is used in either sacrificial or nonsacrificial occasions.[28] The sacrificial use is not relevant to our discussion, but the nonsacrificial use is very enlightening because Abraham's blessing of Pharaoh clearly falls into that category. Thus it is grouped with such incidents as the scapegoat ritual on the Day of Atonement (Leviticus 16:5–10, 21–22), the case of the blasphemer (see Leviticus 24), and Joshua's ordination by Moses (see Numbers 27:18–23). In each of these occasions *sămak* is used to indicate not a blessing but the transference of something from the officiator to the recipient. In the case of the scapegoat, Aaron symbolically transferred the iniquities of Israel to the goat. In the story of a man who blasphemed during an altercation, Moses was instructed to have those who heard the offense "lay *[sămak]* their hands upon his head, and let all the congregation stone him" (Leviticus 24:14). Although there is considerable scholarly debate concerning the nature of the laying on of hands in this instance,[29] it appears that the laying on of hands represents a retransference of the impurity back to the offender. The third example occurred when Moses set Joshua apart as the next Israelite leader (see Numbers 27:23). In that instance, Moses symbolically transferred his honor, or authority, to Joshua (see Numbers 27:20).[30]

In all three of these cases, the verb *sămak* was chosen instead of *šît*. It is clear that it had a specialized meaning in association with nonsacrificial rituals. Unfortunately, though, there is no Old Testament instance where the ritual of the laying on of hands was associated with healing. As Mackay points out, that lack is "understandable since the O. T. is almost entirely the record of the House of Israel under the Law of Moses, that is, without the Melchizedek Priesthood."[31] It was not until the dawning of the Christian era, and hence the return of the Melchizedek Priesthood through the Savior, that the practice was generally associated with the healing of the sick. But Latter-day Saints know that Abraham did hold the Melchizedek Priesthood. The Doctrine and Covenants tells us that he received it from Melchizedek (see D&C 84:14). Therefore, it is certainly not out of place to find in the Genesis Apocryphon that Abraham lays *(sămak̲)* his hands upon the head of Pharaoh to heal him from the plagues sent by the Lord.

The Laying On of Hands and the Genesis Apocryphon

As mentioned previously, the discovery and translation of the Genesis Apocryphon provided scholars with the first Jewish source where healing was achieved by the laying on of hands. In response to Hirqanos's plea for help, Abraham's nephew, Lot, responded that Abraham could not pray for the Pharaoh until he returned Sarah (1QapGen. XX:22–23). When Pharaoh acted accordingly, the author recorded Pharaoh's plea and Abraham's response as follows: "But now pray for me and for my house that this evil spirit will be rebuked from us. So I [Abraham] prayed [. . .] and I laid *[sămak̲]* my hands upon his head and the plague fell from him and the evil spirit was rebuked and he lived" (1QapGen. XX:28–29). It is significant that Abraham did not initiate this scene with Pharaoh. Instead, he waited for Pharaoh to approach him. In fact, this whole episode appears to have been orchestrated so that Pharaoh would seek out Abraham's assistance.

Although the biblical account of this incident does not mention Abraham's praying for the Pharaoh, it is mentioned in the similar account with the king of Gerar, Abimelech. Here we are informed that "Abraham prayed unto God: and God healed Abimelech, and his wife, and his maidservants; and they bare children" (Genesis 20:17). Then the plague which Jehovah had sent upon them is explained: "for the Lord had fast closed up all the wombs of the house of Abimelech, because of Sarah Abraham's wife" (Genesis 20:18). The Genesis Apocryphon gives no indication of the nature of the plague against Pharaoh, and although scholars have suggested numerous hypotheses,[32] it is at least possible, given the corresponding circumstances, that Pharaoh experienced problems similar to those of Abimelech.

Noteworthy in both the passages from the Genesis Apocryphon is the use of *sămak̲* rather than *šîṯ* to indicate the laying on of hands. From the parallel passages in the Old Testament, it appears that the author chose the word *sămak̲* to indicate a transference of something to Pharaoh. In both instances in the Genesis Apocryphon, *sămak̲* is found in connection with *ṣᵉlā,* the verb for praying. The two words seems to be integrally connected. It was not Abraham's power that cured Pharaoh; it was the power of Jehovah, with Abraham as a conduit, that effected the cure. The concept of having a priesthood holder act as a conduit for divine purposes is certainly not unfamiliar to Latter-day Saints. In the Doctrine and Covenants, we read of Jehovah's telling Edward Partridge that "I will lay my hand upon you by the hand of my servant Sidney Rigdon, and you shall receive my Spirit, the Holy Ghost, even the Comforter, which shall teach you the peaceable things of the kingdom" (D&C 36:2). In a similar way, priesthood holders lay their hands upon the sick to invoke the power of God. Brigham Young once declared: "When I lay hands on the sick, I expect the healing power and influence of God to pass through me to the patient, and the disease to give way. . . . When we are prepared, when we are holy vessels before the Lord, a stream of power from the Almighty can pass through the tabernacle of the administrator to the system of the patient, and the sick are made whole."[33] Abraham performed in a similar manner as he approached Pharaoh.

But was the actual healing of Pharaoh the principal reason behind Abraham's actions? I believe that Abraham's actions have a much more significant purpose than the mere healing of Pharaoh. Abraham brought about something that the Egyptians could not do for themselves, even though they were the leading authorities in ancient medical practices and even though they possessed their own pantheon of gods. Those gods failed to cure Pharaoh, but Abraham and his God were successful. This was a contest between man's knowledge—man's gods—and Jehovah, the God of Abraham. Therefore, in recording that Abraham laid his hands upon Pharaoh, the author of the Genesis Apocryphon used the verb *sămak̲* to convey a message to his readers—one that is not readily evident in the English translation but that was very significant to a Hebrew audience. In using the language of the Torah, the author conveyed the idea of a transference of power from Jehovah (through Abraham) to Pharaoh. Could there now be any doubt in Pharaoh's mind concerning the jurisdiction and strength of Jehovah's power? This incident was only the first of a number of contacts between Egypt and Abraham and his descendants. The contest between Pharaoh's wise men and Abraham's God to secure a cure parallels the events some centuries later when Abraham's successor, Moses, also confronted an Egyptian Pharaoh. Once again, Jehovah orchestrated the events so that His power was manifested both to the Pharaoh and to the children of Israel.[34]

CONCLUSION

The prophet Abraham stands uncontested in history as the father of three monotheistic religions: Judaism, Christianity, and Islam. While the people in the world around him worshipped a plethora of deities, Abraham stood firm in his commitment to Jehovah. Whenever Abraham journeyed throughout Chaldea, Canaan, or Egypt, he proclaimed the power of Jehovah. His allegiance did not shift from one country to another. In examining the controversial incident in Egypt, the book of Abraham and the Genesis Apocryphon help us to see Abraham continuing his missionary activities. When Abraham responded to God's commandment to call Sarah his sister, he acted with immediacy and unquestioned obedience. One of the great characteristics of such individuals as Abraham, Nephi, and Peter was their commitment to God's current commandments, not just his previous ones. As we go through life, we also encounter times when we are given commandments that seem strange or that are difficult to understand. We may not always see their immediate purpose, but if we respond as Abraham did, then we can also experience the power of God in our lives and in the lives of those around us. Surely that is one of the great lessons to learn from our mighty ancestor, Abraham.

NOTES

1. Utterance 317, in *The Ancient Egyptian Pyramid Texts,* trans. R. O. Faulkner (Oxford: Clarendon Press, 1969), p. 99.
2. "Tale of Two Brothers," in Miriam Lichtheim, *Ancient Egyptian Literature: A Book of Readings* (Berkeley: University of California Press, 1976), 2:207–8.
3. Josephus, *Jewish Antiquities* 1.8.1, trans. H. St. J. Thackeray, in *Loeb Classical Library,* ed. E. H. Warmington (Cambridge, Mass.: Harvard University Press, 1967), p. 81.
4. For example, Josephus substitutes the name of Sarah for that of Iscah by saying that Sarai and Milcah were Haran's daughters (*Jewish Antiquities* 1.6.5 [Thackeray, p. 75]). A footnote to this episode notes that in making the connection between Sarai and Iscah, Josephus is following rabbinical tradition. Later Augustine also equates the two women. See *City of God* 16.12, in *A Select Library of the Nicene and Post-Nicene Fathers of the Christian Church,* First Series, ed. Philip Schaff (Grand Rapids, Mich.: Eerdmans Publishing, 1956), 2:318. Similarly, the *Targum Jonathan* Genesis 11:29 qualifies the name of Iscah by adding the phrase "who is Sarai" (*Targum du Pentateuque,* trans. Roger Le Déaut, *Sources Chrétiennes 245* [Paris: Les Éditions du Cerf, 1978], p. 147).
5. See Adam Clarke, *The Holy Bible: Containing the Old and New Testaments* (New York: Eaton and Mains, 1883), 1:93–94; and J. Skinner, *Genesis,* in *International Critical Commentary,* ed. Samuel R. Driver, Alfred Plummer, and Charles A. Briggs (New York: Scribner's Sons, 1910), 1:238. Since that time

scholars have insisted on a distinction between Sarah and Iscah. See Claus Westermann, *Genesis 12–36: A Commentary,* trans. John J. Scullion (Minneapolis: Augsburg Publishing, 1984), pp. 137–38; and Victor P. Hamilton, *The Book of Genesis Chapters 1–17,* in *The New International Commentary on the Old Testament,* ed. R. K. Harrison (Grand Rapids, Mich.: Eerdmans Publishing Co., 1990), p. 362.

6. Josephus, *Jewish Antiquities* 1.6.5 (Thackeray, p. 75); and G. Weil, *The Bible, the Koran, and the Talmud; or, Biblical Legends of the Mussulmans* (New York: Harper, 1855), p. 79.
7. For example, see Thomas Whitelaw, *Genesis and Exodus,* in *The Pulpit Commentary,* ed. H. D. M. Spence and Joseph S. Exell (New York: Funk and Wagnalls, 1950), 1:187–88.
8. *The Book of the Cave of Treasures,* trans. E. A. Wallis Budge (London: The Religious Tract Society, 1927), p. 149.
9. *The Book of the Bee,* trans. E. A. Wallis Budge (Oxford: Clarendon Press, 1886), p. 42.
10. Ephraim A. Speiser, "The Wife-Sister Motif in the Patriarchal Narratives," *Biblical and Other Studies,* ed. Alexander H. Altmann (Cambridge, Mass.: Harvard University Press, 1963), pp. 15–28.
11. John Van Seters, *Abraham in History and Tradition* (New Haven: Yale University Press, 1975), p. 74. For further arguments, see S. Greengus, "Sisterhood Adoption at Nuzi and the 'Wife-Sister' in Genesis," *HUCA* 46 (1975): 5–31; and Thomas L. Thompson, *The Historicity of the Patriarchal Narratives: The Quest for the Historical Abraham* (New York: de Gruyter, 1974), pp. 234–48.
12. Translation from Joseph A. Fitzmyer, *The Genesis Apocryphon of Qumran Cave 1: A Commentary* (Rome: Biblical Institute Press, 1966), pp. 51, 53.
13. Stephen D. Ricks, "The Early Ministry of Abraham," *Studies in Scripture, Volume 2: The Pearl of Great Price,* ed. Robert L. Millet and Kent P. Jackson (Salt Lake City: Randall Book, 1985), pp. 221–22.
14. For a discussion of some of the legal implications of Nephi's'action, see John W. Welsh, "Legal Perspectives on the Slaying of Laban," *Journal of Book of Mormon Studies* 1 (Fall 1992): 119–41.
15. Joseph Smith, *Teachings of the Prophet Joseph Smith,* sel. Joseph Fielding Smith (Salt Lake City: Deseret Book Co., 1938), p. 256.
16. Walter Russell Bowie, "Genesis," in *The Interpreter's Bible,* ed. George Arthur Buttrick, et al. (New York: Abingdon Press, 1952), 1:579–80.
17. Homer, *Odyssey* 4.231–32, trans. A. T. Murray, in *Loeb Classical Library,* ed. E. H. Warmington (Cambridge, Mass.: Harvard University Press, 1974), 1:123.
18. Herodotus 2.84, trans. A. D. Godley, in *Loeb Classical Library* (Cambridge, Mass.: Harvard University Press, 1966), 1:369.
19. Miriam Stead, *Egyptian Life* (London: British Museum, 1986), p. 70.
20. E. Brunner-Traut, as cited in Klaus Seybold and Ulrich B. Mueller, *Sickness and Healing,* trans. Douglas W. Stott (Nashville: Abingdon, 1978), p. 33.
21. Donald J. Wiseman, "Medicine in the Old Testament World," *Medicine and the Bible,* ed. Bernard Palmer (Exeter: Paternoster Press, 1986), p. 14.

22. Ebers 1, as cited in P. Ghalioungui, *The House of Life,* Per Ankh: *Magic and Medical Science in Ancient Egypt* (Amsterdam: B. M. Israël, 1973), p. 1.
23. J. V. K. Wilson, "Medicine in the Land and Times of the Old Testament," in *Studies in the Period of David and Solomon and Other Essays,* ed. T. Ishada (Tokyo: Yamakawa-Shuppansha, 1982), p. 338.
24. Wiseman, "Medicine in the Old Testament World," p. 16.
25. Joseph A. Fitzmyer, "Some Observations on the *Genesis Apocryphon,*" *The Catholic Biblical Quarterly* 22 (1960): 283–84.
26. This difference between the two Hebrew verbs is also found in the Septuagint, where *šîṯ* is translated as *epiballo* and *sămaḵ* is translated as *epitithe mi.*
27. David Daube, *The New Testament and Rabbinic Judaism* (London: Athlone Press, 1956), pp. 225–26.
28. Réne Péter, "L'imposition des mains dans l'Ancien Testament," *Vetus Testamentum* 27 (1977): 48–55.
29. Jacob Milgrom, after reviewing the arguments, cogently argues in favor of a transferral ritual in this passage. He believes that "those who heard the blasphemy were contaminated by it and, via the hand-leaning, they effectively transferred the pollution back to the blasphemer and eliminated it by executing him outside the camp." See *Leviticus 1–16,* in *The Anchor Bible,* ed. William Fox Albright and David Noel Freedman (New York: Doubleday, 1991), 3:1041. This is in contrast to David P. Wright, "The Gesture of Hand Placement in the Hebrew Bible and in Hittite Literature," *Journal of the American Oriental Society,* vol. 106, no. 3 (1986): 435. This author argues against the "transferral theory" and instead supports a legal interpretation whereby the witnesses proclaim the guilt of the accused.
30. See Péter, "L'imposition," p. 54.
31. Thomas W. Mackay, "Abraham in Egypt: A Collection of Evidence for the Case of the Missing Wife," *Brigham Young University Studies* 10 (Summer 1970): 436.
32. Two midrashic traditions identify the plague as leprosy. See Lech Lecha 41.2 and Vayera 52.13 in *Midrash Rabba: Genesis,* 3d ed., trans. Rabbi Dr. H. Freedman (New York: Soncino Press, 1939), 1:334, 460. Hugh Nibley, in the forthcoming volume, *Abraham in Egypt,* argues that Pharaoh was afflicted with impotence. That both these incidents should be associated with the creation of offspring is important, given the nature of the Abrahamic covenant that should pass through Abraham's lineage. During these accounts Abraham and Sarah were still awaiting the time when they would be given a son to carry on the covenant. It should also be noted that although many scholars believe that the incidents with Pharaoh and Abimelech are two versions of the same story (see W. W. Sloan, *A Survey of the Old Testament* [New York: Abingdon Press, 1957], pp. 43–44; and Robert Davidson, *Genesis 12–50, Cambridge Bible Commentary,* ed. P. R. Ackroy, A. R. C. Leaney, and J. W. Packer [New York: Cambridge University Press, 1979], 2:4), it is clear from the Joseph Smith Translation of the Bible that the Prophet Joseph Smith

considered them to be two separate events: "and when Abraham said *again* of Sarah his wife, She is my sister" (JST Genesis 20:2; emphasis added).

33. Brigham Young, in *Journal of Discourses* (London: Latter-day Saints Book Depot, 1854–86), 14:72.
34. See John S. Kselman, "Genesis," *Harper's Bible Commentary,* ed. James L. Mays (San Francisco: Harper and Row, 1988), p. 95; and Meredith G. Kline, "Genesis," in *Eerdmans Bible Commentary,* ed. D. Guthrie and J. A. Motyer (Grand Rapids, Mich.: Eerdmans Publishing Co., 1987), p. 93.

CHAPTER TWELVE

THE PROVOCATION IN THE WILDERNESS AND THE REJECTION OF GRACE

M. CATHERINE THOMAS

Camped in the hot, waterless wilderness of southern Palestine, the Israelites challenged Moses, saying, "Wherefore is this that thou hast brought us up out of Egypt, to kill us and our children and our cattle with thirst?" (Exodus 17:3). This complaint might have been understandable had these people never seen the hand of God in their lives, but this incident occurred after the miraculous Passover, after their passage through the Red Sea dry shod, and after the outpouring of manna and quail from heaven. In response to the Israelites' faithlessness, an exasperated Moses cried out to the Lord, "What shall I do unto this people? they be almost ready to stone me" (Exodus 17:4). The Lord answered: "Behold, I will stand before thee there upon the rock in Horeb; and thou shalt smite the rock, and there shall come water out of it, that the people may drink. And Moses did so in the sight of the elders of Israel. And he called the name of the place Massah, and Meribah" (Exodus 17:6–7).

Psalm 95 provides the linguistic link that identifies this incident as the Provocation: "To day if ye will hear his voice, Harden not your heart, as in the *provocation* [Heb., *Meribah*], and as in the day of temptation [Heb., *Massah*] in the wilderness: When your fathers tempted me, proved me, and saw my work. Forty years long was I grieved with this generation, and said, It is a people that do err in their heart, and they have not known my ways: Unto whom I sware in my wrath that they should not enter into my rest" (Psalm 95:7–11; emphasis added; see also Hebrews 3:8–11, 15).

The event at Meribah is the Provocation mentioned throughout the

□ □ □ □ □

M. Catherine Thomas is assistant professor of ancient scripture at Brigham Young University.

Bible. In that incident, the Lord tested the faith of the children of Israel and their willingness to accept his love and grace. Grace is the Lord's divine enabling power, given to humankind to help them with all the challenges of their lives; grace ultimately empowers them to lay hold on heaven itself. But the Israelites' response to the Lord's abundant generosity illustrates a religious paradox: God offers his children grace, but the children will not seek it; God offers his children heaven, but the children will not enter in.

We shall see that the Provocation refers not only to the specific incident at Meribah but to a persistent behavior of the children of Israel that greatly reduced their spiritual knowledge (see Psalm 95:10: "they have not *known* my ways"; emphasis added) and thus removed them from sublime privileges. After a succession of provocations, the Israelites in time rejected and lost the knowledge of the anthropomorphic nature of the Gods, the divine relationship of the Father and the Son, as well as the great plan of grace inherent in the doctrine of the Father and the Son.

The Israelites sought to be self-prospering and became angry when the God of Israel tested or tried them. The Provocation constitutes a recurring theme in the Old Testament, and indeed, in every extant scripture since. The pages of Exodus and Deuteronomy, which narrate the history of the Israelites in the wilderness, describe three additional incidents of provocation. First, at the foot of Sinai, where the Lord tried to sanctify his people and to cause them to come up the mountain and enter his presence and behold his face, the Israelites refused to exercise sufficient faith to overcome their fear and enter into the fire, smoke, and earthquake that lay between them and the face of God. They said to Moses, "Speak thou with us, and we will hear: *but let not God speak with us*, lest we die" (Exodus 20:19; emphasis added). Moses responded, "Fear not" (Exodus 20:20). Nevertheless, "the people stood afar off, and Moses drew [alone] near unto the thick darkness where God was" (Exodus 20:21).

Second, when the Israelites were camped at Kadesh Barnea in the wilderness, the Lord tried to bring them into the promised land, but they were so frightened by the report of giants in the land that neither Moses nor Caleb and Joshua could not get them to exercise enough faith to enter and conquer the land (see Deuteronomy 9:22–23). Again, as at Massah and Meribah, they refused the grace of the Lord.

Third, again at Sinai, when Moses went up to receive the fulness of the gospel from the Lord on the first set of plates, the Israelites made and set up the golden calf. Their rejection of the Lord in the very moment that Moses was receiving the fulness of the gospel for them was a most serious provocation. When he discovered what they had done, Moses broke the tables before the children of Israel. A second, lesser set of plates was made, but they were missing "the words of the everlasting covenant of the holy priesthood" (JST Deuteronomy 10:2), meaning the higher, sanctifying ordinances of the Melchizedek Priesthood. Those were the very ordinances that gave access to the presence of the Lord (see JST Exodus 34:1–2).

With their rejection of the higher priesthood, Israel began to lose the true doctrine of the Father and the Son.[1] The Lord gives the reason: "This greater priesthood administereth the gospel and *holdeth the key* of the mysteries of the kingdom, *even the key of the knowledge of God*. Therefore, in the ordinances thereof, the power of godliness is manifest. And *without the ordinances thereof*, and the authority of the priesthood, the power of godliness is not manifest unto men in the flesh; For without this no man can see the face of God, even the Father, and live. Now this Moses plainly taught to the children of Israel in the wilderness, and sought diligently to sanctify his people that they might behold the face of God; But they hardened their hearts and could not endure his presence; therefore, the Lord . . . swore that they should not enter into his rest while in the wilderness, which rest is the fulness of his glory. Therefore, he took Moses out of their midst, and the Holy Priesthood also" (D&C 84:19–25; emphasis added).

The Prophet Joseph Smith observed: "God cursed the children of Israel because they would not receive the *last law* from Moses. . . . when God offers a blessing or knowledge to a man and he refuses to receive it he will be damned. . . . the Israelites [prayed] that God would speak to Moses [and] not to them in consequence of which he cursed them with a carnal law. . . . [The] law revealed to Moses in Horeb . . . never was revealed to the [children] of Israel."[2] Thus, the children of Israel wandered an unnecessary forty years in the wilderness, as God tried to teach them to rely on him.

We really begin to appreciate the Old Testament when we realize that Israel's experiences in the wilderness are both literal and allegorical of our own experiences. Moses, speaking of manna as a symbolic teaching device, said, "[God] humbled thee, and suffered thee to hunger, and fed thee with manna . . . *that he might make thee know* that man doth not live by bread only, but by every word that proceedeth out of the mouth of the Lord" (Deuteronomy 8:3; emphasis added).

The apostle Paul spoke similarly of the manna and the water and the rock: "Brethren, I would not that ye should be ignorant, how that all our fathers were under the cloud, and all passed through the sea; And were all baptized unto Moses in the cloud and in the sea; And did all eat the same *spiritual meat* [manna]; And did all drink the same *spiritual drink* [water at Meribah]: for they drank of that *spiritual Rock* that followed them: and that Rock was Christ" (1 Corinthians 10:1–4; emphasis added). The Savior called himself manna, or the bread of life (see John 6:51, 54), indicating mankind's persisting need for divine nourishment.

Exploring scriptural symbols further, in both the Old Testament and the Book of Mormon a *wilderness* symbolizes any place in which the people are tested, tried, proven, refined by trials, taught grace, and prepared to meet the Lord (see Alma 17:9; cf. Christ's preparations in the wilderness, Matthew 4:1–2). Scriptural *journeys* often symbolize man's earthly walk from birth through the spiritual wildernesses of a fallen world (see Ether 6:4–7 for the ocean allegory of man's journey; see also 1 Nephi 8 for the *path* leading to the tree of life). God seeks to teach that his children cannot be self-prospering and thereby fulfill the purposes of their earthly lives. They must learn to seek and accept his grace to reach their destinations, which are *promised lands* or places of deliverance and spiritual peace where Zion can be established. The Lord speaks to modern Israel: "Zion cannot be built up unless it is by the principles of the law of the celestial kingdom; otherwise I cannot receive her unto myself. And my people must needs be chastened until they learn obedience, if it must needs be, by the things which they suffer" (D&C 105:5–6). Therefore, the Lord provides in our lives wildernesses and waterlessness and overwhelming challenges to entice his children to involve him as they struggle through life.

The Book of Mormon supplies further insight into what the Provocation actually refers to. Jacob referred to Psalm 95 (the plates of brass) when he wrote: "Wherefore we labored diligently among our people, that we might persuade them *to come unto Christ,* and *partake* of the goodness of God, that they might *enter into his rest,* lest by any means he should swear in his wrath they should not enter in, as in the *provocation* in the days of temptation while the children of Israel were in the wilderness" (Jacob 1:7; emphasis added).

Alma enlarged the implications still further in speaking of the first provocation, or man's first spiritual death at Adam's fall, and the second provocation, or man's continuing spiritual death that comes through rejecting the Lord: "If ye will harden your hearts ye shall not enter into the rest of the Lord . . . as in the *first provocation*, yea, according to his word in the *last provocation*. . . . let us repent, and harden not our hearts, that we provoke not the Lord our God . . . but *let us enter into the rest of God*, which is prepared according to his word" (Alma 12:36–37; emphasis added).

The Provocation, then, seems to encompass a preference for spiritual death—a preference for a return to Egypt—rather than the demanding trek through repentance to sanctification. The Provocation, in all its manifestations, implies a refusal to come to Christ to exercise faith in the face of such a daunting call, a refusal to partake of the goodness of God, a refusal to accept the restoration to God's presence or rest, a refusal to allow the Savior to work his mighty power in one's life, a refusal to enter into the at-one-ment for which he suffered and died, a refusal to be "clasped in the arms of Jesus" (Mormon 5:11). The Provocation is anti-Atonement and anti-Christ. Abinadi laments over men and women who have "gone according to their own carnal wills and desires; having never called upon the Lord while the arms of mercy were extended towards them; for the arms of mercy were extended towards them, and they would not" (Mosiah 16:12).

But who, indeed, was the God who had stood before Moses upon the rock at Meribah? (see Exodus 17:6–7). That God had revealed himself to our fathers Abraham, Isaac, and Jacob as a glorified, exalted man, that is, as an anthropomorphic (in the form of man) God who had created male and female in the image of heavenly parents.[3] This God sought a constant interaction with and a response from his children. He spoke of himself as father and Israel as his children (see Malachi 2:10). He spoke of the covenant people as bride and himself as bridegroom (see Hosea 2:19–20). The scriptures ring with manlike descriptions of an interactive God: "The eyes of the Lord" (Psalm 34:15), the ears of the Lord, and the mouth of the Lord; the heavens as the works of his fingers (see Psalm 8:3); the tablets of the covenant "written by the finger of God" (Exodus 31:18). We read of "his countenance" (Numbers 6:26), which he causes to shine or which he hides. We read of his "right hand" (Psalm 118:16), his arm stretched out in mercy and invitation. In Genesis he walks about in the garden (see Genesis 3:8), he goes down to Sinai or to his temple (see Genesis 11:5; 18:21) to reveal himself (see Exodus 19:18, 34:5) and to dwell in the midst of the children of Israel, and he goes up again (see Genesis 17:22; 35:13). He sits on a throne (see Isaiah 6:1) and causes his voice to be heard among the cherubim (see Numbers 7:89). Moses sees not only the Lord's back (see Exodus 33:23) but speaks to him face to face and mouth to mouth (see Numbers 12:8). Among several emotions, the Lord expresses tenderness, mercy, love, joy, delight, and pity, as well as sadness, frustration, and anger.

With the loss of the Melchizedek Priesthood, however, and the Jews' resulting vulnerability to Greek and other cultural and philosophical influences, there arose among the Jews a resistance to the idea of an anthropomorphic God. At least by the intertestamental period (the period following Malachi, between the Old Testament and the New), the scribes and rabbis found the anthropomorphisms in the Hebrew Bible offensive and made small textual changes, which they described as "biblical modifications of expression."[4] (See Jacob 4:14 for Jacob's acknowledgment of Israel's deliberate mystification of God.) For example, in place of "I [God] will dwell in your midst," they substituted, "I shall cause you to dwell," avoiding the idea that God would dwell with men. The text of Exodus 34:24 was subtly altered from "to see the face of the Lord" *(lir'ot 'et-pene yhwh)* to the phrase "to appear before the Lord" *(lera'ot 'et-pene yhwh)*. Again, the effect is to distance and dematerialize God.

It appears that the Jewish translators of the Septuagint Bible (from Hebrew to Greek; abbreviated LXX) also attempted to dematerialize God.[5] An example is Exodus 29:45 (KJV): "I will dwell among the children of Israel, and will be their God." Instead of, "I will dwell," the Septuagint reads: "And I shall be called upon [or named] among the children of Israel and will be their God" (Exodus 29:45).[6] The effect of the change from *to dwell* to the phrase *to be called upon* is to distance God from his children.[7]

This attempt to dematerialize God is found also among the Israelite apostates in the Book of Mormon. Ammon and Aaron had to teach that God, the Great Spirit, would not always be spirit, but would tabernacle himself in the flesh (see Alma 18:34–35; 22:8–14; see also Mosiah 3:5). Abinadi, in fact, was martyred for his very declaration that this spirit God would take on Him the form of man in order to perform the great Atonement (see Mosiah 13:32–35). The apostate Zoramites' belief that God is a spirit and never would be anything else really meant they believed there would be no Christ, no incarnation of God on earth, and thus, no Atonement (see Alma 31:15–16).

A Jewish scholar named Philo lived in the period just prior to Jesus' advent. His writings, which influenced Judaism as well as Christianity, taught that the physical and emotional references in the scriptures to God were allegorical, not literal. He wrote that when Moses described God with human emotions, the reader needed to know that "neither the . . . passions of the soul, nor the parts and members of the body in general, have any relation to God."[8] Philo explained that Moses used these expressions as an elementary way to teach those who could not otherwise understand. Thus, when the Savior came to the Jews in the meridian of time, he found many of them obsessed with religion, with purity, and with scrupulous observance of law, but he found few who knew God.

Removing the body, parts, and passions from God also removes his ability to suffer and thus obscures the real meanings behind the Atonement. The Book of Mormon, however, teaches that among the several reasons the Savior came to earth was his desire to "take upon him [mankind's] infirmities, that his bowels may be filled with mercy, according to the flesh, that he may know according to the flesh how to succor his people according to their infirmities" (Alma 7:12). Alma quotes Zenos on the accessibility of the Father's grace through the atonement of the Son: "And thou didst hear me because of mine afflictions and my sincerity; and it is because of thy Son that thou hast been thus merciful unto me, therefore I will cry unto thee in all mine afflictions, for in thee is my joy; for thou has turned thy judgments away from me, because of thy Son" (Alma 33:11). Alma then quotes Zenock on the nature of Israel's Provocation: "Thou art angry, O Lord, with this people, because they will not understand thy mercies which thou hast bestowed upon them because of thy Son" (Alma 33:16).

Related to God's nature is God's name. The reluctance to offend God by anthropomorphic references grew stronger with time, so that even the use of the name *YHWH* (Yahweh or Jehovah) was avoided. At least by the third century B.C., *adonai*, meaning "lord," was substituted for the divine name[9] and ultimately to speak the name aloud became both illegal and blasphemous among the Jews, even in the temple or synagogue. One scholar notes: "The divine name, once the 'distinguishing mark' of divine presence and immanence, had become the essence of God's unapproachable holiness so that in the Jewish tradition 'the Name' (*ha shem*) could be synonymous with 'God.'"[10] A moment's reflection leads us to see that since God had ordained his name as a keyword by which a covenant person could gain access to him (Moses 5:8; 1 Kings 8:28–29; Mormon 9:21), to forbid the divine name was to forbid access, through holy ordinances, to God himself.

With the dematerializing of God came the obscuring of the Father-Son relationship. Religious history reveals that one major apostate objective has been to merge the members of the Godhead into one nebulous being. That merging clouds several significant truths, among which I mention two in passing and a third for discussion:

1. The doctrine of a divine Father and Son begins to reveal that there must be family relationships, parents, husbands, and wives, all of which continue in the eternities.

2. Eternal families being possible, there is need for temple ordinances that seal these relationships for eternity.

3. The Son models for humankind the relationship of grace by which one gains exaltation and which men and women must model in order to be like the Gods. It is particularly that last truth that I would like to explore here, but first a word about merging the Gods into one amorphous being. That which set the Israelites apart from all others in the polytheistic Greco-Roman and Near Eastern cultures was their steadfast declaration of one omnipotent God, that is, their belief in monotheism. It was perhaps because they had interpreted Deuteronomy 6:4, "Hear, O Israel: The Lord our God is one Lord" to mean that there was only one God, that the later Jews rejected Christ (see John 8:41, 58–59). After all, Christ taught that he is the Son of God, and so, they said, he made himself equal with God and seemed, in fact, to be multiplying Gods (see John 5:18).[11] Nevertheless, although it is true that there is one omnipotent God, that truth is not the whole truth. When the Savior came to the earth in the meridian of time, one of his tasks was to restore the Melchizedek Priesthood and thus restore the *knowledge of the Father.* Jesus taught that he, the Son, is the only avenue to exaltation or reunion with the Father.

But one of the most important revelations from the divine Father/Son relationship is the model it provides of the *nature of a saving relationship* with God. The Savior showed us how to live in total submission; he drew continually on his Father's grace. He says, "The Son can do *nothing* of himself, but what he seeth the Father do: for *what things soever* he doeth, these also doeth the Son . . . For the Father loveth the Son, and sheweth him all things that himself doeth (John 5:19–20; emphasis added). And again, "As the living Father hath sent me, and *I live by the Father:* so he that eateth me [reference to the sacrament], even *he shall live by me*" (John 6:57; emphasis added). And again, "I do *nothing* of myself; but as my Father hath taught me, I speak these things. And he that sent me is with me: the Father hath not left me alone; for I do always those things that please him" (John 8:28 29; emphasis added). Further, he said, "Believest thou not that I am in the Father, and the Father in me? the words that I speak unto you I speak not of myself: but the Father that dwelleth in me, *he doeth the works*" (John 14:10; emphasis added). Ultimately, Christ will even deliver up the kingdom, for which he died, to his Father (see D&C 76:107). This relationship of the at-one-ment of the Father and the Son is the divine model for the Saints of God and was revealed that we might emulate it.

The Savior taught this at-one-ment relationship to his disciples and, indeed, to all who become his disciples. The means of at-one-ment with the Son and the Father is the Holy Ghost. It is through cultivating the Holy Ghost that we enter into at-one-ment with the Son and the Father. Jesus told his disciples: "I will pray the Father, and he shall give you another Comforter, that *he may abide with you* for ever; Even the Spirit of truth . . . for *he dwelleth with you*, and *shall be in you*" (John 14:16–17; emphasis added; see also John 17:20–23).[12]

The apostle Paul experienced this relationship of oneness with the Savior; he wrote to the Galatians: "I am crucified with Christ: nevertheless I live; yet not I, but Christ liveth in me: and the life which I now live in the flesh I live by the faith of the Son of God, who loved me, and gave himself for me" (Galatians 2:20).

In scenes recorded in 3 Nephi, the resurrected, perfected Christ gave abundant evidence of his continuing dependence on his Father. He makes frequent reference to the commandments and will of his Father. He seems very eager to return to the full presence of his Father (3 Nephi 17:4); we see him kneel and bow himself to the earth, pouring out both his troubled heart (3 Nephi 17:14) as well as his joy (3 Nephi 17:20–21), his thanks (3 Nephi 19:20, 28), and his needs (3 Nephi 19:21, 29). Perhaps this relationship of divine dependence and at-one-ment continues far into the eternities. It is revealed to us in this life so we can learn to live in that relationship and thus gain admission to that community of grace-linked Gods.

The relationship of grace helps us understand more fully this passage in Doctrine and Covenants 93: "[Christ] received not of the fulness at the first, but received grace *for* grace; And he received not of the fulness at first, but continued from grace *to* grace, until he received a fulness. . . . I give unto you these sayings that you may understand and know how to worship, and know what you worship, that *you* may come unto the Father in my name, and in due time receive of his fulness. For if you keep my commandments you shall receive of his fulness, and be glorified in me as I am in the Father; therefore, I say unto you, you shall receive grace *for* grace" (D&C 93:12–13, 19–20; emphasis added).

By this scripture we understand that as Christ gave grace to those around him, he received from his Father increasingly more grace to give. Thus, receiving grace *for* grace, Jesus grew from grace *to* grace: a model for us. "Freely ye have received, freely give," the Savior told his disciples (Matthew 10:8). The Lord has blessed each of us individually many times over with many more forms of grace than we now know or could count. Perhaps all of the Lord's grace to us—his many kindnesses to each of us, our talents, our gifts of spirit and personality, our bodies, our material resources—is given to us so that we will have something to give one another. As we give of this grace in countless ways to those around us, especially where it may not seem to be merited the Lord increases his gifts of grace to us; in this process of our receiving grace *for* the grace we give, we grow from grace *to* grace, as Christ did, until we obtain a fulness.

Living in such a relationship as the Father and the Son's, either on earth or in heaven, requires a total willingness to dethrone oneself as the regent in one's own kingdom and to enthrone Christ as he enthroned the Father. President Ezra Taft Benson observed that "Christ removed self as the force in His perfect life. It was not *my* will, but *thine* be done."[13]

How privileged we are to know about the relationship of grace and to know of the divine possibilities for ourselves through connection with the Father and the Son, to experience the exquisitely loving and personal nature of the Gods in their great chains of light and grace.

In various forms, the Provocation continues with us today. One recognizes in oneself the rejection of grace as one keeps trying to struggle through life on one's own judgment and power, keeping one's own personal agenda on the throne. Mormon described the philosophy of the anti-Christ Korihor as the belief that man prospers and conquers by his own strength and genius, not through dependence on a greater divine being (see Alma 30:17). Thus, struggling alone without calling on God reflects the doctrine of the anti-Christ. It is apparent that even the Son of God could not have prospered without his Father's grace.

Moroni also emphasizes grace: "And now, I would commend you to *seek this Jesus* of whom the prophets and apostles have written, that the *grace of God the Father*, and also *the Lord Jesus Christ*, and the Holy Ghost . . . abide in you forever" (Ether 12:41; emphasis added; see also Moroni 10:32).

We see in Israel's provocations a key to understanding nearly every interaction between God and Israel recorded in the pages of the Bible. On the one hand, God's whole efforts are bent toward helping the covenant people to prosper through his grace; on the other hand, Israel strives to be self-prospering. In the midst of abundant miracles and divine gifts, the persistent rejection of God's grace is Israel's Provocation.

NOTES

1. Of course, all the prophets had the Melchizedek Priesthood, but their right to confer it or teach its mysteries was restricted. See Joseph Smith, *Teachings of the Prophet Joseph Smith*, sel. Joseph Fielding Smith (Salt Lake City: Deseret Book Co., 1938), p. 181.
2. Andrew F. Ehat and Lyndon W. Cook, eds., *The Words of Joseph Smith* (Provo, Utah: Religious Studies Center, BYU, 1980), pp. 244, 247; emphasis added.
3. Because God created man in His own image, it is more accurate to speak of man as *theomorphic* (in the form or image of God) than to speak of God as anthropomorphic.
4. "Anthropomorphism," *Encyclopaedia Judaica,* 17 vols. (Jerusalem: Keter, 1982), 3:54.
5. Perhaps it is helpful to note here, with respect to apostate movements, that in any apostasy there are the *deliberate* initiators and perpetrators of lies (see 1 Nephi 13:27; Jacob 4:14; Moses 1:41); but there is usually also a larger group of innocent and well-intentioned victims (see 1 Nephi 13:29; D&C 123:12). Not all promoters of false ideas have malignant intent; most are to some extent the victims of those who have gone before.
6. Another example is found in Numbers 12:8. The Hebrew version reads: "With [Moses] will I speak mouth to mouth, even apparently, and not in dark speeches; and the *image* (or *form*) of the Lord shall he behold." The Greek version reads: "Mouth to mouth will I speak to him, in his sight and not in riddles, and he shall see *the glory* of the Lord." The change from *image* to *glory* is from the specific to a more nebulous description of God.
7. For a fuller discussion of the apostasy of the doctrine of God during the intertestamental period, see the author's chapter entitled "From Malachi to John the Baptist: The Dynamics of Apostasy," *Studies in Scripture, Volume 4: 1 Kings to Malachi,* ed. Kent P. Jackson (Salt Lake City: Deseret Book Co., 1993), pp. 471–83. See also an in-depth study of the dematerializing of God in the author's "The Influence of Asceticism on the Rise of Christian Text, Doctrine, and Practice in the First Two Centuries," Ph.D. diss. Brigham Young University.

8. Philo, "The Unchangeableness of God," *Loeb Classical Library* (Cambridge, Mass.: Harvard University Press, 1930), 3:37.
9. "God, Name of," *Encyclopaedia Judaica,* 7:680.
10. Another scholar suggests that, with ascendancy of the law in Israel and the need to buffer the law against violations, *any* use of the divine name had to be denied. The prohibition was motivated by a desire to ensure that the name would not be used "in vain" (Exodus 20:7) either by Jews or non-Jews. The name in the temple or the synagogue was eventually affected by this fear. In the Septuagint the name of Yahweh was rendered throughout with *kyrios* ("Lord"), following the Jewish preference for *adonai.* Martin Rose, "Names of God in the OT," *The Anchor Bible Dictionary* (New York: Doubleday, 1992), p. 1010.
11. An extension of this merging of Gods occurred in the early period of the Christian Church at the Council of Nicea (A.D. 325) when the decision to fabricate a trinity of three beings into one made it possible to make Christianity securely monotheistic, again in a threateningly pagan environment. Both of these beliefs, monotheism and trinitarianism, did violence to the full truth about the true nature of the Godhead and of godliness itself.
12. Joseph Smith, *Lectures on Faith,* comp. N. B. Lundwall (Salt Lake City: N. B. Lundwall, n.d.), Lecture 5, pp. 48–49, explains how the Father and the Son are one through the medium of the Spirit, and how all the Saints may in the same manner come into at-one-ment with them: "The Only Begotten of the Father, full of grace and truth, and having overcome, received a *fullness* of the glory of the Father, *possessing the same mind* with the Father, which *mind is the Holy Spirit,* that bears record of the Father and the Son, and these three are one; or, in other words, these three constitute the great, matchless, governing, and supreme power over all things . . . the Father and the Son possessing the same mind, the same wisdom, glory, power, and fullness—filling all in all; the Son being filled with the fullness of the mind, glory, and power; or, in other words, the *spirit,* glory, and power, of the Father . . . which Spirit is shed forth upon all who believe on his name and keep his commandments[.] . . . all those who keep his commandments shall grow up from grace to grace, and become heirs of the heavenly kingdom, and joint heirs with Jesus Christ; possessing the same mind, being transformed *into the same image* or likeness, even *the express image* of him who fills all in all; being filled with the fullness of his glory, and become one in him, even as the Father, Son and Holy Spirit are one." (Emphasis added.)
13. Ezra Taft Benson, in Conference Report, Apr. 1986, p. 6.

CHAPTER THIRTEEN

THE EXODUS: PROPHETIC TYPE AND THE PLAN OF REDEMPTION

THOMAS R. VALLETTA

Among the events recorded in sacred writ, few have had greater effect on the house of Israel than the exodus from Egypt, the glorious Sinai revelations, the wearying wilderness wanderings, and the dramatic entry into the promised land. One commentator aptly noted: "It was that faith received in the exodus which shaped all of Israel's understanding of history. It was only in light of the exodus that Israel was able to look back into the past and piece together her earlier history. It was also the exodus which provided the prophets with a key to the understanding of Israel's future. In this sense, the exodus stands at the center of Israel's history."[1]

Modern western scholarship has tended to focus on the secular history surrounding the events of the Exodus. The ancient writers had a different agenda. One noted Jewish biblical scholar observed: "The biblical narratives are essentially documents of faith, not records of the past; that is to say, the verities of faith are communicated through the forms of history, but these latter are not presented for their own sake. They are employed only insofar as they serve the purposes of the former."[2] That does not mean that modern historical and archeological methods and concerns are irrelevant or even unfruitful. To the contrary, they have yielded much toward our understanding of the scriptures. Still, the question must be posed as to the intended purpose and use of these sacred writings. President Brigham Young asked: "Do you read the Scriptures, my brethren and sisters, as though you were writing them a thousand, two thousand, or five thousand years ago? Do you read them as though you stood in the

□ □ □ □ □

Thomas R. Valletta is an instructor at the Ogden, Utah, LDS Institute of Religion.

place of the men who wrote them? If you do not feel thus, it is your privilege to do so. . . . When you can thus feel, then you may begin to think that you can find out something about God, and begin to learn who he is."[3]

Reading the scriptures as the inspired authors intended involves, among other things, approaching them with an "eye of faith" and "by the power of the Holy Ghost" (Ether 12:19; Moroni 10:5). This includes acknowledging that the scriptures are the prophetic statements of "holy men of God [who] spake *as they were* moved by the Holy Ghost" and that they constitute "the words of Christ" (2 Peter 1:21; 2 Nephi 32:3). It also includes approaching the scriptures as testimony of Jesus Christ and the plan of redemption. The Lord himself declared that "all things have their likeness, and all things are created and made to bear record of me" (Moses 6:63).

One of the many ways the scriptures testify of Christ is through the use of "types and shadows, figures and similitudes . . . revealing [that which is holy] to those whose hearts were prepared for that light and knowledge which leads to salvation."[4] According to Joseph Fielding McConkie, "symbols are the timeless and universal language in which God, in his wisdom, has chosen to teach his gospel and bear witness of his Son. They are the language of the scriptures, the language of revelation, the language of the Spirit, the language of faith."[5]

In his omniscience and foreknowledge, Heavenly Father has long employed sacred history as a teaching tool. He gives us "a pattern in all things, that [we] may not be deceived" (D&C 52:14). In the scriptures, these patterns are often presented as types. A type may be defined as is "a person, event, or ritual with likeness to another person, event, or ritual of greater importance which is to follow." Further, "true types will have noticeable points of resemblance, show evidence of divine appointment, and be prophetic of future events."[6] Many events, objects, persons, and ceremonies recorded in the scriptures are types of Jesus Christ and the plan of redemption. The Lord himself declared that "all things have their likeness, and all things are created and made to bear record of me, both things which are temporal, and things which are spiritual; things which are in the heavens above, and things which are on the earth, and things which are in the earth, and things which are under the earth, both above and beneath: all things bear record of me" (Moses 6:63; see also Moses 5:7; 2 Nephi 2:11; Mosiah 3:15; 13:30–31; Alma 37:38–45). The Exodus "was not only a real event, but also 'a type and a shadow of things,' representing both escape from the wicked world and redemption from the bondage of sin."[7] As a type, the Exodus not only had value in its distinctive lessons but it also testified of greater events, patterns, and persons far beyond its own historical bounds. It is one of the most prevalent typological motifs employed by the prophets throughout the scriptures.[8]

THE OLD TESTAMENT

The Old Testament prophets focused on both the theological and the typological meaning of the Exodus. Often they did so through ceremonializing the experience for purposes of instruction. Even before the escape of the children of Israel from Egypt, the Lord instituted the Passover and the Feast of Unleavened Bread "for a memorial . . . throughout your generations . . . by an ordinance for ever" (Exodus 12:14). Moses directed the people to catechize the Exodus for their children to teach eternal principles (see Deuteronomy 6:20–25). The Lord instituted special days of remembrance even before the Israelites entered the promised land (see Deuteronomy 26). An aged Joshua, in his final public discourse, led his people into a renewal of the covenant to remember the Exodus always (see Joshua 24:1–18). The Exodus, particularly the Sinai covenant, was later remembered regularly in the temple liturgy. "The tribes of Israel came together periodically to one of the sanctuaries to renew the covenant. We do not know all the particulars of the rite of covenant renewal, but a number of biblical texts enable us to discern the main lines of the celebration. Israel was reminded of Yahweh's gracious deeds on their behalf, and then the words of God's law were read to the people. The people responded: 'All that the Lord had said we will do.' Much of the ceremony recalled the original theophany at Sinai."[9]

Isaiah clearly had the Exodus in mind as he prophesied that "the Lord shall set his hand again the second time to recover the remnant of his people." He declared that "the Lord shall utterly destroy the tongue of the Egyptian sea; and with his mighty wind shall he shake his hand over the river, and shall smite it in the seven streams, and make *men* go over dryshod." Isaiah continued using Exodus typology with his prophecy of "an highway for the remnant of his people, which shall be left, from Assyria; like as it was to Israel in the day that he came up out of the land of Egypt" (Isaiah 11:11, 15–16). In another example, Jeremiah described the miraculous gathering of Israel in the last days by comparing it to God's delivering "the children of Israel out of the land of Egypt." The events in the last days would be even more dramatic (Jeremiah 16:12–15).

THE BOOK OF MORMON

The Exodus was no less ingrained in the identity and instruction of the ancient Israelites of the Book of Mormon lands. The Book of Mormon contains an abundance of Exodus motifs.[10] From parallels with Lehi's family's exodus to their promised land (Mosiah 7:18–20) to direct declarations from Book of Mormon prophets, echoes of the Exodus resonate in the pages of the stick of Joseph. As early as 1 Nephi 4, in the effort to obtain the plates of brass, Nephi pleaded with his faithless brothers to "be strong like unto Moses; for he truly spake unto the waters of the Red Sea and they divided hither and thither, and our fathers came through, out of captivity, on dry ground, and the armies of Pharaoh did follow and were drowned in the waters of the Red Sea." Nephi added that "the Lord is able to deliver us, even as our fathers." Ironically but predictably, his brothers "murmured," following the pattern of Moses' murmuring followers (1 Nephi 4:2–4; cf. 16:19–20; Exodus 16:1–8).

Book of Mormon prophets used imagery of the Exodus to teach and illustrate numerous truths, including trusting in God (see 1 Nephi 17:23–35), the final gathering (see 2 Nephi 6:14–18), spiritual bondage and deliverance (see 2 Nephi 9:8–11), the resurrection (see Alma 36:28–29), and the power of God (see Helaman 8:11–15). The early American prophets also referred to various aspects of the Exodus as types of the Savior. Alma cited Zenock as proclaiming that Moses prophesied of Jesus Christ when "a type was raised up in the wilderness, that whosoever would look upon it might live. And many did look and live" (Alma 33:19; see also Helaman 8:11–15; cf. Numbers 21:9). Crowning the Exodus types of the Book of Mormon was the Savior's own declaration during his glorious appearance to the ancient Americans: "Behold, I am he of whom Moses spake, saying: A prophet shall the Lord your God raise up unto you of your brethren, like unto me; him shall ye hear in all things whatsoever he shall say unto you. And it shall come to pass that every soul who will not hear that prophet shall be cut off from among the people" (3 Nephi 20:23; see also 3 Nephi 23:1–3).

THE NEW TESTAMENT

Scholars have previously demonstrated that a "typological understanding of Scripture governed the interpretation of N[ew] T[estament] writers."[11] They relied heavily upon typology of the Exodus to illustrate Jesus Christ and the plan of redemption. "The New Testament writers were convinced that in Jesus Christ God had brought to accomplishment all the prophecies and unfulfilled hopes of Israel's long history. The sacred authors were never content simply to recount the external facts of the ministry of Jesus Christ. They wanted those for whom they wrote to understand that all Scriptures had been fulfilled in what Jesus had said and done, and above all in what he was. He was the New Adam in whom the shattered order of the first Creation would be restored. He was the New Israel in whom the new exodus, the definitive passover from slavery to the freedom of the sons of God, would be accomplished. He was the New David in whom the disappointed hopes of the Israelite monarchy would at last be realized. Jesus Christ, appearing in 'these last days,' recapitulated in himself all of salvation history and brought it to fulfillment. The pages of the New Testament are therefore often a fabric of allusions to Old Testament themes. The 'New Exodus' theme, however, is not just one among many aspects of New Testament theology. Because the exodus from Egypt with the Sinai covenant was the central event of Israel's history, the 'New Exodus' appears as the most fundamental and all-embracing theme in New Testament theology."[12]

The pages of the New Testament abound with more Exodus imagery and similitudes than can be discussed adequately here. A list of some of them follows.

TABLE 1

NEW TESTAMENT APPLICATION OF EXODUS TYPOLOGY

The Ancient Exodus of Israel	New Testament Typology
Moses (Deuteronomy 18: 15–19)	Christ (Acts 3:22–23; 7:37)
Baby Moses Rescued from Pharaoh	Jesus Saved from Herod (Matthew 2:16)
Pharaoh	Satan and His Servants (Romans 9:17)
I AM that I AM (Exodus 3:14)	I AM (John 8:58)
Passover Lamb	Christ's Sacrifice (John 1:29, 36)
Crossing the Red Sea	Christ's Burial and Resurrection (Romans 6:4); Baptism (1 Corinthians 10:2)
Tree Sweetened Bitter Waters (Exodus 15)	I Will Give the Tree of Life (Revelation 2:7)
Manna (Exodus 16:15)	Christ Is the Bread of Life (John 6:31–35)

Moses Fasts 40 Days and Nights (Deuteronomy 9:9)	Jesus Fasts 40 Days and Nights (Matthew 4:2)
Sinai Theophany (Exodus 24:13–16; 29–31)	Mount of Transfiguration (Mark 9:2–8)
Sinai Law and Covenant (Exodus 19ff)	Christ's Sermon on the Mount (Matthew 5)
Plague—Graves of Lust (Numbers 11:31–34)	Lust Brings Death (James 1:15)
Water from Rock (Exodus 17:6; Numbers 20:11)	Christ Is the Living Water (John 4:6–14);Christ, the Rock (John 7:37–40; 1 Corinthians 10:1–5, 11)
Brazen Serpent (Numbers 21:4–9)	Christ Lifted Up (John 3:14–15)
40 Years of Israel's Wanderings	Christ's 40 Days in the Wilderness (Mark 1)
Joshua Crosses Jordan into Canaan	Jesus Baptized at Bethabara (John 1:28)
Joshua Leads Israel into the Promised Land	Jesus Is the Way (John 6:21; 14:6)

THE TESTIMONIES OF MATTHEW AND JOHN

Some of the most spiritually enlightening uses of Exodus typology in the New Testament are the deliberately accentuated literary patterns prevalent in the testimonies of Matthew and John. Particularly edifying is the sixth chapter of John, wherein the entire story of the multitude following Jesus into the wilderness, the miraculous multiplication of loaves and fishes, Jesus retiring to the mountain, the crossing of the sea, the murmuring crowd, and the deeply spiritual Bread of Life discourse are clearly paralleled with the ancient Exodus.[13] The structure of Matthew's gospel suggests that he, too, carefully composed his testimony of Jesus Christ to reveal fulfillment of Exodus typology.[14] It seems that Matthew intentionally crafted his work to show that Jesus Christ fulfilled the Mosaic prophecy that "I will raise them up a Prophet from among their brethren, like unto thee [Moses]" (Deuteronomy 18:18). Table 2 briefly summarizes the common themes in both Exodus and the first five chapters of Matthew.[15]

TABLE 2

COMPARISON OF THE BOOK OF EXODUS AND THE EARLY CHAPTERS OF MATTHEW

The Book of Exodus	**The Testimony of St. Matthew**
Genealogy (Exodus 1)	Genealogy of Jesus (Matthew 1)
Special Role of Women in Moses' Birth and Preparation (Exodus 2)	Special Role of Women in Jesus' Birth and Preparation (Matthew 1)
Pharaoh's Edict to Kill Sons (Exodus 1)	Herod's Infanticide (Matthew 2)
Escape from Egypt (Exodus 12)	Escape into Egypt (Matthew 2)
Crossing the Red Sea; River Jordan (Exodus 14; Joshua 4)	Baptism of Jesus (Matthew 3)
Led by Cloud by Day, Pillar of Fire by Night (Exodus 13)	Sign of the Holy Ghost Given (Matthew 3)
Wilderness Temptations (Exodus 15–18)	40 Days of Temptations (Matthew 4)
Law from Sinai (Exodus 19ff)	Sermon on the Mount (Matthew 5)

EXODUS TYPOLOGY AND THE PLAN OF REDEMPTION

A review of the ancients' penchant for Exodus typology raises the important question of why such typology was used. It has earlier been suggested that the Exodus was a central and crucial point in Israel's history. The Exodus was catechized and ceremonialized so as to never be forgotten. Virtually all of Israel shared the common bond of the Exodus. A constant review of that event could cement the people into a unified people and even a nation. The Exodus also taught important teachings that the prophets wanted passed on to the children. God's omniscience and omnipotence, history's divine design, the critical role of living prophets, the weakness of the natural man, the dangers of pride, and the importance of trusting in God are among the many powerful truths the Exodus teaches.

An important reason for the abundant use of Exodus themes and symbols throughout the scriptures is that the Exodus presents, in pattern and type, the eternal plan of redemption and the central role of Jesus Christ the Redeemer within that plan.[16] Every aspect of the story of Moses and the Exodus of Israel typifies Jesus Christ and Heavenly

Father's plan (see Deuteronomy 18:15; John 6; Acts 7:25–35; 1 Corinthians 5:7–8; 10:1–5; 1 Nephi 17:41; Mosiah 13:30–31; Alma 36:28; see Table 3).

In the Exodus itself, events actually began as early as Abraham and his children receiving and inhabiting the covenant land (see Genesis 15–25). Centuries later, there was dissension among the covenant family, which caused the righteous son, Joseph, to be sold into Egypt (see Genesis 37). Although Israel was temporally saved by Joseph's going down to Egypt, ultimately "there arose up a new king over Egypt, which knew not Joseph" (Exodus 1:8). The new rulers of Egypt enslaved Israel and "made their lives bitter with hard bondage" (Exodus 1:14). But "God remembered his covenant with Abraham, with Isaac, and with Jacob. And God looked upon the children of Israel, and God had respect unto them" (Exodus 2:24–25). He prepared Moses as a deliverer and told him to "say unto the children of Israel, I am the Lord, and I will bring you out from under the burdens of the Egyptians, and I will rid you out of their bondage, and I will redeem you with a stretched out arm, and with great judgments" (Exodus 6:6).

With great power and might, culminating with the death of "all the firstborn in the land of Egypt" (Exodus 11:5), Israel was delivered from bondage (see Exodus 12). They were led miraculously across the Red Sea to escape their Egyptian enemies (see Exodus 15). They were not left alone after the crossing, but "the Lord went before them by day in a pillar of a cloud, to lead them the way; and by night in a pillar of fire, to give them light; to go by day and night" (Exodus 13:21). Israel was nourished by manna from heaven in their time of need (see Exodus 16). Moses "sought diligently to sanctify his people that they might behold the face of God" (D&C 84:23). When they got to Mount Sinai, the Israelites "hardened their hearts and could not endure his [God's] presence; therefore, the Lord in his wrath, for his anger was kindled against them, swore that they should not enter into his rest while in the wilderness, which rest is the fulness of his glory" (D&C 84:24). Covenants, laws, and ordinances were given to Israel. A lesser law was given to school them for the greater (see Exodus 19; cf. Galatians 3:24–25). Part of Israel's preparatory process was to "wander in the wilderness forty years, until all the generation, that had done evil in the sight of the Lord, was consumed" (Numbers 32:13). When the old generation was purged, Joshua (Hebrew, meaning "Jehovah is Salvation," a form of the later proper name translated into Greek as *Jesus)* led the children of Israel miraculously across the

River Jordan, back home into the promised land (Joshua 3:10–17; cf. Acts 7:45).

The plan of salvation reveals the unmistakable parallels with the Exodus. Prior to mortality, we lived with our Heavenly Father as his spirit children (see Abraham 3:22–28; D&C 93:21–29). According to the Prophet Joseph Smith, Heavenly Father "saw proper to institute laws whereby the rest could have a privilege to advance like himself."[17] This plan for our exaltation was presented at a great heavenly council, but opposition soon became evident (see Moses 4:1–4). Under the direction of Lucifer, those in rebellion to Father's plan "sought to destroy the agency of man" (Moses 4:3; see also Abraham 3:24–28; D&C 29:36–38; Isaiah 14:12–20; Luke 10:18). Their opposition to the terms and conditions set forth in the Father's plan and their struggle against truth and light are called the war in heaven by John the Revelator (see Revelation 12:4–9). Lucifer was "cast down; And he became Satan, yea, even the devil, the father of all lies, to deceive and to blind men, and to lead them captive at his will, even as many as would not hearken unto my voice" (Moses 4:3–4). "A third part of the hosts of heaven" followed Lucifer's deception and "were thrust down, and thus came the devil and his angels" (D&C 29:36–37; see also Revelation 12:4–9; Abraham 3:27–28).

An important part of Heavenly Father's plan involved sending his children to earth to "prove them herewith, to see if they will do all things whatsoever the Lord their God shall command them" (Abraham 3:25.) Adam and Eve led the way into mortality for all of us by accomplishing the Fall (see 2 Nephi 2:24–25). That was an important step toward our salvation, but it was not without consequences, which included being shut off from the presence of God. Without a deliverance, all of the spirits sent down to earth would have become subject to the devil forever.

In the wisdom of God, the Atonement was provided as a means of escape (see 2 Nephi 9:6–10). Through the resurrection, we overcome physical death. We can also overcome spiritual bondage and death through following our Deliverer's lead. He is "the way, the truth, and the life: no man cometh unto the Father, but by me [Jesus Christ]" (John 14:6). His way involves obedience to his principles and ordinances (see D&C 136:2, 4), one of which is baptism by immersion for the remission of sins (see D&C 20:68–74; 2 Nephi 9:23–24). With this ordinance, we symbolize burying the old man of sin and begin the process of building "the new man" in the image of Christ (see Ephesians 4:21–24; Colossians 2:12; 3:8–11; Romans 6:4). After baptism, we must receive the gift of the Holy Ghost. "The presentation or 'gift' of the Holy Ghost," President Joseph F. Smith said, "simply confers upon a man the right to receive at any time, when he is worthy of it and desires it, the power and light of truth of the Holy Ghost, although he may often be left to his own spirit and judgment."[18] Elder Boyd K. Packer has explained that to help us along the path, the Lord has blessed us with Prophets, the Holy Scriptures, and a church organization with a mission to "prepare all of Heavenly Father's children to receive the ordinances and covenants associated with immortality and eternal life." Further, "a good and useful and true test of every major decision made by a leader in the Church is whether a given course leads toward or away from the making and keeping of covenants."[19] Ultimately, these teachings, ordinances, and covenants lead us to the house of the Lord, where further preparations are made to overcome the temptations and trials of this life and to enter into God's presence. Of course, tribulations and tests do not end when we enter the temple; rather, The glorious teachings, covenants, and ordinances of the temple aid us in overcoming all things. Most of all, we are reminded that "there shall be no other name given nor any other way nor means whereby salvation can come unto the children of men, only in and through the name of Christ, the Lord Omnipotent" (Mosiah 3:17). "The words of Christ, if we follow their course, carry us beyond this vale of sorrow into a far better land of promise" (Alma 37:45).

TABLE 3

THE EXODUS PATTERN OF THE PLAN OF REDEMPTION

Exodus	**Plan of Redemption**
Israel in the Promised Land	Premortality with Father
Dissension	War in Heaven
Joseph and Israel into Egypt	Sent to Earth to Be Proven
Pharaoh Who Knew Not Joseph	Satan Seeks Our Misery
Israel in Bondage in Egypt	Captive of the Devil
Moses Called to Help Deliver Us	Christ Is Our Redeemer
Israel Is Liberated through Death of the Firstborn	Jesus Christ, the Firstborn of the Father, Liberates Mankind through the Atonement

Crossing of the Red Sea; Burying the Pharaoh's Forces	Baptism and Other Ordinances; Begin Putting Off the World
Cloud and Pillar of Fire	Guided by the Holy Ghost
Manna from Heaven	Sustained by the Word of God
Mount Sinai and the Tabernacle	Temple Worship
Covenants, Ordinances, and Law of Moses	Covenants, Ordinances, and Higher Law of Christ
Forty Years of Wilderness: Old Generation Dies Off	Trials and Tests of Life: The Process Continues of Putting Off the World and Becoming a New Creature in Christ
Joshua Leads Israelites into Canaan	Jesus Leads Us Home

Realizing that the Exodus pattern typifies the plan of redemption helps explain its prevalent use throughout the scriptures. Is it really any wonder why it is such a beloved motif among the prophets? Church leaders have long emphasized the need for the Saints to study, ponder, and teach the plan of redemption. President Ezra Taft Benson has indicated: "I am deeply concerned about what we are doing to teach the Saints at all levels the gospel of Jesus Christ as completely and authoritatively as do the Book of Mormon and the Doctrine and Covenants. By this I mean teaching the 'great plan of the Eternal God,' to use the words of Amulek (Alma 34:9). . . . Brethren and sisters, we all need to take a careful inventory of our performance and also the performance of those over whom we preside to be sure that we are teaching the 'great plan of the Eternal God' to the Saints."[20]

Recently, the prophet's desire that teachers teach the plan of salvation was reaffirmed by Elder Boyd K. Packer in a symposium for Church educators. After listing many scriptural names for the plan of redemption, Elder Packer instructed: "A brief overview of the 'plan of happiness' (which is my choice, my favorite title, in talking of the plan), if given at the very beginning and revisited occasionally, will be of immense value to your students. . . . You will not be with your students or your own children at the time of their temptations. At those dangerous moments they must depend on their own resources. If they can locate themselves within the framework of the gospel plan, they will be immensely strengthened. The plan is worthy of repetition over and over again. Then the purpose of life, the reality of the Redeemer, and the reason for the commandments will stay with them."[21]

That may be one reason why the Exodus pattern is repeated and echoed throughout the scriptures. It is a type of the "great plan of happiness." The Exodus and the plan of salvation are both reminders that there is a way out of darkness and bondage, and that way is by the design and power of God. Our Heavenly Father loves us and has sent his Son, our Redeemer, to show us the way back home, "beyond this vale of sorrow into a far better land of promise" (Alma 37:45).

NOTES

1. James Plastaras, *The God of Exodus: The Theology of the Exodus Narratives* (Milwaukee: Bruce Publishing Co., 1966), p. 7.
2. Nahum M. Sarna, *Exploring Exodus: The Heritage of Biblical Israel* (New York: Schocken Books, 1986), p. 7.
3. Brigham Young, in *Journal of Discourses* (London: Latter-day Saints' Book Depot, 1854–86), 7:333.
4. Bruce R. McConkie, *The Promised Messiah: The First Coming of Christ* (Salt Lake City: Deseret Book Co., 1978), pp. 43–44.
5. Joseph Fielding McConkie, *Gospel Symbolism* (Salt Lake City: Bookcraft, 1985), p. 1.
6. McConkie, *Gospel Symbolism,* p. 274.
7. Hugh Nibley, *An Approach to the Book of Mormon,* 2d ed. (Salt Lake City: Deseret Book Co., 1976), p. 116.
8. See George S. Tate, "The Typology of the Exodus Pattern in the Book of Mormon," in *Literature of Belief: Sacred Scripture and Religious Experience,* ed. Neal E. Lambert (Provo: Religious Studies Center, Brigham Young University, 1981), pp. 245–62.
9. Plastaras, *God of Exodus,* p. 20.
10. See, for example, S. Kent Brown, "The Exodus Pattern in the Book of Mormon," *Brigham Young University Studies* 30 (Summer 1990): 111–26; Terrence L. Szink, "Nephi and the Exodus," in *Rediscovering the Book of Mormon,* ed. John L. Sorenson and Melvin J. Thorne (Salt Lake City: Deseret Book Co. and F.A.R.M.S., 1991), pp. 38–51; and Tate, "Typology of the Exodus Pattern in the Book of Mormon," pp. 245–62.
11. Leonhard Goppelt, *Typos: The Typological Interpretation of the Old Testament in the New* (Grand Rapids, Mich.: Eerdmans Publishing Co., 1982), p. 1.
12. Plastaras, *The God of Exodus,* p. 313.
13. See my paper, "John's Testimony of the Bread of Life," in *The Lord of the Gospels: The 1990 Sperry Symposium on the New Testament* (Salt Lake City: Deseret Book Co., 1991), pp. 173–88.
14. See Plastaras, *God of Exodus,* pp. 319–22; and Peter F. Ellis, *Matthew: His Mind and His Message* (Collegeville, Minn.: Liturgical Press, 1985), p. 10.

15. Table 2 is based upon Lee Donaldson, "Gospel Portraits of the Messiah," United States Central States Area Church Educational System Symposium, Sept. 1988, unpublished ms. in possession of author.
16. See S. Kent Brown, "The Exodus: Seeing It as a Test, a Testimony, and a Type," *Ensign,* Feb. 1990, pp. 54–57. This article powerfully recounts how the prophets employed the Exodus as an affirmation of God's power to carry out his promises and to deliver his children from both temporal and spiritual bondage.
17. Joseph Smith, *Teachings of the Prophet Joseph Smith,* sel. Joseph Fielding Smith (Salt Lake City: Deseret Book Co., 1938), p. 354.
18. Joseph F. Smith, *Gospel Doctrine* (Salt Lake City: Deseret Book Co., 1939), pp. 60–61.
19. "June Videoconference: 'Accomplishing the Mission of the Church,'" *Ensign,* Sept. 1987, p. 74.
20. Ezra Taft Benson, "The Book of Mormon and the Doctrine and Covenants," *Ensign,* May 1987, pp. 84–85.
21. Boyd K. Packer, "The Great Plan of Happiness," *Doctrine and Covenants/Church History Symposium Speeches, 1993* (Salt Lake City: The Church of Jesus Christ of Latter-day Saints, 1993), pp. 2–3.

INDEX